PENGUIN CLASSICS

POEMS, PROTEST, AND A DREAM

Sor Juana Inés de la Cruz was born Juana Ramírez de Asbaje in 1648 at the hacienda of San Miguel Nepantla, not far from present-day Mexico City. She was an illegitimate child, and until relatively recently, 1651 was widely accepted as the year of her birth. Called by her contemporaries "the Tenth Muse" and "the Phoenix of Mexico," she became a favorite in the viceregal court before entering the convent in 1669. She joined a Convent of the Barefoot Carmelites but remained only a short time before settling in the more liberal Convent of Santa Paula of the order of San Jerónimo. Her most famous work is *La Respuesta de la poetisa a la muy ilustre Sor Filotea de la Cruz* (*Response to the Most Illustrious Poetess Sor Filotea de la Cruz*, 1691), the first document written in the Western Hemisphere to defend the rights of women to study, to teach, and to write. Renowned as the finest Latin American poet of the Baroque period, Sor Juana also composed numerous songs, devotional exercises, and plays written in verse form. Although many of these works were commissioned, she also wrote intensely personal poetry, including her masterpiece, the 975-line *silva* "El Sueño" or "Primero Sueño" (The Dream or First [I] Dream). In 1695, Sor Juana died in the convent while nursing her sister nuns during a devastating plague.

Margaret Sayers Peden is Professor Emerita of Spanish at the University of Missouri, Columbia. She is a recipient of Rockefeller, National Endowment for the Arts, and National Endowment for the Humanities fellowships, co-recipient of the PEN Gregory Kolovakos Award, and an honorary life member of the American Literary Translators Association. Among her translations are works by Isabel Allende, Carlos Fuentes, Pablo Neruda, Octavio Paz, and Juan Rulfo.

Ilan Stavans, a novelist and critic, teaches at Amherst College. His books include *Growing Up Latino* (1993); *Tropical Synagogues* (1994); *The Hispanic Condition* (1995); *The One-Handed Pianist and Other Stories* and *Art and Anger: Essays on Politics and the Imagination* (both 1996); and *The Oxford Book of Latin American Essays* (1997). He has been a National Book Critics Circle Award nominee and the recipient of the Latino Literature Prize.

POEMS, PROTEST, AND A DREAM

SELECTED WRITINGS

SOR JUANA INÉS DE LA CRUZ

TRANSLATED WITH NOTES BY
MARGARET SAYERS PEDEN
INTRODUCTION BY ILAN STAVANS

PENGUIN BOOKS

PENGUIN BOOKS
Published by the Penguin Group
Penguin Books USA Inc., 375 Hudson Street,
New York, New York 10014, U.S.A.
Penguin Books Ltd, 27 Wrights Lane,
London W8 5TZ, England
Penguin Books Australia Ltd, Ringwood,
Victoria, Australia
Penguin Books Canada Ltd, 10 Alcorn Avenue,
Toronto, Ontario, Canada M4V 3B2
Penguin Books (N.Z.) Ltd, 182–190 Wairau Road,
Auckland 10, New Zealand

Penguin Books Ltd, Registered Offices:
Harmondsworth, Middlesex, England

First published in Penguin Books 1997

7 9 10 8

Margaret Sayers Peden's translation of *La Respuesta a Sor Filotea*,
the first translation of the work into the English language, was originally
commissioned by a small independent press, Lime Rock Press, Inc.,
Salisbury, CT. It appeared in 1982 in a limited edition entitled *A Woman
of Genius: The Intellectual Autobiography of Sor Juana Inés de la Cruz*,
with photographs by Gabriel North Seymour. Copyright © 1982 by
Lime Rock Press, Inc. Reprinted with permission.

Dr. Peden's translation of a portion of "Primero Sueño" and the other poems
in this book formed the volume, *Sor Juana Inés de la Cruz: Poems*, published
by Bilingual Press/Editorial Bilingue. © 1985 by Bilingual Press/Editorial
Bilingue. Reprinted by arrangement with the publisher.

LIBRARY OF CONGRESS CATALOGING IN PUBLICATION DATA
Juana Inés de la Cruz, Sister, 1651–1695.
[Selections. English & Spanish. 1997]
Poems, protest, and a dream : selected writings / Sor Juana Inés
de la Cruz ; translated with notes by Margaret Sayers Peden ;
introduction by Ilan Stavans.
p. cm.
Includes bibliographical references.
ISBN 0 14 04.4703 2 (pbk.)
1. Juana Inés de la Cruz, Sister, 1651–1695—Translations into
English. I. Peden, Margaret Sayers. II. Title.
PQ7296.J6A25 1997
861—dc20   96–30638

Printed in the United States of America
Set in Stempel Garamond
Designed by Virginia Norey

TRANSLATOR'S NOTE

Why translate Sor Juana Inés de la Cruz? One can only state the obvious: out of love and fascination. It is the rare individual who, once exposed to the mind and persona of this "woman of genius," is not eager to linger in her presence. And for a translator, what closer communion than to attempt what Jorge Luis Borges called an "approximation" of her words?

When in 1982 Lime Rock Press published *A Woman of Genius,* my English version of *La Respuesta a Sor Filotea,* it was the first full-length translation of this incredible document. Why had there not been a dozen before it? Here was the first statement in our hemisphere to argue a woman's right to study and teach and learn. A later bilingual anthology of Sor Juana's poems offered me an opportunity to explore Sor Juana in a different way. For me, each of the poems suggests additional facets of her amazingly complex mind, from generally acknowledged autobiographical pieces, such as the sonnet to her portrait and Doña Leonor's monologue from *Los empeños de una casa,* to the love poems that may or may not echo real emotions, the ribald burlesque sonnets, the militant praise of the martyr Saint Catherine, and Sor Juana's defense of the peoples and customs of her hemisphere.

In that selection of poems I included a hundred or so lines of Sor Juana's master poem, "Primero sueño," referring to it as "the Mount Everest of Sor Juana's writing," and expressing my desire to return to it and attempt to scale it "simply because it is there." More than that brought me back to it, and now I have the opportunity to combine it with earlier translations in *Poems, Protest, and a Dream.* I am extremely grateful for that privilege.

My philosophy in translating all these works has remained constant, and I merely repeat what I wrote earlier in the Bilingual Press anthology of poems included in this volume. "In *After Babel* George Steiner accurately depicts the act of translation as 'a transparent absurdity, an endeavor to go backwards up the escala-

tor of time. . . . Art dies,' he says, 'when we lose or ignore the conventions by which it can be read.' He suggests that in rereading the baroque, we must extend the 'backward reach of our senses.' I have experienced the weight of this truth. The baroque cannot come to us. We must go to the baroque; we must attempt to recreate it by means of that backward reach." This is why I have chosen to translate Sor Juana's poems using variations on meter and verse, and her prose with a suggestion of time past. Sor Juana's world, her very reality, is represented in the strict hierarchy of her forms and the elegance of her rhetoric. My admiration and respect cause me to move backward toward her. And it is my hope that in some places we meet.

Finally, a word about the title of Sor Juana's masterwork, the long epistemological poem known as "Primero sueño" ("First Dream") or, more simply, "El sueño" ("The Dream"). We can never know with certainty which of the titles Sor Juana preferred, although it seems apparent that she used both. We know that in the *Respuesta a Sor Filotea*, she called the poem "a *papellilo* [a scribble, a trifle] they call 'El sueño,'" which may have been a desire to be offhand about a work that mattered greatly to her, or perhaps a simplification of the title, her personal name for the poem. We also know that in the first edition of her complete works the poem was entitled "Primero sueño." We must assume that Sor Juana suggested that title to her editors in Spain. Certainly she knew of it.

All the resonances of the title "First Dream" have been well explored: that the title was Sor Juana's nod to the *Soledades* of a poet she much admired, Luis de Góngora y Argote; or that, not foreseeing that she would be silenced, Sor Juana thought of this "dream" as the "first," to be followed by a "second," and perhaps more. Both these possibilities are logical, and I have no quarrel with them. Titles are very difficult for translators because their purpose is so encompassing, both to convey within a few words the content of a book and, at the same time, to carve a niche within the broader context of contemporaneous, past, and future literatures. With this translation I use a title that I like to think would have pleased Sor Juana, one sufficiently Baroque, and sub-

versive, to resonate with her time, her world, and her place in both: "First I Dream."

This title presented itself to me not precisely in a dream but sometime during the stage that Sor Juana describes as "not awake, but neither somnolent." I awoke with the thought that in Spanish there are *two* possible readings of the words *primero sueño*. In the one we are familiar with, the noun "dream," *sueño*, is modified by the adjective "first," *primero*. But in a felicitous ambiguity, *primero* may also serve as an adverb and *sueño* as the first person of the verb *soñar*, "to dream." "First Dream," then, is also "First *I* Dream."

Given Sor Juana's love of wordplay, of conceits and puns and sly allusions, I take great delight from the possibility that in the same way she "responded" to her superior, the Bishop of Puebla, by ironically addressing him as her "sister," so, too, in this poem she was able to insinuate her voice into explorations and arguments reserved for male scholars. In this poem, as in the *Respuesta*, Sor Juana is challenging the wrath of the male establishment. She is asserting her right as a woman to explore the very foundations of knowledge, the world of the intellect, the sphere from which a mere nun should have been excluded. We find in the poem itself that despite Sor Juana's attempts to maintain an anonymous, genderless voice—the neuter state that allowed her to soar toward, though fail to achieve, the ecstasy of union with the omniscient cosmos—the first-person *yo* does occasionally escape to identify the yearning, questing mind that seduces us today. It is present in the Spanish title "Primero sueño." We need to hear it in the English as well.

I wish to thank all my friends who have read and commented on these translations through the years, and especially the following: Claribel Alegría, Emilio Carballido, Magdalena García Pinto, Larry Kart, Gary Keller, Gregorio Luke, the Seymour family, and Caroline White. My gratitude to them, and, of course, to "the Tenth Muse," the *sor-presa* (captive nun), the Mexican sphinx, the incomparable Sor Juana Inés de la Cruz.

MARGARET SAYERS PEDEN

CONTENTS

INTRODUCTION

"What . . . is the devil in my being a woman?" Sor Juana Inés de la Cruz asked this question in her famous epistolary memoir, *Response to the Most Illustrious Poetess Sor Filotea de la Cruz*. And then she wondered: Am I, by virtue of my gender, condemned to eternal silence, as "is intended not only for women, but for *all* incompetents"? Isn't silence a form of compliance, the art of saying without saying? These queries are the vertebrae of her literary contribution and sit perfectly well in a courageous document that serves both as a mirror to her overall odyssey and as a farewell letter. In poor health and besieged by the merciless campaign of intimidation her superiors were orchestrating, she drafted her uneasy lines meticulously, as if aware that she was signing her own death sentence. She was then forty-three.

Until a few months earlier, her star had shone bright and high. Time and again she had challenged the male-dominated intellectual milieu, emerging triumphant to the applause of one viceregal court after another. While she was occasionally confronted by a prioress, cautioned by her confessor against sacrilegious misconduct, and reprimanded by a representative of the Archbishop of Mexico, Francisco Aguiar y Seijas, her position in the Convent of Santa Paula was secure. And her reputation as the premier Baroque poet in New Spain, as Mexico was known in the seventeenth century, reached far beyond—from Quito to Lima, from the Philippines to the Iberian peninsula.

But now, sequestered in her convent cell, she was alone and lonely. As she drafted her response, dated March 1, 1691, she knew her fate was no longer in her own hands. The delicate balance that she had successfully maintained most of her adult life had finally collapsed. Envy and resentment surrounded her. So she made sure her double message was unclouded. She confessed her "insignificance" as a woman, her "vile nature," her "unworthiness." She did so mainly because she wished "no quarrel with

the Holy Office, for I am ignorant, and I tremble that I may express some proposition that will cause offense or twist the true meaning of some scripture." However, she seized the occasion to denounce openly the repressive, misogynistic atmosphere that surrounded her and the criticism that had targeted her as a poet. She first used her response to articulate a persuasive manifesto in favor of intellectual rights for women, a topic that had preoccupied her since childhood; and then, so as not to alienate her superiors, she promised to entrust her future to her addressee: "You will command what I am to do," she told Sor Filotea de la Cruz, aware, no doubt, that complete silence and a full abstention from all literary endeavors would be requested of her. And she would comply. "I will weaken and dull the workings of my feeble reason," she wrote; that is, not a single *redondilla* more would come out of her pen, not a single epigraph more. Never again would she participate in poetry contests, never would she accept commissions to celebrate a government official. Eventually this silence also meant selling her much-admired collection of indigenous and imported musical instruments and dismantling her considerable library, which contemporary scholars, including Pedro Henríquez Ureña, Dorothy Schons, Ermilo Abreu Gómez, and Francisco de la Maza, have estimated to comprise 1,500 to 4,000 volumes, no small number for a time when book publishing was still a most elitist affair and the circulation of works of literature, religion, and philosophy was restricted in the Spanish colonies.

Judging by the standards of conformity and resignation, Sor Juana's letter is incredibly candid. She is neither sorry nor remorseful. She drafts it as a *"j'accuse,"* a map to the many obstacles she has found on the road to knowledge and self-assertion. And time has added relevance to her double message, turning the document into a cornerstone of Hispanic-American identity: it is at once a chronicle of the tense gender relations in the Western Hemisphere, a rich portrait of the social behavior that prevailed more than a century before independence from Spain was gained in 1810, and the very first intellectual autobiography written by a *criolla* in a hemisphere known for its solipsism, introversion, and allergy to public confessions. While she wrote it as a private letter, she had reason to believe it would become a civic affront, and so

she let herself go. Sick, anxious, persecuted by visible ghosts, Sor Juana allowed herself a final scream, a shriek of desperation, promising afterward to lose herself forever in the passive piety forced by the Catholic Church on scores of anonymous nuns.

Although the roots of Sor Juana's serious quarrels can be traced back to more than a decade earlier, her discontent reached an apex in 1690, as she sat down to write an argument against a celebrated Portuguese Jesuit, Father Antonio de Vieyra, one of the most eloquent and distinguished Christian thinkers and orators of the seventeenth century, admired especially in Spain and Mexico. On Holy Thursday of 1650, at the Royal Chapel in Lisbon, Vieyra had delivered an erudite sermon on one of Jesus Christ's important *finezas,* a term often used to describe divine acts of loving kindness toward humankind. Such speculative topics were often at the center of heated theological debates in Spain and Portugal and, as in Father Vieyra's case, these debates produced decades-long repercussions in their American colonies.

Even a quick glance at the sermon makes Father Vieyra's narrative and rhetorical talents clear: he is lucid yet verbose, insightful yet manipulative in regard to the information he is handling. He quotes generously from Saint John Chrysostom, Saint Thomas Aquinas, and Saint Augustine, but takes issue with each and every one of these thinkers, claiming they failed to understand the meaning behind Christ's decisive *fineza:* his washing, toward the end of his days, the feet of his disciples, including those of Judas. On the other side of the Atlantic, almost four decades later, Sor Juana discussed Father Vieyra's thesis during an academic gathering in a cloister of her Convent of Santa Paula of the Order of San Jerónimo, located in the southern section of today's Mexico City, then a placid urban center with a population of some one hundred thousand. She praised Father Vieyra's wisdom and applauded his scope but sharply criticized his understanding of Christ's love for humanity. She accused him of misunderstanding Christ's most important *fineza:* according to Father Vieyra, Christ had washed his disciples' feet for love's own sake; Sor Juana, on the other hand, viewed the act as evidence of Christ's love for humanity. This distinction might seem insignificant, especially to contempo-

rary readers, but in seventeenth-century Mexico it was extremely controversial. Sor Juana embellished her quasi-heretical argument with Greek and Latinate quotes and biblical references; she placed it in the context of other crucial arguments, such as the distinction between love and utility and the theme of "negative favors." In her characteristic Baroque style, in which appearances are deceitful and light and shadow are versions of each other, she claims: "We appreciate and we ponder the exquisiteness of divine love, in which to reward is a benefaction and to chastise is a benefaction, and the absence of benefaction is the greatest benefaction, and the absence of a *fineza* is the greatest *fineza*."

Don Manuel Fernández de Santa Cruz y Sahagún, the Bishop of Puebla, a clergyman close to Sor Juana and a rival of Francisco Aguiar y Seijas, Archbishop of Mexico since 1681 and known for his relentless misogyny, asked her to write down her thoughts; the result was the *Athenagoric Letter,* as elegant, punctilious, and exhausting an address as she was capable of and among her most lucid pieces of writing, a treatise not only on theology but on ecclesiastical politics as well. It circulated unofficially for a short while until the Bishop of Puebla, without Sor Juana's permission, had the treatise titled and privately printed, at his own expense, in late November 1690. He even sent a copy to Sor Juana herself, with a personal dedication. Because of her celebrity, news of her critique of Father Vieyra was soon widespread. Her supporters applauded her audacity and determination, but her opponents accused her of insolence and disrespect to a luminary whose authority could not be denied. Her straightforward commentary generated an atmosphere of fear. Rumors and insinuations abounded, while the specter of the Holy Office loomed in the background. Her superiors were not impressed: they judged her female imprudence regrettable and looked for ways to punish her.

Soon the Bishop of Puebla himself, either by his own personal choice or encouraged by higher authorities, decided to write a letter to Sor Juana. The epistle is short, strong, and uncompromising. He asks her to give up her secularism, to devote herself to faith and abandon the careless roads of reason. His comments, surprisingly, are less threatening than they might appear at first sight. Maintaining a correspondence, as Sor Juana did with innu-

merable people in Mexico and beyond, was not the private affair
we have grown accustomed to. Letters easily reached more eyes
than those of the parties involved, so the correspondent was usu-
ally compelled to manipulate language and meaning, to insinuate
and allude, to hide behind formulaic jargon—in short, to apply a
self-censoring device so as not to become the subject of public
embarrassment. Fernández de Santa Cruz addresses Sor Juana as
Señora mía and *Vuestra merced,* i.e., [Y]our [R]everence. He
grants her respect and distinction, and shows a high degree of ad-
miration for and familiarity with her work, but he also wants her
rebellious spirit brought under control and alludes to the fragility
of her situation as a woman in a male-controlled environment. In
spite of the fact that her *Athenagoric Letter* is a religious disquisi-
tion, the Bishop of Puebla asks her to put aside her nearsighted
scientific pursuits in favor of what nuns ought to do: devote
themselves to the purest of spiritual practices—their marital love
for Jesus Christ. "I don't pretend, in this epistle, for Y.R. to
change your talents by renouncing books, but to improve them
by occasionally reading that of Jesus Christ," writes Fernández de
Santa Cruz, so that Sor Juana's nature, "well-endowed by the
Almighty with many positive aspects on this earth, will not have
to grant her a negative condemnation in the world to come." The
last paragraph is a display of sexual innuendo: "These [improve-
ments] I wish to Y.R., for since I kissed your hand many years
ago, I live in love with your soul, and this love has not been
cooled by time or distance, because spiritual love is not overcome
by transitoriness, and is recognizable only when it is focused to-
ward growth. Let my supplications be heard by Y.R. May they
mark you a saint and keep you for all posterity."

On the surface Fernández de Santa Cruz's letter seems cordial:
he is at once tolerant and reprimanding, lenient and severe; on a
deeper level, however, the text is a more sophisticated strata-
gem—an authoritarian masquerade, an attack on Sor Juana's over-
all character, an accusation vibrating with sexual transgression. To
be more comfortable, to express himself without inhibition, the
Bishop of Puebla chose to write under a pseudonym: Sor Filotea
de la Cruz. The irony could not be more obvious: he attacks Sor
Juana at her most vulnerable point, her womanhood, but from a

woman's perspective; that is, he suggests she has trespassed into the male order and he in turn must stop her by entering the female realm. One can say, of course, that Fernández de Santa Cruz, sympathetic as he is to Sor Juana, is tempering the severity of his message by pretending to be a sister nun instead of a male superior. But this argument misses the irony behind the masquerade: the accuser assumes the voice of the accused in order to punish her; he impersonates a woman to stop her own move toward the male world. Sor Juana surely knew the true identity of her interlocutor; nevertheless, she chose to play the game. "My most illustrious *señora* . . . ," she begins her *Response to Sor Filotea.* "And thus say I, most honorable lady. Why do I receive such favor?" Since Fernández de Santa Cruz had already transgressed her right to privacy by printing the *Athenagoric Letter,* she would respond by exhibiting her guilt in public, by detailing her torturous journey, by openly discussing her lifelong impersonations.

This elaborate prank is at the center of Sor Juana's career. The environment had forced a thespian defense mechanism upon her. She had become an impersonator of masculinity, an actress pretending to be someone other than herself. To allow her intellectual talents to flourish, she had to revamp, even reinvent, her feminine side. This, of course, has generated a flurry of modern psychological studies. The most controversial is by a German scholar, Ludwig Pfandl, whose 1946 book, *Juana Inés de la Cruz, die zehnten Muse von Mexiko,* drew on the theories of Sigmund Freud to offer a range of reductive explanations of Sor Juana's conduct. Pfandl described her as a "neurotic with an Oedipal complex," a frustrated woman, vengeful, jealous, and malign. Others have ventured similar, if not quite so extreme, interpretations, portraying the nun as hysterical and sexually repressed. These simplistic views reflected the times in which they were concocted. Certainly, Sor Juana's lifelong struggle for individual expression evidenced admirable equanimity. Given the limited space she had in which to act, she was both ingenious and astute about finding alternative strategies of fulfillment. In fact, one could even claim she was at times too tame, too cautious, too conscious of her limits and limitations, too conservative in her approach to truly defy the ecclesiastical status quo. Her confronta-

tion with the Church is not unlike that which artists and intellectuals experience when denouncing the nearsightedness of the society in which they live. While in her *Response to Sor Filotea* she articulated a clear defense of secularism, she was also careful not to become a dissident, an apostate, a Joan of Arc facing an inevitable death by burning. The epistle might have been an occasion for self-reflection, but it wasn't a threat to secede. Sor Juana was too subtle, too docile, too submissive at heart; she was aware of the wide attention she attracted from various segments of society, but was careful not to turn her performance into a public scandal. Had she been more radical, less conciliatory, she could have provided a catalyst to reform and an invitation to secularism. But many factors impeded her. First and foremost is the fact that New Spain lacked a critical tradition. The Spanish-speaking Americas were not born in a struggle for liberalism and democracy. They inherited the Iberian philosophy of timidity and intolerance. Sor Juana challenged this philosophy, but ultimately gave up her struggle.

Modern feminist criticism of Sor Juana disagrees. For example, Georgina Sabat de Rivers, Marie-Cécile Bénassy-Berling, and Stephanie Merrim, three leading *sorjuanistas,* believe the tragic journey of the Mexican nun is attributable less to her own personal weakness than to the force of patriarchal structures. They appreciate Sor Juana's twisting literary course as weaving a "uniquely deviant, convoluted pathway between masculine and feminine modes." The *Response to Sor Filotea,* they argue, is about balancing recognition and rejection. What matters is not the limits of her rebelliousness but the strategies she adopted in order to find what Virginia Woolf calls "a room of one's own" in her male-dominated society. Sor Juana should not be perceived as submissive, a flaccid promoter of enlightenment, since no clear reform could be attained in New Spain from *within* the ecclesiastical hierarchy.

The issue of Sor Juana's public scandal and the extent of her courage have gained clarity as a result of a major scholarly breakthrough. For a long time scholars believed the *Response to Sor Filotea* was her only overtly autobiographical work, but that view changed in 1981, when Father Aureliano Tapia Méndez published

a booklet entitled *Sor Juana: A Spiritual Self-Defense,* in which he included a five-and-a-half-page letter he had uncovered in the Seminario Arquidiocesano of Monterrey, in northern Mexico. The letter, undated but probably written in 1681, was from Sor Juana to her confessor, Father Antonio Núñez de Miranda. At first its authenticity was questioned, but the style of the epistle and crucial information contained in it confirm its credibility and its relevance. Far more candid than the *Response to Sor Filotea,* if less poetic, it shows that Sor Juana's confrontation with the Church hierarchy predated the Vieyra controversy. In addition, it evidences the degree of intimacy she had with her confessor, who, as is clear in *A Spiritual Self-Defense,* had disparaged her in the circles of power; and it fully illustrates Sor Juana's changing steadfastness in that, probably a result of the support she had earlier received from the viceregal court, she was far more confrontational, more self-assured and uncompromising, in 1681 than in 1690.

Sor Juana also addresses Father Núñez de Miranda as Y[our] R[everence]. "For some time now," she writes, "various persons have informed me that I am singled out for censure in the conversations of Y.R., in which you denounce my actions with such bitter exaggeration as to suggest a *public scandal.*" The basis for his complaint: her poetry, a most unworthy and profane endeavor in the eyes of the Catholic Church. Her defense is clear-cut. "On which . . . occasions was the transgression of having written them so grave?" Sor Juana wonders. She then describes the pressure she experiences: "Women feel that men surpass them, and that I seem to place myself on a level with men; some wish that I did not know so much; others say that I ought to know more to merit such applause; elderly women do not wish that other women know more than they; young women, that others present a good appearance; and one and all wish me to conform to the rules of their judgment; so that from all sides comes such a singular martyrdom as I deem none other has ever experienced." Her solution can be read as a diatribe against dogmatism in that it suggests an individualistic stand that, taken a step further, would bring laissez-faire reform. "I beg of Y.R.," Sor Juana writes, "that if you do not wish or find it in your heart to favor me (for that is voluntary) you think of me no more, for though I shall regret so great a loss, I

shall utter no complaint, because God, Who created and redeemed me and Who has bestowed so many mercies on me, will supply a remedy in order that my soul, awaiting His kindness, shall not be lost even though it lack the direction of Y.R., for He has made many keys to Heaven and has not confined Himself to a single criterion; rather, there are many mansions of people of as many different natures, and in the world there are many theologians, but were they lacking, salvation lies more in the desiring than in the knowing, and that will be more in me than in my confessor."

Less than a decade later, though, her approach would be less defiant. While in both works Sor Juana claims to have built her literary career on the requests of others, in the *Response to Sor Filotea* she has become aware of her vulnerability and thus writes a self-portrait designed to highlight her talents and scope. One of her mythological heroes, she notes, is Phaëthon, son of Helios, the sun god, and the heroine Clymene, who wants only to drive his father's sun chariot for a day. Unable to control the horses that pull the chariot across the sky, he is killed and falls to earth when Zeus hurls a thunderbolt at him. The story of Phaëthon's over-reaching ambition is an allegory, of course, a mirror in which Sor Juana saw her own reflection. Her hunger for wisdom brought her glory; but it also, and she always knew it, would precipitate her downfall.

Very few oil portraits of Sor Juana survive, all of them derivative and not fully reliable, in that they were painted after her death in 1695. Three stand out: those by the Mexican artists Juan de Miranda and Miguel Cabrera hang in the Universidad Nacional Autónoma de México and the fortress of Chapultepec, respectively; an anonymous third portrait now belongs to the Philadelphia Museum of Art. The impression given by the three is that of a proud elitist, a stoic, serious learner, a distinguished woman of substance and vision. Sor Juana is invariably at the center of the composition, immobile, serious, wearing a habit resembling that of a Sister of the Immaculate Conception: a white tunic with full but cuffed sleeves, and a white coif, black veil, and scapular whose coif completely conceals her hair; she wears a huge metal or parchment medallion below her chin, nearly covering her neck, il-

lustrated with a religious scene incorporating an angel; a black thong of the order of San Agustín encircles her waist, and a rosary dangling from her neck almost reaches her knees. In Miranda's portrait she is standing and writing; in Cabrera's she sits, her right hand resting on a large book.

Her religious attire and her crucifix are standard features in portraits of the time. Still, the fact that only her face is exposed is significant. Male religious icons in Mexican art, from Jesus Christ to the crowded pantheon of saints and child angels, are often half-naked, as if male flesh needed to be displayed, represented, to convey the ethos of these figures. But their female counterparts, from the Virgin of Guadalupe to Hernán Cortés's mistress, La Malinche, almost without exception are totally dressed; their pure, virginal flesh is both threatening and threatened when exposed to the public eye. In the backdrop of each painting of Sor Juana, society and nature play absolutely no role. Neither animals nor people surround her, only books, ink, and pens. In fact, modern scholars and biographers, such as Ermilo Abreu Gómez, have made inventories of Sor Juana's library based in part on the content of her work and on the portraits of her that survive. We know, for instance, how well versed she was in Golden Age Spanish poetry, particularly Luis de Góngora, whom she so admired. Also, the Baroque period in which she lived celebrated a handful of Hellenistic classics, most particularly Ovid's *Metamorphoses,* and she was certainly well acquainted with Neoplatonic and Scholastic texts, most of which she probably read in anthologies, compendiums, encyclopedias, and dictionaries of deities and symbols of antiquity. She was familiar with Avicenna, Aquinas, and Maimonides. Her poem "El Sueño," as Octavio Paz has shown in his magisterial biography of 1982, *Sor Juana or, The Traps of Faith* (translated 1988), manifests her considerable knowledge of Cicero and particularly of Athanasius Kircher's *Iter exstaticum coeleste.* She also read Macrobius, Baltasar de Vitoria, Juan Pérez de Moya, Boethius, and Boccaccio, as well as Pico della Mirandola, Pierio Valeriano's dictionary of symbols, the *Hieroglyphica,* and Bartholomeus Garzoni's *Piazza universale di tutte le professioni del mondo, e nobili e ignobili,* among others.

Books, Sor Juana claims in the *Response to Sor Filotea,* were her

lifelong passion and her best, most loyal companions. In her eyes they were instruments of knowledge and control devised by mankind to make order from chaos. Her love for them was maternal: she embraced and collected them, and gave birth to several poetry pamphlets circulated among friends and fans, and a set of three printed volumes, all published in Spain: *Castalian Inundation* (1689), *Works* (1692), and *Fame and Posthumous Works* (1700). This was no small achievement when one considers, as Asunción Lavrin has shown, the minimal publishing rate by women in the seventeenth century. Which does not mean that nuns in New Spain didn't write. On the contrary, they wrote at the instigation of their male superiors so as "to refine the self and ultimately achieve perfection," but never for sheer pleasure. "*Abstention, mortification, renunciation,* and *humiliation* are all key words in the religious vocabulary of the colonial period," Lavrin states, and they color the legacy of these sisters. What makes Sor Juana stand out is her literary power, the subtlety of her subversion, and her pursuit of secular forms of knowledge. She was and was not a typical nun: she obeyed her superiors and performed her conventual duties, but at the same time, she didn't seem to have a clear sense of religious vocation, as most of her companions did. Sor Juana was a contemporary of other remarkable women, such as Sor Marcela de San Félix and Luisa Roldán of Spain, the Mesdames de Sévigné and de Lafayette of France, and Sor María de San José of colonial Mexico, a self-flagellating mystic who was requested by the Bishop of Puebla to record her visions; but they were all exceptions to the norm. To make a wide range of books a part of her being, to inhabit them, Sor Juana had to become an anomaly—in her own words, a *rara avis*. The *Response to Sor Filotea* is filled with delicious anecdotes about her love affair with books. "I was not yet three years old," she writes, "when my mother determined to send one of my elder sisters to learn to read at a school for girls. . . . Affection, and mischief, caused me to follow her, and when I observed how she was being taught her lessons I was so inflamed with the desire to know how to read, that deceiving—for so I knew it to be—the mistress, I told her that my mother had meant for me to have lessons too. She did not believe it, as it was little to be believed, but, to humor

me, she acceded." Sor Juana goes on to describe how she "abstained from eating cheese because I had heard that it made one slow of wits, for in me the desire for learning was stronger than the desire for eating." And she establishes a pattern when, sometime later, "being six or seven, and having learned how to read and write, along with all other skills of needlework and household arts that girls learn, it came to my attention that in Mexico City there were schools, and a University, in which one studied the sciences. The moment I heard this, I began to plague my mother with insistent and importunate pleas: she should dress me in a boy's clothing and send me to Mexico City to live with relatives, to study and be tutored at the University. She would not permit it." The connection between her thirst for knowledge and her female body is quite strong. "I began to study Latin grammar . . . and so intense was my concern that though among women (especially a woman in the flower of her youth) the natural adornment of one's hair is held in such high esteem, I cut off mine to the breadth of some four to six fingers, measuring the place it had reached, and imposing upon myself the condition that if by the time it had again grown to that length I had not learned such and such a thing I had set for myself to learn while my hair was growing, I would again cut it off as punishment for being so slow-witted. And it did happen that my hair grew out and still I had not learned what I had set for myself—because my hair grew quickly and I learned slowly—and in fact I did cut it in punishment for such stupidity: for there seemed to me no cause for a head to be adorned with hair and naked of learning."

The precise circumstances of Sor Juana's birth are still somewhat obscure. She was born at the hacienda of San Miguel Nepantla, in the shadow of the volcano Popocatépetl, not far from what is today Mexico City, on either December 2, 1648, or November 12, 1651. Since Father Diego Calleja, her first biographer (or, better, hagiographer), a Jesuit and Sor Juana's contemporary who saw her life as an act of ascendancy, an allegory of sublime spirituality, introduced the latter date, it was accepted as correct for decades; but modern scholars have unraveled records that appear to establish her baptism three years earlier. Juana

Ramírez de Asbaje was Sor Juana's given name. Hers was a family of small landowners of modest means. What is certain is that, just like her two sisters, Sor Juana was a "natural" child—that is, born out of wedlock. How this fact marked her vision of the world and her standing in society is a controversial issue among *sorjuanistas*. Apparently she repeatedly tried to hide her illegitimacy. Indeed, several critics believed it was at the core of Sor Juana's existential dilemma and is the main reason for her becoming a nun. But this might be an exaggeration. "Natural" children were common in New Spain, not only among the lower classes but among nuns and viceroys. (Fray Payo Enríquez de Rivera, a.k.a. Don Payo, appointed viceroy of New Spain in 1674 and one of Sor Juana's protectors, for instance, was also illegitimate.) Not only could one find all sorts of ways to ameliorate the impact of one's "natural" birth, but the fact that this was a common occurrence reduces its stigmatization.

Sor Juana's father, Pedro Manuel de Asbaje, was a Basque frequently absent from the household. He goes unmentioned in the *Response to Sor Filotea,* which says something about the family dynamics. Sor Juana is absolutely silent about him, but many questions remain. Did she know him? Did they spend time together? Was he aware of his daughter's extraordinary talents and did he encourage them? Paz suggests the possibility that Sor Juana was the daughter of a certain Friar F. (or H.) de Asvaje, but this is unlikely. In any event, the enigma of the paternal figure is central, not only to her life but to the Mexican psyche. Since the arrival of Hernán Cortés, the father figure has been portrayed as an intruder, a foreigner—the Spanish conquistador interested in gold and power, promiscuous and irresponsible, who propagated the mestizo race. The fact that we know so little about Pedro Manuel de Asbaje has helped turn the model of Sor Juana, the bastard child, into an archetype of the collective Mexican soul.

As for Sor Juana's mother, Isabel Ramírez, she was a *criolla* who seems to have been the center of gravity in her daughter's life. It appears that in the absence of the children's father, she took control of the hacienda in Nepantla, and her strong character kept the family afloat. Sor Juana's love for her is clear in the way she wanted to be known publicly almost as soon as she began writing

poetry: as Juana Ramírez de Asbaje, with her mother's family name first. She seems to have written about her mother regularly; anecdotes and references to her appear in the *Response to Sor Filotea*, in her plays, and in her poetry, testimony, no doubt, to the respect and appreciation she carried with her always. Brilliant and precocious even as a young girl, Sor Juana found refuge and fulfillment in the library of her grandfather, Pedro Ramírez. At eight she wrote a poem about the Eucharist for a religious festival. She had some Latin lessons, but since her formal education ended at the primary level, most of her learning came from her reading. Even the domestic realm was, in her eyes, a laboratory for study. "What shall I tell you, lady, of the natural secrets I have discovered while cooking?" she would write. "I see that an egg holds together and fries in butter or in oil, but, on the contrary, in syrup shrivels into shreds; observe that to keep sugar in a liquid state one need only add a drop or two of water in which a quince or other bitter fruit has been soaked; observe that the yolk and the white of one egg are so dissimilar that each with sugar produces a result not obtainable with both together. I do not wish to weary you with such inconsequential matters, and make mention of them only to give you full notice of my nature. . . . What wisdom may be ours if not the philosophies of the kitchen? . . . Had Aristotle prepared victuals, he would have written more."

The world into which Sor Juana was thrown was obsessed with, and nervous about, race and identity. As a colony, the seventeenth-century viceroyalty of New Spain was totally dependent on the Spanish Crown. Colonial governmental autonomy was minimal, and culture, as well, moved from west to east: Society was organized hierarchically, based on race and birthright. The role of the Holy Office of the Inquisition was that of a brutal police force: it preserved the considerable gap between one group and another by calling attention to an individual's honor and publicly castigating those falsifying an ethnic identity. Since the *Reconquista* of the Iberian peninsula, the concept of *pureza de sangre*, purity of blood, had colored every aspect of life, from food and medicine to diplomacy and the arts. It justified the expulsion of Moors and Jews from Spanish territory by legitimizing the lineage of the *cristianos viejos*, old Christians, and opened up

an acerbic debate around the notion of *el honor,* an individual's honor and moral standing.

This racial craze was at the heart of the colonizing enterprise in the Americas, built on the basis of transculturation. The Spaniards had encountered a strong indigenous population and quickly established a system of castes. At the top of the ladder were the ruling *españoles,* Spanish settlers heading legal and financial institutions. Next came the *criollos,* American-born descendants of the Spaniards. They were followed by the part-European and part-native *mestizos,* and then by the *castizos,* whose heritage was *mestizo* and white. The *indios* followed, and at the bottom of the ladder were *mulattos, zambos,* and other ethnic mixtures of Indians and African slaves. The divisions were not limited to race. Gender played as important a role as skin color in the shaping of society and its worldview. Male rule prevailed, a direct result of the male composition of the army led by Hernán Cortés. Unlike their counterparts in the British colonies to the north, the Iberian conquistadores crossed the Atlantic without spouses. Their goal was not to start from scratch to build an altogether new civilization, to become the new people of Israel in search of a new Canaan this side of the Atlantic. Instead, their objective was encapsulated in the words *oro* and *poder,* gold and power. Leaving their female companions behind, at home in Europe, allowed them to be free, to seek and possess pleasure. Their mandate was to subdue the native population and build a dependency whose riches the Spanish Catholic monarchs could use to enhance their domain.

In Sor Juana's time, women were restricted to three milieus: the domestic, the courtly, and the monastic. All were male-dominated, and the role handed down to the women varied from realm to realm: in the privacy of the homestead, wives were expected to be passive and caring; in the flamboyant corridors of the court, women were objects of adoration; and in the cloister, nuns were silent and contemplative observers. These set social patterns made it difficult for a talented young girl, a hybrid of Spaniard and *criolla,* to live freely without attracting suspicion. Still, Sor Juana managed to move in circles of power, meeting important government and Church officials, seeking the security of their protection while launching a career as an intellectual that would take her far

beyond the limits they set. Thus identity was at the core of Sor
Juana's personal quest. She understood early on that to excel she
would need to arm herself with a sense of security and self-esteem
that precluded all possible doubts about her character. "One truth
I shall not deny," she writes in the *Response to Sor Filotea,* "(first,
because it is well-known to all, and second, because although it
has not worked in my favor, God has granted me the mercy of
loving truth above all else), which is that from the moment I was
first illuminated by the light of reason, my inclination towards
letters has been so vehement, so overpowering, that not even the
admonitions of others—and I have suffered many—nor my own
meditations—and they have not been few—have been sufficient
to cause me to forswear this natural impulse that God placed in
me." And the admonitions were indeed many. Her autobiograph-
ical letters enumerate the countless obstacles placed before her.
But giving up was not an option. She was a woman born out of
wedlock, a double handicap, but perhaps she could turn it to her
advantage if her achievements could overwhelm her critics. Ap-
pearances, contrived and authentic, a favorite Baroque theme in
the Spanish Golden Age, are the vertebrae unifying her entire
body of work. Her poems deal with hypocrisy and pretense, with
mirrors and original models, with the shallowness of social be-
havior and the vulnerability of women to male demands. Her
cloak-and-dagger 1683 comedy *The Trials of a Noble House* and
her mythological love-intrigue play *Love Is a Greater Labyrinth*
deal with the confusing effects of choice. Unlike those Iberian
dramatists she clearly imitated (Lope de Vega, Tirso de Molina,
Calderón de la Barca, and others), she wrote not for the public
stage but for the palace—that is, for an aristocratic audience—and
her dramas offer no clear solutions to the mysteries of identity.

There is little extant information about Sor Juana's entrance to
the viceregal court. Her *Response to Sor Filotea* jumps abruptly
from her childhood to her convent life, leaving the years in be-
tween, roughly from 1656, when her grandfather died, to 1669,
when she entered the convent, in the dark. Her biographers have
thus been forced to speculate, to fill in the gaps by way of infer-
ence. We know that while she was still at home, a new lover,
Diego Ruíz Lozano, came into her mother's life. Then, at age thir-

teen, Sor Juana moved to the capital, into the house of a wealthy uncle and aunt, Juan de Mata and Doña María Ramírez, who presented her at the viceregal court. Father Calleja observes that the urban elite were immediately entranced by her. Her cleverness, intelligence, and beauty made her an instant sensation. In 1664, after eight years with her relatives, she met the newly arrived vicereine, Doña Leonor Carreto, Marquesa de Mancera, who quickly admitted Sor Juana to her service.

Judging by the sonnets, *décimas, seguidillas,* epigrams, *redondillas, romances,* and other poetry Sor Juana produced, she was fascinated by the flirtations, the sensuous codes, and the secret provocations of courtly manners. But life at court was not pure leisure, and her duties were fixed: she would be both companion and confidante of her patrons and write under their commission in exchange for a routine that allowed her to cultivate her intellectual interests and escape marital responsibilities. Some of her poetry written under the patronage of various vicereines is intense, candid, burning with passion, qualities that have invited speculation: was she sentimentally involved with some of them? Her loyalty and gratitude to the Marquesa de Mancera, known as "Laura" in her work, is expressed in the three funerary sonnets on the marquesa's death, in which Sor Juana thanks her patroness for encouraging and supporting her poetic drive. According to historical data, the Marquesa de Mancera was around thirty years of age when the two women met. Father Calleja believes the Marquesa "could not live without her servant," and Paz describes their liaison as "a composite of selfishness and admiration, sympathy and pity . . . a relationship of superior to inferior, of protectress to protégée, but one in which there was also recognition of an exceptional young woman's worth." Sor Juana also had relationships with three viceroys: Fray Payo de Rivera; Don Tomás Antonio de la Cerda, the Marqués de la Laguna; and Don Gaspar de Sandoval Cerda Silva y Mendoza, the Conde de Galve, whose wife was the subject of a set of poems Sor Juana wrote between 1688 and the time of her death.

Of all of her patronesses, María Luisa Manrique de Lara y Gonzaga, Condesa de Paredes and Marquesa de la Laguna, known as "Lysis" in Sor Juana's writing, was probably the dearest. Their

friendship was colored by tacit eroticism, as is clear in the poems written in the condesa's honor between 1680 and 1685, three of which are included in this volume: *décimas* 126, 130, and 132 in the modern edition of Sor Juana's *Complete Works*, edited in 1951 by Father Alfonso Méndez Plancarte with the assistance of Alberto G. Salceda. Intelligent, energetic, and extremely beautiful, the Condesa de Paredes encouraged Sor Juana to compose what some consider her best work, *The Divine Narcissus*, a sacramental play full of allegorical references, possibly written in 1688. The subject matter of its *loa*, a small dramatic scene that serves as an introduction and is often performed on its own, is of great importance: the Indian population in New Spain and the birth of a new civilization. The main characters are Occident, personified by a stately Indian wearing a crown, and America, a noble Indian woman. Together with her friend and devotee Carlos Sigüenza y Góngora, Mexico's leading man of letters in the seventeenth century, who in 1668 wrote *Primavera indiana*, a long poem in honor of the Virgen de Guadalupe, Sor Juana was among the first to juxtapose Christianity and native pagan mythology and to reflect on the encounter between the two civilizations. The *loa* is structured as a debate between European monotheism and Aztec idolatry; although the latter refuses to accept the Christian doctrine, by the end it understands, in a syncretistic view, that the faiths have much in common. The Condesa de Paredes also helped Sor Juana pay for her first published collection of poems: *Castalian Inundation*, which appeared in Madrid and was dedicated to her patroness. Did they share a lesbian love? Should we consider the risks Sor Juana took in her poems as a token of gratitude and affection typical of the time? The answers to these questions are elusive. They have generated bewilderment and confusion among cultural historians and biographers, some of whom are ready to venture risky hypotheses whereas others prefer a more conservative, less speculative stand. For instance, María Luisa Bemberg's film of 1990, *I, the Worst of All*, with Dominique Sanda and Assumpta Serna, underscores erotic elements in their relationship by having the condesa visit Sor Juana's convent cell, ask her to uncover her hair, and eventually kiss her on the mouth. That such an encounter took place is highly improbable. It is true that there

was a constant flow of gifts between the viceregal palace and the Convent of Santa Paula. Furthermore, the condesa is known to have paid innumerable visits to Sor Juana. But strict rules forbade visitors, no matter how powerful and well connected they were, to enter a nun's cell, let alone engage in physical love with her.

Sor Juana wrote most of her poetry after she took the veil, but for her nonreligious stanzas she always drew on her life at court. Is she exaggerating when she states in the *Response to Sor Filotea* that "I have never written on my own choice, but at the urging of others, to whom with reason I might say, *You have compelled me*"? Similarly, she claims, in *A Spiritual Self-Defense,* "I have extremely resisted in writing [the miserable verses] and have excused myself in every possible way." Almost everything she wrote, with the exception of "El Sueño," was commissioned by and dedicated to important personalities of her time, not only patrons. Between 1671 and 1680, for instance, she composed a couple of *romances* to Don Payo; she also wrote homages to the Duque de Veragas, her Latin teacher Martín de Olivas, Philip IV and Charles II, and Sigüenza y Góngora. The selection translated by Margaret Sayers Peden in this volume, from *Castalian Inundation,* illustrates her style and themes. It opens with three examples of the *romance*, a simple and widely used Spanish ballad written in octosyllabic verse in which the even-numbered lines rhyme with the same assonance and the odd-numbered are left free. "Prologue to the Reader," with which Sor Juana began her first book of poetry, is a standard introduction filled with a modesty customary in her time but absurd in ours: she offers her poems with a de rigueur sense of hesitation, "though all that may speak well of them / is that I know them to be poor." "In Reply to a Gentleman from Peru," another invaluable document on her status as a woman in colonial Mexico, is an epistolary *romance* addressed to a certain Señor Navarrete, who sent Sor Juana a set of clay vessels from Chile and some original poems in which, by way of commending her, he suggested "she would better be a man." Her response is a brief manifesto on the value of women's roles as pleasure objects and wives, neither of which she accepts for herself. She adds:

So in my case, it is not seemly
that I be viewed as feminine,
as I will never be a woman
who may as woman serve a man.
I know only that my body,
not to either state inclined,
is neuter, abstract, guardian
of only what my Soul consigns.

The third *romance,* "While by Grace I am inspired," has a sa-
cred theme. Included in Volume 3 of the edition by Méndez Plan-
carte, it chronicles the ongoing antagonism between faith and
reason, neither of which can cure the suffering of her soul. The di-
chotomy in this poem can serve to underscore the main motifs of
el barroco hispano, a Baroque style in fashion in the Spanish
Golden Age until roughly 1680, the latest date of Calderón de la
Barca's *autos,* and, with renewed intensity in the New World,
from early colonial times through the age of independence in the
early eighteenth century and onward into the present. Its prime
objective is to call attention to the artificiality of human endeav-
ors by accentuating their unnatural character. Baroque art abounds
in conceits and counterfeits, in theatricality and obsessive sophis-
tication, to the extent that, as Borges once put it, these endeavors
"run the risk of becoming caricatures of themselves." In Baroque
poetry, verbal puns are ubiquitous, designed to call attention to
the fragile line between reality and fantasy, between beauty and
ugliness, and, as in Sor Juana's *romance,* between faith and reason.
Why *lo barroco,* although practiced all over Europe from 1580,
ended up becoming a signature of Hispanic-American culture at
large is still a subject of heated debate. Such a style is likely to
flourish in environments where a variety of diverse, often antago-
nistic ethnic, linguistic, and religious backgrounds clash, generat-
ing a state of impurity and contamination, an atmosphere of
hybridization like that on the Iberian peninsula after the expul-
sion of the Jews in 1492. In the Americas, the mingling of various
backgrounds—Indian, Iberian, African—resulted in what the
Cuban ethnographer Fernando Ortíz once called "a transcultural

milieu." But other factors also contributed to its reign in Spain and its dissemination in the colonies across the Atlantic: the struggle between Reformation and Counter-Reformation, the defeat of the Spanish Armada, and the crisis of Catholicism.

Baroque Spanish poetry developed two alternative modes: the *culteranismo* of Luis de Góngora y Argote (1561–1627), infatuated with learned words and a labyrinthine syntax, and the *conceptismo* of Francisco Gómez de Quevedo y Villegas (1580–1645), characterized by ingenious conceits. Whereas the former embellishes by means of verbal pyrotechnics, the latter makes poetry an instrument for investigating existential dilemmas. In New Spain, where the Spanish Baroque was taken to its limits, Góngora was seen as the more admirable of the two, but Quevedo was also influential, as were Lope de Vega, Calderón, and Baltazar Gracián. Probably nobody has studied these links with the vision and perseverance of Octavio Paz, who in 1958 compiled an important anthology, *Mexican Poetry*, which includes many well- and lesser-known literary figures of colonial Mexico (Francisco de Terrazas, Bernardo de Balbuena, Juan Ruiz de Alarcón, Miguel de Guevara, Luis de Sandoval y Zapata, and others). In *The Traps of Faith*, Paz places them in context. "It has often been said—both in praise and deprecation—that the Mexican baroque was an exaggeration of the Spanish models," he observes. "Indeed, like all imitative art, the poetry of New Spain attempted to surpass its models: it was the extreme of baroqueness, the apogee of strangeness. This excess is proof of its authenticity." Nevertheless, amid this strangeness, Sor Juana has a room of her own: her Baroque voice is neither misguided nor excessive, and by virtue of her status as a colonial woman, the dichotomies she writes of in *romances* like "While by Grace I am inspired" and sonnets such as "In my pursuit, World, why such diligence?" possess an urgency no Spanish poet could dream of.

By definition, all of Latin American literature written in the Spanish language is derivative: Spanish is a foreign artifact adapted to native needs, an import, a hand-me-down. But Sor Juana, much like Borges nearly three centuries later, found originality in imitation. While Góngora's fingerprints, and a certain Quevedian

mood, lurk in many corners of her work, she is never so deriva-
tive as to lose her own personality. What distinguishes her from
the Spanish masters is her political agenda: not only is she a poet,
but she is a female poet; not only is she Catholic, but she is a
Catholic nun living under strict male rule within the confines of
the Church in New Spain; not only is she infatuated with neolo-
gisms and other precious words, but she uses them to call atten-
tion to the artificiality of the Spanish language in the colonies,
where all sonnets are echoes of other sonnets. In short, Sor Juana
is wise enough to turn her status as a colonial woman poet to her
advantage: if she is derivative, it is because she must depend on
others. And she did more than incorporate Mexican motifs into
her writings. She was also among the first to experiment with
Nahuatl ballads, known as *tocotines,* traditional Indian-style dance
songs of which she wrote two: one mixes Nahuatl and Spanish;
the other, composed in 1676, is in Nahuatl in its entirety. Its sub-
ject is the Assumption of the Virgin; it makes fun of the way blacks
and Indians react to the ascension of the Virgen de Guadalupe.
This poem is of enormous relevance. Dependent as it was on Eu-
rope, the *criollo* intelligentsia of seventeenth-century New Spain
denigrated indigenous folklore. But Sor Juana's scope was much
larger: in her work one witnesses the metamorphosis of the po-
etry of New Spain into the poetry of Mexico.

Her overall ideological stance is nowhere clearer than in her
philosophical satire "Misguided men, who will chastise a woman
when no blame is due," her most famous *redondilla,* an indict-
ment that goes beyond class lines, criticizing men for manipulat-
ing women, and reprimanding women for their passivity and
submission to men. Sor Juana includes references to Thais, the
Athenian mistress of Alexander the Great and Ptolemy and
known as a symbol of liberalism; and to Lucretia, a Roman exem-
plar of "the virtuous wife" who, raped and betrayed by the son of
Tarquin the Proud, ultimately committed suicide. Shaped as a
Spanish stanza in octosyllabic quatrains rhymed *abba,* it is even
today memorized in part by schoolchildren in Mexico and
throughout Latin America who grasp only a fragment of its over-
all meaning and thus simplify the poetess's message. Its popular-

ity might well be based, as Electra Arenal and Amanda Powell claim, on "the suppressed anger it reveals in women and the giddy catharsis it permits men." This *redondilla* is both endearing and accessible, at least when one compares it to Sor Juana's epigrams and *décimas,* stanzas of ten octosyllabic lines with a rhyme scheme of *abbaa/aaddc,* and particularly to her sonnets with Italianate rhyme scheme. In the sonnets her talent is at its apex: she displays a perfect grasp of her theme as well as astonishing stylistic control. The selection in this book is representative, including classics such as "This that you gaze on, colorful deceit," "In my pursuit, World, why such diligence?," and "Stay, shadow of contentment too short-lived." They have recurrent themes: love and indiscretion, individual honor, and, her favorite dichotomy, female vanity versus female intellect.

The variety of the selection affirms her versatility and her genius, but she was comfortable in other literary forms, and wrote medleys, panegyrics, devotional exercises, riddles for parlor guessing games, even a treatise on musical methods (now lost), entitled *The Conch Shell.* One could ascribe to Sor Juana a psychological urgency to excel against all odds. Her road to success was blocked by obstacles, not the least of which was her gender. Father Aguiar y Seijas, the Archbishop of Mexico, disliked her to such a degree that after she died, he confiscated her belongings and fought to erase her from human memory. Father Aguiar y Seijas had arranged for the publication in Mexico of Father Vieyra's sermon, and so may have taken Sor Juana's critique of it as an indirect attack on himself. Sor Juana's willingness to face the likes of the archbishop shows how courageous she was, how she needed to test herself constantly, to surpass her male competitors, to call attention to their mediocrity and signal their shortcomings. Since her achievements generated envy, she handled herself with discretion, scattering clues to her existential dilemma in various parts of her oeuvre. One such clue is the famous monologue of Doña Leonor, a young woman trapped in the crossroads where female beauty and intellectual talents meet, in the play *The Trials of a Noble House,* also included here. In Act I, Scene II, Doña Leonor tells her confidantes Doña Ana and Cecilia:

> To tell you I was born with beauty
> is something you may well forgive,
> this truth is witnessed by your eyes
> as well as hardships I have lived.
> I merely state, I did not wish
> to be the one to tell this tale,
> in telling or in keeping still
> two difficulties I detail:
> if I say that I was known
> and celebrated for discretion,
> I prove the very opposite
> by the folly of narration;
> but if silent, none will know
> the truth of me; you see the question,
> in silence, you are uninformed,
> in speaking, I betray discretion.

And a few lines later:

> I was, through all my native land,
> recipient of praise and laud,
> the quality of veneration
> formed by communal acclaim;
> and as the things that all were saying,
> to good purpose, or in vain,
> by elegance of face and bearing
> were not in any way gainsaid,
> too soon, a general superstition
> was so insistent and widespread
> that the idol they'd created
> now the people deified.

Sor Juana's life and career drastically changed in 1669, when, all of a sudden, after enjoying enormous success in the viceregal court, she chose the contemplative environment of the convent. She gave up earthly pleasures for a life of meditation. The transformation was amazing: she switched identities; she became somebody altogether different. The metamorphosis began with

changing her name: she ceased to be Juana Ramírez de Asbaje and became Sor Juana Inés de la Cruz, and, by virtue of her talents, was nicknamed by her contemporaries "the Tenth Muse" and "the Mexican Phoenix." First she joined a Convent of the Bare-foot Carmelites, but after three months she found the regime and routine too dogmatic, too strict. After a brief return to her life at court, she finally joined the more liberal Convent of Santa Paula, where she would stay for her remaining twenty-six years.

This decision by Sor Juana is also surrounded by mystery. "And so I entered the religious order," she writes in her *Response to Sor Filotea*, "knowing that life there entailed certain conditions (I refer to superficial, and not fundamental, regards) most repug-nant to my nature; but given the antipathy I felt for marriage, I deemed convent life the least unsuitable and the most honorable I could elect if I were to insure my salvation." But why did she quit the comfort of aristocratic circles so abruptly? Why become a nun? Was her faith strong enough to handle a daily routine of prayer and devotion? Or was she running away from scandal? Was a love affair the reason behind her escape? Sor Juana might have seen marriage as the expected objective of her period at court and wanted to escape it; she might have begun to perceive the court as too frivolous an atmosphere for serious thinking; and she might simply have imagined the reclusiveness of nuns as the best context in which to pursue her intellectual quest.

Mexico City had some twenty-nine religious institutions for nuns at the end of the seventeenth century. They were semi-autonomous and self-sufficient, dependent on the support of a centralized ecclesiastical organization, and surviving by means of educational as well as agricultural and commercial activities. Many of these convents ran girls' schools, hospitals, and orphan-ages. Young daughters, brought by their fathers, took refuge in them from the responsibilities of society. Every act, though, came under male supervision. Enraptured by the voice of Christ, nuns were often forced by their confessors to write down these blissful communications.

Entering one of these convents wasn't easy: a dowry and proof of genealogical purity were required. The latter condition perhaps

explains why, when Sor Juana entered Santa Paula, she falsified her background by declaring herself legitimate; otherwise, despite her reputation, she would have been rejected. A hierarchical structure organized different types of nuns according to their mystical elevation, degree of devotion, and administrative responsibilities. The Convent of Santa Paula had a girls' school that offered music, dance, and theater classes, in which Sor Juana participated by writing lyrics. Nuns were expected to follow a strict schedule of meals and prayers, but they joined in all sorts of activities, such as poetry tournaments, musical concerts, theatrical events, masquerades, and other happenings. On occasion lay visitors were allowed in, even invited to participate in conventual convocations, but only in restricted areas. As the critic Luis Harss states in *Sor Juana's Dream,* "It was an age of great pageantry, given to grand entries through ceremonial arches, majestic Te Deums with ringing church bells, allegorical floats and fireworks, dramatic mystery plays, rousing popular farces. Although the conventual ideal was still sacrificial self-denial, many nuns, like vestal courtesans, led quite luxurious lives, with slaves and servants. They dressed in finery, wore jewelry, enjoyed comfortable furniture, and collected valuable ornaments."

The Convent of Santa Paula was founded in 1586 by a nun from the Royal Convent of the Immaculate Conception and intended only for *criolla* women. There Sor Juana led a rather comfortable life, unlike anything modern readers might visualize when invoking images of flagellant nuns in states of mystical ecstasy. Her cell was a large apartment with sitting room and kitchen. Given considerable space for books, musical instruments, maps and other research material, she frequently found herself surrounded by silence and tranquillity conducive to writing at her leisure. She had other conveniences as well, including part-time domestic help—a servant to wash, cook, and attend to her earthly needs. A wealthy benefactor had endowed her with enough money to carry on a luxurious existence, and, judging by the accounts of her possessions, she amassed a distinguished collection of indigenous musical and scientific instruments, folk art, and other paraphernalia. Like other nuns, Sor Juana was forbidden to leave the convent's four walls, but through her reading and

artistic endeavors she was able to travel in her imagination to distant places and to seek knowledge well beyond the confines of the convent, which she often found suffocating. She served as the convent's accountant, an elective position. Her relationships with various authorities within and outside the institution, mainly men, had many ups and downs: at one point, for instance, she was forced by the prioress, in response to Father Aguiar y Seijas, to abandon her studies for several months; and she was also tormented by Father Núñez de Miranda, who constantly cautioned her against "sacrilegious paths."

Overall, the convent period was the most productive of Sor Juana's career. She was prolific, versatile, and challenging as a poet. Her thirst for knowledge was insatiable. "I myself can affirm," she wrote in the *Response to Sor Filotea,* "that what I have not understood in an author in one branch of knowledge I may understand in a second in a branch that seems remote from the first." She also was guileful, retaining her ties to the viceregal court in spite of the changing political climate. A sign of her status and influence was the commission she received in 1680 to write a poem celebrating a triumphal cathedral arch to honor the advent of a new viceregal period, that of the Marqués de la Laguna. Sor Juana composed "Allegorical Neptune" as a dedication to the architectural structure and an explanation of its allusions, which included the figure of Neptune as a reference to the marqués. The poem itself is a web of biblical and mythological references, all of which reflect the defiant idea that male power depends on female wisdom.

Such works were a source of both pride and nervousness; they kept her in the public eye. And there is the question of her faith: as seen in her *romance* "While by Grace I am inspired," belief in Christ generated suffering and confusion within her, and this hint of skepticism would increase, and be fought against, as her years in Santa Paula went on. She would fight not to be perceived as superior to the other nuns, and would visit them to comfort them, to discuss their pain, to be helpful. At the same time, though, she was quite aware that her fame and privileged position made her a target of animosity and envy, both within and without the convent, of those who, in her own words, "abhor one who excels."

This led her more than once to compare her fate to that of Jesus persecuted by the Pharisees.

Proud of her body of work, she made sure no stanza of hers was "unbecoming." But only a single poem made her truly proud, "a little trifle . . . called "El Sueño," which stands, indeed, as her most astonishing creation. Written around 1685, this long epistemological poem is Sor Juana's most intellectually challenging legacy. Also known as "Primero Sueño" (First Dream), it comprises 975 lines arranged in the free Italian form known in Spanish as *silvas*. The adjective *primero* has been taken to suggest that Sor Juana, emulating Góngora's two-part *Las Soledades* (1613), was planning to write a sequel; however, no record of a companion poem has ever been found. In this volume the translator suggests a different semantic approach: Sor Juana isn't really numbering her poem; instead, she is assuming full responsibility for the act of dreaming: "First I Dream" implies that the anonymous protagonist of the poem, the Soul, is not an abstract entity but a facet of her own self. Sor Juana's piece is about an actual dream and a symbolic one, an intellectual and a poetic quest. Moreover, her quest is multifaceted: a dream about dreaming; a dream about the limits of knowledge; a dream about the possibilities of poetry; and a dream about the antagonism between faith and reason, between received and acquired knowledge, between science and doctrine.

Much has been written about "The Dream" since Ermilo Abreu Gómez's first modern edition of 1928. It is crucial to note that Sor Juana is not actually inventing a new poetic tradition. In fact, epistemological literature in which a dream serves as an excuse to visit the concrete and abstract confines of the universe was common in antiquity. Sor Juana's points of departure and arrival, studied in detail by José Pascual Buxó, Paz, Harss, and Sabat de Rivers, were Cicero's *De re publica*, Book VI; Scipio's *Dream*; Kepler's *Somnium, Sive Astronomia Lunaris*; and, most notably, Anastasio Kircher's *Iter exstaticum coeleste*. After studying Cicero, the early-fifth-century Neoplatonist Ambrosius Macrobius established five categories for dreams: enigmatic, prophetic or visionary, oracular, insomniac, and phantasmal. Most literary quests were based on the prophetic and the oracular and followed a pat-

tern not unlike that of Dante's *Divine Comedy,* metamorphosed in modern times into what became the *Bildungsroman:* a lost soul first finds a Virgil; together they descend to the underworld; subsequently, they ascend to heaven, where they find enlightenment and peace. Sor Juana's is also a dream of *anabasis,* or "going up," but is distinct in that the human soul embarks on a solitary journey. The Soul, an androgynous entity represented by a "mournful shadow," separates itself from the bodily prison and travels around and across the earth: first it wanders in the mineral realm; then through the natural; and finally it reaches the celestial spheres, following a Neoplatonist structure, a "pyramidal" pattern in creation, from the simplest item to the most complex. Since the original text is lost, the issue of how to divide the poem has preoccupied many scholars: some divide it into twelve major progressive sections, made to resemble the twelve nocturnal hours; others suggest three: sleep, voyage, and awakening. Any way we look at it, faith in a universal order drives the quest, but the end brings only darkness, a clear sign of Sor Juana's increasing skepticism.

The poem has a strong Scholastic, Gnostic, and mystical foundation, but it doesn't parade its erudition in a presumptuous manner. Sor Juana was obviously quite familiar with a vast array of sources. From the scholastic tradition she drew on Thomism, which sought to reconcile Aristotelian philosophy and Christianity and understood that the order of universal things could be inferred by studying earthly matters; the teachings of Ramon Llull, who portrayed science as an extension of theology and believed science to be as essential as intuition, and empirical and scientific knowledge to be complements of each other; and other Jewish, Muslim, and Christian systems of thought, including those of Averroës, Maimonides, Duns Scotus, and Peter Abelard. In the Gnostic tradition, Sor Juana was well acquainted with Plotinus, who articulated a vastly influential philosophy based on the linkage and harmonious structure of earthly and celestial realms and whose concepts of "transcendence" and "emanence," approaching creation as a descendant order of things, are pervasive in "The Dream." And in the mystical tradition she made use of Kabbalah and Sufism, as well as types of Hermetic Christian systems, posit-

ing the link between the divine and human realms by way of arcane connections. Add to these astronomy and the indigenous beliefs Sor Juana derived from the Aztecs and other native Mexican peoples and the end product is quite an aggregation. But Sor Juana refuses to endorse any single approach; instead, in a twist suitable to her Baroque Latin American spirit, she adds and multiplies them, and this syncretism is her signature. Acknowledging this syncretism is crucial to our understanding the poem's overall place in world literature: its originality is not to be found in the renewal of the literary tradition of dream voyages; instead, what Sor Juana offers in "The Dream," with a Baroque style more conceptual than that of the rest of her poetry, is a silent challenge to the traditional concept of the Catholic Church. She follows her reason and trusts her faith, but the end result is disappointment: as in the myth of Phaëthon, the more we strive to know, the less we understand.

So the question emerges: Was Sor Juana a heretic? The answer is yes and no. Yes, because she dared to question faith at a time and place where Catholic dogma remained intact; no, because she failed to articulate a reformist worldview, a critical argument capable of exposing the sham. But it was never her goal to do so. As a masterpiece of art, "The Dream" could be written only far from the centers of European knowledge; it is a peripheral work of art generated by the declining echoes of Renaissance thought. Its syncretism is the colonial mask under which it hides: no original philosophical system is offered, only a quilt made of bits and pieces, a sum of disparate parts. At the same time, Sor Juana comes close to suggesting a type of vision the Enlightenment would deliver in the eighteenth century and beyond: human reason is partial, limited, relative, and unscrupulous; faith, on the other hand, is a palliative to existential doubt, but it offers no real explanation of the ways and mysteries of the cosmos. All this makes the poem unlike anything Santa Teresa de Jésus could deliver: an accumulative premodernist artifact. What's more, for Sor Juana only one aspect of human endeavor emerges triumphant in its quest: poetry. No concrete reference to it appears, but its power palpitates in each of the poem's words: both *credo* and *episteme,* belief and knowledge, are destined to fail, and divine light

cannot cure a broken soul, but the act of writing can bring happiness: poetry is survival, poetry is the only true redemption, poetry is the door to individualism and self-affirmation. In many ways, "The Dream" is a companion to Sor Juana's *Response to Sor Filotea:* a manifesto promoting freedom of expression and elevating literature to a status higher than all other human affairs, a modernist document transforming poetry into a new type of religion. This subversiveness explains why Sor Juana is a favorite today: she challenged the ecclesiastical status quo, but with a subtlety that confused her contemporaries; she fought for women's rights not with weapons but with poetry.

The period between 1691 and 1693 in Mexico City was marked by heavy rains, floods, famine, and plague. The population blamed the viceroy for their suffering, and Indians stormed the viceregal palace, setting fire to it and to nearby buildings. In an important biographical essay of 1926, Dorothy Schons writes that on June 8, 1692, "The Viceroy and his wife took refuge in the monastery of St. Francis. Everybody sought monasteries and other places of security. The soldiers were helpless. Hordes of Indians pillaged the plaza and the surrounding neighborhood. Nothing could be done to stop the terrible riot. Bells rang all night. In the nunneries and monasteries prayer was said. Jesuits and Franciscans went in procession to the plaza in an effort to quiet the rioters, but they were hissed and their images were treated with disrespect. After days and nights of terror, during which the churches ceased to function, the civil government succeeded in restoring order. Weeks and months of *azotados* [whippings] and *ahorcados* [hangings] kept alive the memory of the tumult." While in retrospect this explosion of violence can be related to the social injustice and racial repression that reigned in New Spain at the end of the seventeenth century, the consensus at the time related the events of "the apocalypse" to "our collective sins." Schons suggests that Sor Juana blamed herself for the sad state of affairs: she turned her energy to prayer and to helping convalescent nuns in Santa Paula.

The end of Sor Juana's life brought some surprises. Having given up everything, she apparently had nothing to lose. Some-

time in 1694 she signed a couple of documents of abjuration—one in blood—and thereby officially renounced humane letters, declared her loyalty to the Catholic faith, repented her sinful actions, and asked the Holy Spirit for forgiveness. "I beg your Sacramental Majesty to grant me license, to all Saints and Angels I ask for mercy, especially those assigned for voting, so that I can be proposed and received by the vote of the entire Celestial Community." Was it another theatrical ploy? Was she truly ashamed? Did she simply accept her fate? The inventory at the Convent of Santa Paula evidences a puzzling fact: at the time of her death, Sor Juana, despite her public protestations, still owned about 100 books and some 185 bundles of manuscripts and letters, signaling her ongoing defiance of the Catholic hierarchy. Obviously her spirit had not full taken *el camino de la perfección,* the road to Christ, as is also indicated by another fact: as the convent's accountant, apparently she had secretly and illegally invested her own funds and those of the institution with a banker. Rebellion, Albert Camus loved to say, is to say no. And that "no" would soon turn Sor Juana into a patriotic emblem: her portraits would be ubiquitous on stamps and on thousand-peso notes and coins, her memory repeatedly evoked in operas, films, science-fiction stories, murals, music videos, poems, studies and eulogies of all sorts, and tributes by literati in Mexico and beyond, such as Gabriela Mistral, Amado Nervo, Xavier Villaurrutia, and José Lezama Lima.

Father Calleja describes Sor Juan's final days: "The illness was extremely contagious and Sister Juana, by nature compassionate and charitable, attended all [her fellow nuns] without rest and without fear of their proximity. . . . Finally she fell ill . . . but the severity of the sickness, so extreme as to claim her life, had not the least effect on her mind." She died on April 17, 1695, at the age of forty-six. Her body was buried in the convent's graveyard, accompanied by a medallion like the one in the portraits by Miranda and Cabrera.

As she remarked in *A Spiritual Self-Defense,* she had zestfully antagonized the status quo: "Like men, do women not have a rational soul? Why then shall they not enjoy the privilege of the enlightenment of letters? Is a woman's soul not as receptive to God's

grace and glory as a man's? Then why is she not able to receive learning and knowledge, which are the lesser gifts? What divine revelation, what regulation of the Church, what rule of reason framed for us such a severe law?" And she concluded: "I have this nature; if it is evil, I am the product of it; I was born with it and with it I shall die." But the significance of Sor Juana's journey is best captured by what may be the most memorable sentence she wrote in the *Response to Sor Filotea:* "I suffer no blame, as I have no obligation; no discredit, as I have no possibility of triumphing and *ad impossibilita neme tenetur.*" No one is obliged to do the impossible.

ILAN STAVANS

Since the bibliography on Sor Juana Inés de la Cruz is incredibly vast, I limit myself to highlighting important editions, scholarly studies, essays, and biographies, as well as anthologies and translations available in English. Readers interested in more complete listings should consult Anita Arroyo's *Razón y pasión de Sor Juana* (Mexico: Editorial Porrúa, 1971), Francisco de la Maza's *Sor Juana Inés de la Cruz ante la historia,* revised by Elías Trabulse (Mexico: Universidad Nacional Autónoma de Mexico, 1980), Georgia Sabat de Rivers's entry on Sor Juana in vol. 1 of *Historia de la literatura hispanoamericana,* Luis Iñigo Madrigal, ed. (Madrid: Ediciones Cátedra, 1982), and Margo Glantz's *Obra selecta de Sor Juana Inés de la Cruz,* with a bibliography by María Dolores Bravo (Caracas: Biblioteca Ayacucho, 1994).

Abreu Gómez, Ermilo. "Iconografía de Sor Juana Inés de la Cruz," *Anales del Museo Nacional de Arqueología, Historia y Etnología* 1. Mexico: Museo Nacional de México, 1935.

———. *Sor Juana Inés de la Cruz: Biografía y biblioteca.* Mexico: Secretaría de Relaciones Exteriores, 1934.

Arenal, Electra, with Amanda Powell, trans. *Sor Juana Inés de La Cruz: Respuesta and Selection of Poems.* Critical edition, annotated and introduced. New York: Feminist Press at the City University of New York, 1994.

Arenal, Electra, with Stacey Schlau, eds. *Untold Sisters: Hispanic Nuns in Their Own Works.* Translated by Amanda Powell. Albuquerque: University of New Mexico Press, 1989.

Bénassy-Berling, Marie-Cécile. *Humanisme et religion chez Sor Juana Inés de la Cruz: La femme et la culture au XVIIième siècle.* Paris: Sorbonne, Editions Hispaniques, 1982.

Benítez, Fernando. *Los demonios en el convento: Sexo y religión en la Nueva España.* Mexico: Editorial Era, 1985.

"Building a Translation, the Re-Construction Business: Poem 145 of Sor Juana Inés de la Cruz," *Symposium,* Summer 1984. Reprinted in *The Craft of Translation,* edited by John Biguenet and Rainer Schulte. Chicago: University of Chicago Press, 1989.

Buxó, José Pascual. *Sor Juana Inés de la Cruz en el conocimiento de su sueño.* Mexico: Universidad Nacional Autónoma de Mexico, 1984.

Calleja, Diego. Biographical essay in Sor Juana's *Fama y obras póstumas.* Madrid, 1700. Reprinted in Francisco de la Maza's *Sor Juana Inés de la Cruz ante la historia.*

Franco, Jean. *Plotting Women: Gender and Representation in Mexico.* New York: Columbia University Press, 1989.

Galve, Gelvira de Toledo. *Two Hearts, One Soul: The Correspondence of the Condesa de Galve, 1688–96.* Edited, annotated, and translated by Meredith D. Dodge and Rick Hendricks. Albuquerque: University of New Mexico Press, 1993.

Harss, Luis, trans. *Sor Juana's Dream.* Bilingual edition. New York: Lumen Books, 1986.

Henríquez Ureña, Pedro. *Literary Currents in Hispanic America.* Cambridge: Harvard University Press, 1945.

Jiménez Rueda, Julio. *Santa Teresa y Sor Juana: Un paralelo imposible.* Mexico, 1942.

Lafaye, Jacques. *Quetzalcóatl and Guadalupe: The Formation of Mexican National Consciousness 1531–1813.* Translated by Benjamin Keen. Chicago: University of Chicago Press, 1974.

Lavrin, Asunción, ed. *Latin American Women: Historical Perspectives.* Westport, Conn.: Greenwood Press, 1978.

———, ed. *Sexuality and Marriage in Colonial Latin America.* Lincoln: University of Nebraska Press, 1989.

Leonard, Irving A. *Baroque Times in Old Mexico.* Ann Arbor: University of Michigan Press, 1959.

Lezama Lima, José. "La curiosidad barroca," in *La expresión americana.* Madrid: Alianza Editorial, 1969.

Ludmer, Josefina. "Las tretas del débil," in *La sartén por el mango.* Edited by Patricia Elena González and Eliana Ortega. Río Piedras, Puerto Rico: Ediciones Huracán, 1984.

Méndez Plancarte, Alfonso, with Alberto G. Salceda, eds. *Sor Juana Inés de La Cruz: Obra Completa*. Introduced and annotated. 4 vols. México: Fondo de Cultura Económica, 1951.

Menéndez y Pelayo, Marcelino. *Historia de la poesía hispano-americana*. Madrid, 1911.

Merrim, Stephanie, ed. *Feminist Perspectives on Sor Juana Inés de La Cruz*. Detroit, Mich.: Wayne State University Press, 1991.

Mistral, Gabriela. "Silueta de Sor Juana Inés de la Cruz," *Abside* 15 (1951): 501–6. Reprinted in *Lecturas para mujeres*. Mexico: Editorial Porrúa, 1967.

Nervo, Amado. *Juana de Asbaje*. Madrid, 1910.

Oviedo, Juan de. *Vida ejemplar, heroicas virtudes y apostólico ministerio del venerable padre Antonio Núñez de Miranda de la Compañía de Jesús*. Mexico, 1702.

Paz, Octavio. *Sor Juana: or, The Traps of Faith*. Translated by Margaret Sayers Peden. Cambridge: Harvard University Press, 1988.

———. "Sor Juana Inés de la Cruz (1651–1695)," *Sur* 206 (1951): 27–40. Reprinted in *Las peras del olmo*. Mexico: Universidad Nacional Autónoma de México, 1965.

———, ed. *Mexican Poetry: An Anthology*. Introduced and annotated. Translated by Samuel Beckett. Bloomington: Indiana University Press, 1958. Reprinted by Grove Press, 1985.

Pfandl, Ludwig. *Juana Inés de La Cruz, die zehnten Muse von Mexiko: Ihr Leben, Ihre Dichtung, Ihre Psyche*. Munich: H. Rinn, 1946.

Poot Herrera, Sara, ed. *Sor Juana y su mundo: Una mirada actual*. Mexico: Universidad del Claustro de Sor Juana, 1995.

Puccini, Dario. *Sor Juana Inés de la Cruz. Studio d'una personalità del barroco messicano*. Rome: Edizioni dell'Ateneo, 1967.

Reyes, Alfonso. *Las letras de Nueva España*. Mexico: Fondo de Cultura Económica, 1948.

Royer, Fanchon, trans. *The Tenth Muse*. Paterson, N.J.: St. Anthony Guild Press, 1952.

Sabat de Rivers, Georgina. *El "Sueño" de Sor Juana Inés de la Cruz: Tradiciones literarias y originalidad*. London: Tamesis, 1976.

———. *Estudios de literatura hispanoamericana: Sor Juana Inés de la Cruz y otros poetas barrocos de la Colonia.* Barcelona: PPU, 1992.

Schons, Dorothy. "Nuevos datos para la biografía de Sor Juana," *Contemporáneos* 9 (1969): 161–76.

———. "Some Obscure Points in the Life of Sor Juana Inés de la Cruz," *Modern Philology* 24:2 (November 1926).

Stavans, Ilan. "¿Es *Primero Sueño* la aventura de un fracaso intelectual?" *Exégesis* 3:9 (1990): 48–52.

Tapia Méndez, Aureliano. *Carta de Sor Juana Inés de la Cruz a su Confesor: Autodefensa espiritual.* Monterrey, Mexico: Universidad de Nuevo León, 1981.

Tavard, George Henry. *Juana Inés de La Cruz and the Theology of Beauty.* Notre Dame, Ind.: University of Notre Dame Press, 1991.

Trabulse, Elías. *El hermetismo y Sor Juana Inés de la Cruz: Orígenes e interpretación.* Mexico: Litografía Regina de Los Angeles, 1980.

Trueblood, Alan S., trans. *A Sor Juana Anthology.* Bilingual edition. Foreword by Octavio Paz. Cambridge: Harvard University Press, 1988.

Villaurrutia, Xavier. "Sor Juana Inés de la Cruz," *Obras.* Mexico: Fondo de Cultura Económica, 1966.

Vossler, Karl. *Die Welt im Traum: Eine Dichtung der "Zehten Muse von Mexiko."* Berlin: Ulrich Riemerschmidt, 1941.

Xirau, Ramón. *Genio y figura de Sor Juana Inés de la Cruz.* Buenos Aires: Editorial Universitaria, 1967.

A NOTE ON THE TEXT

The standard text of Sor Juana's works is the four-volume *Obras completas de Sor Juana Inés de la Cruz* (Mexico: Fondo de Cultura Económica, 1951, 1952, 1955, 1957). The first three volumes were edited by Alfonso Méndez Plancarte; at his death the fourth volume was completed by Alberto G. Salceda. Spanish versions of Sor Juana's poems, and the numbers assigned to them, are taken from this source. It should be noted that Sor Juana did not title her poems; titles were added by her editors.

RESPONSE TO THE MOST ILLUSTRIOUS POETESS SOR FILOTEA DE LA CRUZ

Muy ilustre Señora, mi Señora: No mi voluntad, mi poca salud y mi justo temor han suspendido tantos días mi respuesta. ¿Qué mucho si, al primer paso, encontraba para tropezar mi torpe pluma dos imposibles? El primero (y para mí el más riguroso) es saber responder a vuestra doctísima, discretísima, santísima y amorosísima carta. Y si veo que preguntado el Ángel de las Escuelas, Santo Tomás, de su silencio con Alberto Magno, su maestro, respondió que callaba porque nada sabía decir digno de Alberto, con cuánta mayor razón no callaría, no como el Santo de humildad, sino que la realidad es no saber algo digno de vos. El segundo imposible es saber agradeceros tan excesivo como no esperado favor de dar a las prensas mis borrones; merced tan sin medida que aun se le pasara por alto a la esperanza más ambiciosa y al deseo más fantástico, y que ni aun como ente de razón pudiera caber en mis pensamientos; y, en fin, de tal magnitud que no sólo no se puede estrechar a lo limitado de las voces, pero excede a la capacidad del agradecimiento, tanto por grande como por no esperado, que es lo que dijo Quintiliano: *Minorem spei, maiorem benefacti gloriam pereunt.* Y tal, que enmudecen al beneficiado.

Cuando la felizmente estéril, para ser milagrosamente fecundada, madre del Bautista vio en su casa tan desproporcionada visita como la Madre del Verbo, se le entorpeció el entendimiento y se le suspendió el discurso; y así, en vez de agradecimientos, prorrumpió en dudas y preguntas: *Et unde hoc mihi?* ¿De dónde a mí viene tal cosa? Lo mismo sucedió a Saúl cuando se vio electo y ungido rey de Israel: *Numquid non filius Iemini ego sum de minima tribu Israel, et cognatio mea novissima inter omnes de tribu Beniamin? Quare igitur locutus*

My most illustrious *señora,* dear lady. It has not þeen my will, my poor health, or my justifiable apprehension that for so many days delayed my response. How could I write, considering that at my very first step my clumsy pen encountered two obstructions in its path? The first (and, for me, the most uncompromising) is to know how to reply to your most learned, most prudent, most holy, and most loving letter. For I recall that when Saint Thomas, the Angelic Doctor of Scholasticism, was asked about his silence regarding his teacher Albertus Magnus, he replied that he had not spoken because he knew no words worthy of Albertus. With so much greater reason, must not I too be silent? Not, like the Saint, out of humility, but because in reality I know nothing I can say that is worthy of you. The second obstruction is to know how to express my appreciation for a favor as unexpected as extreme, for having my scribblings printed, a gift so immeasurable as to surpass my most ambitious aspiration, my most fervent desire, which even as a person of reason never entered my thoughts. Yours was a kindness, finally, of such magnitude that words cannot express my gratitude, a kindness exceeding the bounds of appreciation, as great as it was unexpected—which is as Quintilian said: *aspirations engender minor glory; benefices, major.* To such a degree as to impose silence on the receiver.

When the blessedly sterile—that she might miraculously become fecund—Mother of John the Baptist saw in her house such an extraordinary visitor as the Mother of the Word, her reason became clouded and her speech deserted her; and thus, in the place of thanks, she burst out with doubts and questions: *And whence is to me* [*that the mother of my Lord should come to me?*][1] And whence cometh such a thing to *me?* And so also it fell to Saul when he found himself the chosen, the anointed, King of Israel: *Am I not a son of Jemini, of the least tribe of Israel, and my kindred the last among all the families of the tribe of Benjamin? Why*

3

es mihi sermonem istum? Así yo diré: ¿de dónde, venerable Señora, de dónde a mí tanto favor? ¿Por ventura soy más que una pobre monja, la más mínima criatura del mundo y la más indigna de ocupar vuestra atención? Pues *quare locutus es mihi sermonem istum? Et unde hoc mihi?*

Ni al primer imposible tengo más que responder que no ser nada digno de vuestros ojos; ni al segundo más que admiraciones, en vez de gracias, diciendo que no soy capaz de agradeceros la más mínima parte de lo que os debo. No es afectada modestia, Señora, sino ingenua verdad de toda mi alma, que al llegar a mis manos, impresa, la carta que vuestra propiedad llamó Atenagórica prorrumpí (con no ser esto en mí muy fácil) en lágrimas de confusión, porque me pareció que vuestro favor no era más que una reconvención que Dios hace a lo mal que le correspondo; y que como a otros corrige con castigos, a mí me quiere reducir a fuerza de beneficios. Especial favor de que conozco ser su deudora, como de otros infinitos de su inmensa bondad; pero también especial modo de avergonzarme y confundirme: que es más primoroso medio de castigar hacer que yo misma, con mi conocimiento, sea el juez que me sentencie y condene mi ingratitud. Y así, cuando esto considero acá a mis solas, suelo decir: Bendito seáis vos, Señor, que no sólo no quisisteis en manos de otra criatura el juzgarme, y que ni aun en la mía lo pusisteis, sino que lo reservasteis a la vuestra, y me librasteis a mí de mí y de la sentencia que yo mismo me daría— que, forzada de mi propio conocimiento, no pudiera ser menos que de condenación—, y vos la reservasteis a vuestra misericordia, porque me amáis más de lo que yo me puedo amar.

Perdonad, Señora mía, la digresión que me arrebató la fuerza de la verdad; y si la he de confesar toda, también es buscar efugios para huir la dificultad de responder, y casi me he determinado a dejarlo al silencio; pero como éste es cosa negativa, aunque explica mucho con el énfasis de no explicar, es necesario ponerle algún breve rótulo para que se entienda lo que se pretende que el silencio diga; y si no, dirá nada el silencio, porque ése es su propio oficio: decir nada. Fue arrebatado el

then hast thou spoken this word to me?[2] And thus say I, most hon-
orable lady. Why do I receive such favor? By chance, am I other
than an humble nun, the lowliest creature of the world, the most
unworthy to occupy your attention? "Wherefore then speakest
thou so to me?" "And whence is this to me?"

Nor to the first obstruction do I have any response other than
I am little worthy of your eyes; nor to the second, other than won-
der, in the stead of thanks, saying that I am not capable of thank-
ing you for the smallest part of that which I owe you. This is not
pretended modesty, lady, but the simplest truth issuing from the
depths of my heart, that when the letter which with propriety you
called *Atenagórica* reached my hands, in print, I burst into tears of
confusion (withal, that tears do not come easily to me) because it
seemed to me that your favor was but a remonstrance God made
against the wrong I have committed, and that in the same way He
corrects others with punishment He wishes to subject me with
benefices, with this special favor for which I know myself to be
His debtor as for an infinitude of others from His boundless
kindness. I looked upon this favor as a particular way to shame
and confound me, it being the most exquisite means of castiga-
tion, that of causing me, by my own intellect, to be the judge who
pronounces sentence and who denounces my ingratitude. And
thus, when here in my solitude I think on these things, I am wont
to say: Blessed art Thou, oh Lord, for Thou hast not chosen to
place in the hands of others my judgment, nor yet in mine, but
hast reserved that to Thy own, and freed me from myself, and
from the necessity to sit in judgment on myself, which judgment,
forced from my own intellect, could be no less than condemna-
tion, but Thou hast reserved me to Thy mercy, because Thou
lovest me more than I can love myself.

I beg you, lady, to forgive this digression to which I was drawn
by the power of truth, and, if I am to confess all the truth, I shall
confess that I cast about for some manner by which I might flee
the difficulty of a reply, and was sorely tempted to take refuge in
silence. But as silence is a negative thing, though it explains a great
deal through the very stress of not explaining, we must assign
some meaning to it that we may understand what the silence is in-
tended to say, for if not, silence will say nothing, as that is its very

Sagrado Vaso de Elección al tercer Cielo, y habiendo visto los arcanos secretos de Dios, dice: *Audivit arcana Dei, quae non licet homini loqui.* No dice lo que vio, pero dice que no lo puede decir; de manera que aquellas cosas que no se pueden decir es menester decir siquiera que no se pueden decir, para que se entienda que el callar no es no haber qué decir, sino no caber en las voces lo mucho que hay que decir. Dice San Juan que si hubiera de escribir todas las maravillas que obró nuestro Redentor, no cupieran en todo el mundo los libros; y dice Vieyra, sobre este lugar, que en sola esta cláusula dijo más el Evangelista que en todo cuanto escribió; y dice muy bien el Fénix Lusitano (pero ¿cuándo no dice bien, aun cuando no dice bien?), porque aquí dice San Juan todo lo que dejó de decir y expresó lo que dejó de expresar. Así yo, Señora mía, sólo responderé que no sé qué responder; sólo agradeceré diciendo que no soy capaz de agradeceros; y diré, por breve rótulo de lo que dejo al silencio, que sólo con la confianza de favorecida y con los valimientos de honrada me puedo atrever a hablar con vuestra grandeza. Si fuere necedad, perdonadla, pues es alhaja de la dicha, y en ella ministraré yo más materia a vuestra benignidad y vos daréis mayor forma a mi reconocimiento.

No se hallaba digno Moisés, por balbuciente, para hablar con Faraón, y después, el verse tan favorecido de Dios, le infunde tales alientos, que no sólo habla con el mismo Dios, sino que se atreve a pedirle imposibles: *Ostende mihi faciem tuam.* Pues así yo, Señora mía, ya no me parecen imposibles los que puse al principio, a vista de lo que me favorecéis; porque quien hizo imprimir la Carta tan sin noticia mía, quien la intituló, quien la costeó, quien la honró tanto (siendo de todo indigna por sí y por su autora), ¿qué no hará?, ¿qué no perdonará?, ¿qué dejará de hacer y qué dejará de perdonar? Y así, debajo del supuesto de que hablo con el salvoconducto de vuestros favores y debajo del seguro de vuestra benignidad, y de que me habéis, como otro Asuero, dado a besar la punta del cetro de oro de vuestro cariño en señal de concederme benévola licencia

office: *to say nothing.* The holy Chosen Vessel, Saint Paul, having been caught up into paradise, and having heard the arcane secrets of God, *heard secret words, which it is not granted to man to utter.*[3] He does not say what he heard, he says that he cannot say it. So that of things one cannot say, it is needful to say at least that they cannot be said, so that it may be understood that not speaking is not the same as having nothing to say, but rather being unable to express the many things there are to say. Saint John says that if all the marvels our Redeemer wrought "were written every one, the world itself, I think, would not be able to contain the books that should be written."[4] And Vieyra says on this point that in this single phrase the Evangelist said more than in all else he wrote; and this same Lusitanian Phoenix speaks well (but when does he not speak well, even when it is not well he speak?) because in those words Saint John said everything left unsaid and expressed all that was left to be expressed. And thus I, lady, shall respond only that I do not know how to respond; I shall thank you in saying only that I am incapable of thanking you; and I shall say, through the indication of what I leave to silence, that it is only with the confidence of one who is favored and with the protection of one who is honorable that I presume to address your magnificence, and if this be folly, be forgiving of it, for folly may be good fortune, and in this manner I shall provide further occasion for your benignity and you will better shape my appreciation.

Because he was halting of speech, Moses thought himself unworthy to speak with Pharaoh, but after he found himself highly favored of God, and thus inspired, he not only spoke with God Almighty but dared ask the impossible: *shew me thy face.*[5] In this same manner, lady, and in view of how you favor me, I no longer see as impossible the obstructions I posed in the beginning: for who was it who had my letter printed unbeknownst to me? Who entitled it, who bore the cost, who honored it, it being so unworthy in itself, and in its author? What will such a person not do, not pardon? What would he fail to do, or fail to pardon? And thus, based on the supposition that I speak under the safe-conduct of your favor, and with the assurance of your benignity and with the knowledge that like a second Ahasuerus you have offered to me to kiss the top of the golden scepter of your affection as a sign of

para hablar y proponer en vuestra venerable presencia, digo que recibo en mi alma vuestra santísima amonestación de aplicar el estudio a Libros Sagrados, que aunque viene en traje de consejo, tendrá para mí sustancia de precepto; con no pequeño consuelo de que aun antes parece que prevenía mi obediencia vuestra pastoral insinuación, como a vuestra dirección, inferido del asunto y pruebas de la misma Carta. Bien conozco que no cae sobre ella vuestra cuerdísima advertencia, sino sobre lo mucho que habréis visto de asuntos humanos que he escrito; y así, lo que he dicho no es más que satisfaceros con ella a la falta de aplicación que habréis inferido (con mucha razón) de otros escritos míos. Y hablando con más especialidad os confieso, con la ingenuidad que ante vos es debida y con la verdad y claridad que en mi siempre es natural y costumbre, que el no haber escrito mucho de asuntos sagrados no ha sido desafición, ni de aplicación la falta, sino sobra de temor y reverencia debida a aquellas Sagradas Letras, para cuya inteligencia yo me conozco tan incapaz y para cuyo manejo soy tan indigna; resonándome siempre en los oídos, con no pequeño horror, aquella amenaza y prohibición del Señor a los pecadores como yo: *Quare tu enarras iustitias meas, et assumis testamentum meum per os tuum?;* esta pregunta, y el ver que aun a los varones doctos se prohibía el leer los Cantares hasta que pasaban de treinta años, y aun el Génesis: éste por su oscuridad, y aquéllos porque de la dulzura de aquellos epitalamios no tomase ocasión la imprudente juventud de mudar el sentido en carnales afectos. Compruébalo mi gran Padre San Jerónimo, mandando que sea esto lo último que se estudie, por la misma razón: *Ad ultimum sine periculo discat Canticum Canticorum, ne si in exordio legerit, sub carnalibus verbis spiritualium nuptiarum Epithalamium non intelligens, vulneretur;* y Séneca dice: *Teneris in annis haut clara est fides.* Pues ¿cómo me atreviera yo a tomarlo en mis indignas manos, repugnándolo el sexo, la edad y, sobre todo, las costumbres? Y así confieso que muchas veces este temor me ha quitado la pluma de la mano y ha hecho retroceder los asuntos hacia el mismo en-

conceding to me your benevolent license to speak and offer judgments in your exalted presence, I say to you that I have taken to heart your most holy admonition that I apply myself to the study of the Sacred Books, which, though it comes in the guise of counsel, will have for me the authority of a precept, but with the not insignificant consolation that even before your counsel I was disposed to obey your pastoral suggestion, as your direction, which may be inferred from the premise and arguments of my Letter. For I know well that your most sensible warning is not directed against it, but rather against those worldly matters of which I have written. And thus I had hoped with the Letter to make amends for any lack of application you may (with great reason) have inferred from others of my writings; and, speaking more particularly, I confess to you with all the candor of which you are deserving, and with the truth and clarity which are the natural custom in me, that my not having written often of sacred matters was not caused by disaffection or by want of application, but by the abundant fear and reverence due those Sacred Letters, knowing myself incapable of their comprehension and unworthy of their employment. Always resounding in my ears, with no little horror, I hear God's threat and prohibition to sinners like myself. *Why dost thou declare my justices, and take my covenant in thy mouth?*[6] This question, as well as the knowledge that even learned men are forbidden to read the Canticle of Canticles until they have passed thirty years of age, or even Genesis—the latter for its obscurity, the former in order that the sweetness of those epithalamia not serve as occasion for imprudent youth to transmute their meaning into carnal emotion, as borne out by my exalted Father Saint Jerome, who ordered that these be the last verses to be studied, and for the same reason: *And finally, one may read without peril the Song of Songs, for if it is read early one may suffer harm through not understanding those Epithalamia of the spiritual wedding which is expressed in carnal terms.* And Seneca says: *In the early years the faith is dim.* For how then would I have dared take in my unworthy hands these verses, defying gender, age, and, above all, custom? And thus I confess that many times this fear has plucked my pen from my hand and has turned my thoughts back toward the very same reason from which they had

tendimiento de quien querían brotar; el cual inconveniente no topaba en los asuntos profanos, pues una herejía contra el arte no la castiga el Santo Oficio, sino los discretos con risa y los críticos con censura; y ésta, *iusta vel iniusta, timenda non est,* pues deja comulgar y oír misa, por lo cual me da poco o ningún cuidado; porque según la misma decisión de los que lo calumnian, ni tengo obligación para saber ni aptitud para acertar; luego si lo yerro, ni es culpa ni es descrédito. No es culpa, porque no tengo obligación; no es descrédito, pues no tengo posibilidad de acertar, y *ad impossibilia nemo tenetur.* Y, a la verdad, yo nunca he escrito sino violentada y forzada y sólo por dar gusto a otros; no sólo sin complacencia, sino con positiva repugnancia, porque nunca he juzgado de mí que tenga el caudal de letras e ingenio que pide la obligación de quien escribe; y así, es la ordinaria respuesta a los que me instan, y más si es asunto sagrado: «¿Qué entendimiento tengo yo, qué estudio, qué materiales, ni qué noticias para eso, sino cuatro bachillerías superficiales? Dejen eso para quien lo entienda, que yo no quiero ruido con el Santo Oficio, que soy ignorante y tiemblo de decir alguna proposición malsonante o torcer la genuina inteligencia de algún lugar. Yo no estudio para escribir, ni menos para enseñar (que fuera en mí desmedida soberbia), sino sólo por ver si con estudiar ignoro menos.» Así lo respondo y así lo siento.

El escribir nunca ha sido dictamen propio, sino fuerza ajena; que les pudiera decir con verdad: *Vos me coegistis.* Lo que sí es verdad que no negaré (lo uno porque es notorio a todos, y lo otro porque, aunque sea contra mí, me ha hecho Dios la merced de darme grandísimo amor a la verdad) es que desde que me rayó la primera luz de la razón, fue tan vehemente y poderosa la inclinación a las letras, que ni ajenas reprensiones —que he tenido muchas—, ni propias reflejas —que he hecho no pocas—, han bastado a que deje de seguir este natural impulso que Dios puso en mí: Su Majestad sabe por qué y para qué; y sabe que le he pedido que apague la luz de mi en-

wished to be born: which obstacle did not impinge upon profane matters, for a heresy against art is not punished by the Holy Office but by the judicious with derision, and by critics with censure, and censure, *just or unjust, is not to be feared*, as it does not forbid the taking of communion or hearing of mass, and offers me little or no cause for anxiety, because in the opinion of those who defame my art, I have neither the obligation to know nor the aptitude to triumph. If, then, I err, I suffer neither blame nor discredit: I suffer no blame, as I have no obligation; no discredit, as I have no possibility of triumphing—*and no one is obliged to do the impossible.* And, in truth, I have written nothing except when compelled and constrained, and then only to give pleasure to others; not alone without pleasure of my own, but with absolute repugnance, for I have never deemed myself one who has any worth in letters or the wit necessity demands of one who would write; and thus my customary response to those who press me, above all in sacred matters, is, what capacity of reason have I? what application? what resources? what rudimentary knowledge of such matters beyond that of the most superficial scholarly degrees? Leave these matters to those who understand them; I wish no quarrel with the Holy Office, for I am ignorant, and I tremble that I may express some proposition that will cause offense or twist the true meaning of some scripture. I do not study to write, even less to teach—which in one like myself were unseemly pride—but only to the end that if I study, I will be ignorant of less. This is my response, and these are my feelings.

I have never written of my own choice, but at the urging of others, to whom with reason I might say, *You have compelled me.*[7] But one truth I shall not deny (first, because it is well-known to all, and second, because although it has not worked in my favor, God has granted me the mercy of loving truth above all else), which is that from the moment I was first illuminated by the light of reason, my inclination toward letters has been so vehement, so overpowering, that not even the admonitions of others—and I have suffered many—nor my own meditations—and they have not been few—have been sufficient to cause me to forswear this natural impulse that God placed in me: the Lord God knows why, and for what purpose. And He knows that I have prayed that He

tendimiento dejando sólo lo que baste para guardar su Ley, pues lo demás sobra, según algunos, en una mujer; y aun hay quien diga que daña. Sabe también Su Majestad que no consiguiendo esto, he intentado sepultar con mi nombre mi entendimiento, y sacrificársele sólo a quien me lo dio; y que no otro motivo me entró en religión, no obstante que al desembarazo y quietud que pedía mi estudiosa intención eran repugnantes los ejercicios y compañía de una comunidad; y después, en ella, sabe el Señor, y lo sabe en el mundo quien sólo lo debió saber, lo que intenté en orden a esconder mi nombre, y que no me lo permitió, diciendo que era tentación; y sí sería. Si yo pudiera pagaros algo de lo que os debo, Señora mía, creo que sólo os pagara en contaros esto, pues no ha salido de mi boca jamás, excepto para quien debió salir. Pero quiero que con haberos franqueado de par en par las puertas de mi corazón, haciéndoos patentes sus más sellados secretos, conozcáis que no desdice de mi confianza lo que debo a vuestra venerable persona y excesivos favores.

Prosiguiendo en la narración de mi inclinación, de que os quiero dar entera noticia, digo que no había cumplido los tres años de mi edad cuando enviando mi madre a una hermana mía, mayor que yo, a que se enseñase a leer en una de las que llaman Amigas, me llevó a mí tras ella el cariño y la travesura, y viendo que la daban lección, me encendí yo de manera en el deseo de saber leer, que engañando, a mi parecer, a la maestra, la dije que mi madre ordenaba me diese lección. Ella no lo creyó, porque no era creíble; pero, por complacer al donaire, me la dio. Proseguí yo en ir y ella prosiguió en enseñarme, ya no de burlas, porque la desengañó la experiencia; y supe leer en tan breve tiempo, que ya sabía cuando lo supo mi madre, a quien la maestra lo ocultó por darle el gusto por entero y recibir el galardón por junto; y yo lo callé, creyendo que me azotarían por haberlo

dim the light of my reason, leaving only that which is needed to keep His Law, for there are those who would say that all else is unwanted in a woman, and there are even those who would hold that such knowledge does injury. And my Holy Father knows too that as I have been unable to achieve this (my prayer has not been answered), I have sought to veil the light of my reason— along with my name—and to offer it up only to Him who bestowed it upon me, and He knows that none other was the cause for my entering into Religion, notwithstanding that the spiritual exercises and company of a community were repugnant to the freedom and quiet I desired for my studious endeavors. And later, in that community, the Lord God knows—and, in the world, only the one who must know—how diligently I sought to obscure my name, and how this was not permitted, saying it was temptation: and so it would have been. If it were in my power, lady, to repay you in some part what I owe you, it might be done by telling you this thing which has never before passed my lips, except to be spoken to the one who should hear it. It is my hope that by having opened wide to you the doors of my heart, by having made patent to you its most deeply-hidden secrets, you will deem my confidence not unworthy of the debt I owe to your most august person and to your most uncommon favors.

Continuing the narration of my inclinations, of which I wish to give you a thorough account, I will tell you that I was not yet three years old when my mother determined to send one of my elder sisters to learn to read at a school for girls we call the *Amigas*. Affection, and mischief, caused me to follow her, and when I observed how she was being taught her lessons I was so inflamed with the desire to know how to read, that deceiving—for so I knew it to be—the mistress, I told her that my mother had meant for me to have lessons too. She did not believe it, as it was little to be believed, but, to humor me, she acceded. I continued to go there, and she continued to teach me, but now, as experience had disabused her, with all seriousness; and I learned so quickly that before my mother knew of it I could already read, for my teacher had kept it from her in order to reveal the surprise and reap the reward at one and the same time. And I, you may be sure, kept the secret, fearing that I would be whipped for having acted without

hecho sin orden. Aún vive la que me enseñó (Dios la guarde), y puede testificarlo.

Acuérdome que en estos tiempos, siendo mi golosina la que es ordinaria en aquella edad, me abstenía de comer queso, porque oí decir que hacía rudos, y podía conmigo más el deseo de saber que el de comer, siendo éste tan poderoso en los niños. Teniendo yo después como seis o siete años, y sabiendo ya leer y escribir, con todas las otras habilidades de labores y costuras que deprenden las mujeres, oí decir que había Universidad y Escuelas en que se estudiaban las ciencias, en Méjico; y apenas lo oí cuando empecé a matar a mi madre con instantes e importunos ruegos sobre que, mudándome el traje, me enviase a Méjico, a casa de unos deudos que tenía, para estudiar y cursar la Universidad; ella no lo quiso hacer, e hizo muy bien; pero yo despiqué el deseo en leer muchos libros varios que tenía mi abuelo, sin que bastasen castigos ni reprensiones a estorbarlo; de manera que cuando vine a Méjico, se admiraban, no tanto del ingenio, cuanto de la memoria y noticias que tenía en edad que parecía que apenas había tenido tiempo para aprender a hablar.

Empecé a deprender gramática, en que creo no llegaron a veinte las lecciones que tomé; y era tan intenso mi cuidado, que siendo así que en las mujeres—y más en tan florida juventud— es tan apreciable el adorno natural del cabello, yo me cortaba de él cuatro o seis dedos, midiendo hasta dónde llegaba antes e imponiéndome ley de que si cuando volviese a crecer hasta allí no sabía tal o tal cosa que me había propuesto deprender en tanto que crecía, me lo había de volver a cortar en pena de la rudeza. Sucedía así que él crecía y yo no sabía lo propuesto, porque el pelo crecía aprisa y yo aprendía despacio, y con efecto le cortaba en pena de la rudeza, que no me parecía razón que estuviese vestida de cabellos cabeza que estaba tan desnuda de noticias, que era más apetecible adorno. Entréme religiosa, porque aunque conocía que tenía el estado cosas (de las accesorias hablo, no de las formales) muchas repugnantes a mi genio,

permission. The woman who taught me, may God bless and keep her, is still alive and can bear witness to all I say.

I also remember that in those days, my tastes being those common to that age, I abstained from eating cheese because I had heard that it made one slow of wits, for in me the desire for learning was stronger than the desire for eating—as powerful as that is in children. When later, being six or seven, and having learned how to read and write, along with all the other skills of needlework and household arts that girls learn, it came to my attention that in Mexico City there were Schools, and a University, in which one studied the sciences. The moment I heard this, I began to plague my mother with insistent and importunate pleas: she should dress me in boy's clothing and send me to Mexico City to live with relatives, to study and be tutored at the University. She would not permit it, and she was wise, but I assuaged my disappointment by reading the many and varied books belonging to my grandfather, and there were not enough punishments, nor reprimands, to prevent me from reading: so that when I came to the city many marveled, not so much at my natural wit, as at my memory, and at the amount of learning I had mastered at an age when many have scarcely learned to speak well.

I began to study Latin grammar—in all, I believe, I had no more than twenty lessons—and so intense was my concern that though among women (especially a woman in the flower of her youth) the natural adornment of one's hair is held in such high esteem, I cut off mine to the breadth of some four to six fingers, measuring the place it had reached, and imposing upon myself the condition that if by the time it had again grown to that length I had not learned such and such a thing I had set for myself to learn while my hair was growing, I would again cut it off as punishment for being so slow-witted. And it did happen that my hair grew out and still I had not learned what I had set for myself—because my hair grew quickly and I learned slowly—and in fact I did cut it in punishment for such stupidity: for there seemed to me no cause for a head to be adorned with hair and naked of learning—which was the more desired embellishment. And so I entered the religious order, knowing that life there entailed certain conditions (I refer to superficial, and not fundamental, regards) most repugnant

con todo, para la total negación que tenía al matrimonio, era lo menos desproporcionado y lo más decente que podía elegir en materia de la seguridad que deseaba de mi salvación; a cuyo primer respeto (como al fin más importante) cedieron y sujetaron la cerviz todas las impertinencillas de mi genio, que eran de querer vivir sola; de no querer tener ocupación obligatoria que embarazase la libertad de mi estudio, ni rumor de comunidad que impidiese el sosegado silencio de mis libros. Esto me hizo vacilar algo en la determinación, hasta que alumbrándome personas doctas de que era tentación, la vencí con el favor divino y tomé el estado que tan indignamente tengo. Pensé yo que huía de mí misma, pero, ¡miserable de mí!, trájeme a mí conmigo y traje mi mayor enemigo en esta inclinación, que no sé determinar si por prenda o castigo me dio el Cielo, pues de apagarse o embarazarse con tanto ejercicio que la religión tiene, reventaba como pólvora, y se verificaba en mí el *privatio est causa appetitus.*

Volví (mal dije, pues nunca cesé); proseguí, digo, a la estudiosa tarea (que para mí era descanso en todos los ratos que sobraban a mi obligación) de leer y más leer, de estudiar y más estudiar, sin más maestro que los mismos libros. Ya se ve cuán duro es estudiar en aquellos caracteres sin alma, careciendo de la voz viva y explicación del maestro; pues todo este trabajo sufría yo muy gustosa por amor de las letras. ¡Oh, si hubiese sido por amor de Dios, que era lo acertado, cuánto hubiera merecido! Bien que yo procuraba elevarlo cuanto podía y dirigirlo a su servicio, porque el fin a que aspiraba era a estudiar Teología, pareciéndome menguada inhabilidad, siendo católica, no saber todo lo que en esta vida se puede alcanzar, por medios naturales, de los divinos misterios; y que siendo monja y no seglar debía, por el estado eclesiástico, profesar letras; y más siendo hija de un San Jerónimo y de una Santa Paula, que era degenerar de tan doctos padres ser idiota la hija. Esto me proponía yo de mí misma y me parecia razón; si no es que era (y eso es lo más cierto) lisonjear y aplaudir a mi propia

to my nature; but given the total antipathy I felt for marriage, I deemed convent life the least unsuitable and the most honorable I could elect if I were to insure my salvation. Working against that end, first (as, finally, the most important) was the matter of all the trivial aspects of my nature that nourished my pride, such as wishing to live alone, and wishing to have no obligatory occupation that would inhibit the freedom of my studies, nor the sounds of a community that would intrude upon the peaceful silence of my books. These desires caused me to falter some while in my decision, until certain learned persons enlightened me, explaining that they were temptation, and, with divine favor, I overcame them, and took upon myself the state which now so unworthily I hold. I believed that I was fleeing from myself, but—wretch that I am!—I brought with me my worst enemy, my inclination, which I do not know whether to consider a gift or a punishment from Heaven, for once dimmed and encumbered by the many activities common to Religion, that inclination exploded in me like gunpowder, proving how *privation is the source of appetite.*

I turned again (which is badly put, for I never ceased), I continued, then, in my studious endeavour (which for me was respite during those moments not occupied by my duties) of reading and more reading, of study and more study, with no teachers but my books. Thus I learned how difficult it is to study those soulless letters, lacking a human voice or the explication of a teacher. But I suffered this labor happily for my love of learning. Oh, had it only been for love of God, which were proper, how worthwhile it would have been! I strove mightily to elevate these studies, to dedicate them to His service, as the goal to which I aspired was to study Theology—it seeming to me debilitating for a Catholic not to know everything in this life of the Divine Mysteries that can be learned through natural means—and, being a nun and not a layperson, it was seemly that I profess my vows to learning through ecclesiastical channels; and especially, being a daughter of a Saint Jerome and a Saint Paula, it was essential that such erudite parents not be shamed by a witless daughter. This is the argument I proposed to myself, and it seemed to me well-reasoned. It was, however (and this cannot be denied) merely glorification and ap-

inclinación, proponiéndola como obligatorio su propio gusto.

Con esto proseguí, dirigiendo siempre, como he dicho, los pasos de mi estudio a la cumbre de la Sagrada Teología; pareciéndome preciso, para llegar a ella, subir por los escalones de las ciencias y artes humanas, porque ¿cómo entenderá el estilo de la Reina de las Ciencias quien aún no sabe el de las ancilas? ¿Cómo sin Lógica sabría yo los métodos generales y particulares con que está escrita la Sagrada Escritura? ¿Cómo sin Retórica entendería sus figuras, tropos y locuciones? ¿Cómo sin Física, tantas cuestiones naturales de las naturalezas de los animales de los sacrificios, donde se simbolizan tantas cosas ya declaradas y otras muchas que hay? ¿Cómo si el sanar Saúl al sonido del arpa de David fue virtud y fuerza natural de la música, o sobrenatural que Dios quiso poner en David? ¿Cómo sin Aritmética se podrán entender tantos cómputos de años, de días, de meses, de horas, de hebdómadas tan misteriosas como las de Daniel, y otras para cuya inteligencia es necesario saber las naturalezas, concordancias y propiedades de los números? ¿Cómo sin Geometría se podrán medir el Arca Santa del Testamento y la Ciudad Santa de Jerusalén, cuyas misteriosas mensuras hacen un cubo con todas sus dimensiones, y aquel repartimiento proporcional de todas sus partes tan maravilloso? ¿Cómo sin Arquitectura, el gran Templo de Salomón, donde fue el mismo Dios el artífice que dio la disposición y la traza, y el Sabio Rey sólo fue sobrestante que la ejecutó; donde no había basa sin misterio, columna sin símbolo, cornisa sin alusión, arquitrabe sin significado; y así de otras sus partes, sin que el más mínimo filete estuviese sólo por el servicio y complemento del Arte, sino simbolizando cosas mayores? ¿Cómo sin grande conocimiento de reglas y partes de que consta la Historia se entenderán los libros historiales? Aquellas recapitulaciones en que muchas veces se pospone en la narración lo que en el hecho sucedió primero. ¿Cómo sin grande noticia de ambos Derechos podrán entenderse los li-

probation of my inclination, and enjoyment of it offered as justi-
fication.

And so I continued, as I have said, directing the course of my
studies toward the peak of Sacred Theology, it seeming necessary
to me, in order to scale those heights, to climb the steps of the hu-
man sciences and arts; for how could one undertake the study of
the Queen of Sciences if first one had not come to know her ser-
vants? How, without Logic, could I be apprised of the general
and specific way in which the Holy Scripture is written? How,
without Rhetoric, could I understand its figures, its tropes, its lo-
cutions? How, without Physics, so many innate questions con-
cerning the nature of animals, their sacrifices, wherein exist so
many symbols, many already declared, many still to be discov-
ered? How should I know whether Saul's being refreshed by the
sound of David's harp was due to the virtue and natural power of
Music, or to a transcendent power God wished to place in David?
How, without Arithmetic, could one understand the computa-
tions of the years, days, months, hours, those mysterious weeks
communicated by Gabriel to Daniel, and others for whose under-
standing one must know the nature, concordance, and properties
of numbers? How, without Geometry, could one measure the
Holy Arc of the Covenant and the Holy City of Jerusalem, whose
mysterious measures are foursquare in all their dimensions, as
well as the miraculous proportions of all their parts? How, with-
out Architecture, could one know the great Temple of Solomon,
of which God Himself was the Author who conceived the dispo-
sition and the design, and the Wise King but the overseer who ex-
ecuted it, of which temple there was no foundation without
mystery no column without symbolism, no cornice without allu-
sion, no architrave without significance; and similarly others of its
parts, of which the least fillet was never intended solely for the
service and complement of Art, but as symbol of greater things?
How, without great knowledge of the laws and parts of which
History is comprised, could one understand historical Books? Or
those recapitulations in which many times what happened first is
seen in the narrated account to have happened later? How, with-
out great learning in Canon and Civil Law, could one understand
Legal Books? How, without great erudition, could one apprehend

bros legales? ¿Cómo sin grande erudición tantas cosas de historias profanas, de que hace mención la Sagrada Escritura; tantas costumbres de gentiles, tantos ritos, tantas maneras de hablar? ¿Cómo sin muchas reglas y lección de Santos Padres se podrá entender la oscura locución de los Profetas? Pues sin ser muy perito en la Música, ¿cómo se entenderán aquellas proporciones musicales y sus primores que hay en tantos lugares, especialmente en aquellas peticiones que hizo a Dios Abraham, por las Ciudades, de que si perdonaría habiendo cincuenta justos, y de este número bajó a cuarenta y cinco, que es sesquinona y es como de mi a re; de aquí a cuarenta, que es sesquioctava y es como de re a mi; de aquí a treinta, que es sesquitercia, que es la del diatesarón; de aquí a veinte, que es la proporción sesquiáltera, que es la del diapente; de aquí a diez, que es la dupla, que es el diapasón; y como no hay más proporciones armónicas no pasó de ahí? Pues ¿cómo se podrá entender esto sin Música? Allá en el Libro de Job le dice Díos: *Numquid coniungere valebis micantes stellas Pleiadas, aut gyrum Arcturi poteris dissipare? Numquid producis Luciferum in tempore suo, et Vesperum super filios terrae consurgere facis?* cuyos términos, sin noticia de Astrología, será imposible entender. Y no sólo estas nobles ciencias; pero no hay arte mecánica que no mencione. Y en fin, ¿cómo el Libro que comprende todos los libros, y la Ciencia en que se incluyen todas las ciencias, para cuya inteligencia todas sirven? Y después de saberlas todas (que ya se ve que no es fácil, ni aun posible), pide otra circunstancia más que todo lo dicho, que es una continua oración y pureza de vida, para impetrar de Dios aquella purgación de ánimo e iluminación de mente que es menester para la inteligencia de cosas tan altas; y si esto falta, de nada sirve lo demás.

Del Angélico Doctor Santo Tomás dice la Iglesia estas palabras: *In difficultatibus locorum Sacrae Scripturae ad orationem ieiunium adhibebat. Quin etiam sodali suo Fratri Reginaldo dicere solebat, quidquid sciret, non tam studio, aut labore suo peperisse, quam divinitus traditum accepisse.* Pues yo, tan distante de la virtud y las letras, ¿cómo había de tener

the secular histories of which the Holy Scripture makes mention, such as the many customs of the Gentiles, their many rites, their many ways of speaking? How without the abundant laws and lessons of the Holy Fathers could one understand the obscure lesson of the Prophets? And without being expert in Music, how could one understand the exquisite precision of the musical proportions that grace so many Scriptures, particularly those in which Abraham beseeches God in defense of the Cities, asking whether He would spare the place were there but fifty just men therein; and then Abraham reduced that number to five less than fifty, forty-five, which is a ninth, and is as Mi to Re; then to forty, which is a tone, and is as Re to Mi; from forty to thirty, which is a diatessaron, the interval of the perfect fourth; from thirty to twenty, which is the perfect fifth, and from twenty to ten, which is the octave, the diapason; and as there are no further harmonic proportions, made no further reductions. How might one understand this without Music? And there in the Book of Job, God says to Job: *Shalt thou be able to join together the shining stars the Pleiades, or canst thou stop the turning about of Arcturus? Canst thou bring forth the day star in its time and make the evening star to rise upon the children of the earth?*[8] Which message, without knowledge of Astrology, would be impossible to apprehend. And not only these noble sciences; there is no applied art that is not mentioned. And, finally, in consideration of the Book that comprises all books, and the Science in which all sciences are embraced, and for whose comprehension all sciences serve, and even after knowing them all (which we now see is not easy, nor even possible), there is one condition that takes precedence over all the rest, which is uninterrupted prayer and purity of life, that one may entreat of God that purgation of spirit and illumination of mind necessary for the understanding of such elevated matters: and if that be lacking, none of the aforesaid will have been of any purpose.

Of the Angelic Doctor Saint Thomas the Church affirms: *When reading the most difficult passages of the Holy Scripture, he joined fast with prayer. And he was wont to say to his companion Brother Reginald that all he knew derived not so much from study or his own labor as from the grace of God.* How then should I—

ánimo para escribir? Y así, por tener algunos principios granjeados, estudiaba continuamente diversas cosas, sin tener para alguna particular inclinación, sino para todas en general; por lo cual, el haber estudiado en unas más que en otras no ha sido en mí elección, sino que el acaso de haber topado más a mano libros de aquellas facultades les ha dado, sin arbitrio mío, la preferencia. Y como no tenía interés que me moviese, ni límite de tiempo que me estrechase el continuado estudio de una cosa por la necesidad de los grados, casi a un tiempo estudiaba diversas cosas o dejaba unas por otras; bien que en eso observaba orden, porque a unas llamaba estudio y a otras diversión; y en éstas descansaba de las otras de donde se sigue que he estudiado muchas cosas y nada sé, porque las unas han embarazado a las otras. Es verdad que esto digo de la parte práctica en las que la tienen, porque claro está que mientras se mueve la pluma descansa el compás, y mientras se toca el arpa sosiega el órgano, *et sic de caeteris;* porque como es menester mucho uso corporal para adquirir hábito, nunca le puede tener perfecto quien se reparte en varios ejercicios; pero en lo formal y especulativo sucede al contrario, y quisiera yo persuadir a todos con mi experiencia a que no sólo no estorban, pero se ayudan dando luz y abriendo camino las unas para las otras, por variaciones y ocultos engarces—que para esta cadena universal les puso la sabiduría de su Autor—, de manera que parece se corresponden y están unidas con admirable trabazón y concierto. Es la cadena que fingieron los antiguos que salía de la boca de Júpiter, de donde pendían todas las cosas eslabonadas unas con otras. Así lo demuestra el R. P. Atanasio Quirquerio en su curioso libro *De Magnete.* Todas las cosas salen de Dios, que es el centro a un tiempo y la circunferencia de donde salen y donde paran todas las líneas criadas.

Yo de mí puedo asegurar que lo que no entiendo en un autor de una facultad lo suelo entender en otro de otra que parece muy distante; y esos propios, al explicarse, abren ejemplos metafóricos de otras artes, como cuando dicen los lógicos que el medio se ha con los términos como se ha una medida con dos

so lacking in virtue and so poorly read—find courage to write? But as I had acquired the rudiments of learning, I continued to study ceaselessly divers subjects, having for none any particular inclination, but for all in general; and having studied some more than others was not owing to preference, but to the chance that more books on certain subjects had fallen into my hands, causing the election of them through no discretion of my own. And as I was not directed by preference, nor, forced by the need to fulfill certain scholarly requirements, constrained by time in the pursuit of any subject, I found myself free to study numerous topics at the same time, or to leave some for others; although in this scheme some order was observed, for some I deigned study and others diversion, and in the latter I found respite from the former. From which it follows that though I have studied many things I know nothing, as some have inhibited the learning of others. I speak specifically of the practical aspect of those arts that allow practice, because it is clear that when the pen moves the compass must lie idle, and while the harp is played the organ is stilled, *et sic de caeteris.* And because much practice is required of one who would acquire facility, none who divides his interest among various exercises may reach perfection. Whereas in the formal and theoretical arts the contrary is true, and I would hope to persuade all with my experience, which is that one need not inhibit the other, but, in fact, each may illuminate and open the way to others, by nature of their variations and their hidden links, which were placed in this universal chain by the wisdom of their Author in such a way that they conform and are joined together with admirable unity and harmony. This is the very chain the ancients believed did issue from the mouth of Jupiter, from which were suspended all things linked one with another, as is demonstrated by the Reverend Father Athanasius Kircher in his curious book, *De Magnate.*[9] All things issue from God, Who is at once the center and the circumference from which and in which all lines begin and end.

I myself can affirm that what I have not understood in an author in one branch of knowledge I may understand in a second in a branch that seems remote from the first. And authors, in their elucidation, may suggest metaphorical examples in other arts: as

cuerpos distantes, para conferir si son iguales o no; y que la oración del lógico anda como la línea recta, por el camino más breve, y la del retórico se mueve, como la corva, por el más largo, pero van a un mismo punto los dos; y cuando dicen que los expositores son como la mano abierta y los escolásticos como el puño cerrado. Y así no es disculpa, ni por tal la doy, el haber estudiado diversas cosas, pues éstas antes se ayudan, sino que el no haber aprovechado ha sido ineptitud mía y debilidad de mi entendimiento, no culpa de la variedad. Lo que sí pudiera ser descargo mío es el sumo trabajo no sólo en carecer de maestro, sino de condiscípulos con quienes conferir y ejercitar lo estudiado, teniendo sólo por maestro un libro mudo, por condiscípulo un tintero insensible; y en vez de explicación y ejercicio, muchos estorbos, no sólo los de mis religiosas obligaciones (que éstas ya se sabe cuán útil y provechosamente gastan el tiempo), sino de aquellas cosas accesorias de una comunidad: como estar yo leyendo y antojárseles en la celda vecina tocar y cantar; estar yo estudiando y pelear dos criadas y venirme a constituir juez de su pendencia; estar yo escribiendo y venir una amiga a visitarme, haciéndome muy mala obra con muy buena voluntad, donde es preciso no sólo admitir el embarazo, pero quedar agradecida del perjuicio. Y esto es continuamente, porque como los ratos que destino a mi estudio son los que sobran de lo regular de la comunidad, esos mismos les sobran a las otras para venirme a estorbar; y sólo saben cuánta verdad es ésta los que tienen experiencia de vida común, donde sólo la fuerza de la vocación puede hacer que mi natural esté gustoso, y el mucho amor que hay entre mí y mis amadas hermanas, que como el amor es unión, no hay para él extremos distantes.

En esto sí confieso que ha sido inexplicable mi trabajo; y así no puedo decir lo que con envidia oigo a otros: que no les ha costado afán el saber. ¡Dichosos ellos! A mí, no el saber (que aún no sé), sólo el desear saber me le ha costado tan grande que

when logicians say that to prove whether parts are equal, the mean is to the extremes as a determined measure to two equidistant bodies; or in stating how the argument of the logician moves, in the manner of a straight line, along the shortest route, while that of the rhetorician moves, as a curve, by the longest, but that both finally arrive at the same point. And similarly, as it is when they say that the Expositors are like an open hand, and the Scholastics like a closed fist. And thus it is no apology, nor do I offer it as such, to say that I have studied many subjects, seeing that each augments the other; but that I have not profited is the fault of my own ineptitude and the inadequacy of my intelligence, not the fault of the variety. But what may be offered as exoneration is that I undertook this great task without benefit of teacher, or fellow students with whom to confer and discuss, having for a master no other than a mute book, and for a colleague, an insentient inkwell; and in the stead of explication and exercise, many obstructions, not merely those of my religious obligations (for it is already known how useful and advantageous is the time employed in them), rather, all the attendant details of living in a community: how I might be reading, and those in the adjoining cell would wish to play their instruments, and sing; how I might be studying, and two servants who had quarreled would select me to judge their dispute; or how I might be writing, and a friend come to visit me, doing me no favor but with the best of will, at which time one must not only accept the inconvenience, but be grateful for the hurt. And such occurrences are the normal state of affairs, for as the times I set apart for study are those remaining after the ordinary duties of the community are fulfilled, they are the same moments available to my sisters, in which they may come to interrupt my labor; and only those who have experience of such a community will know how true this is, and how it is only the strength of my vocation that allows me happiness; that, and the great love existing between me and my beloved sisters, for as love is union, it knows no extremes of distance.

With this I confess how interminable has been my labor; and how I am unable to say what I have with envy heard others state—that they have not been plagued by the thirst for knowledge: blessed are they. For me, not the knowing (for still I do not

pudiera decir con mi Padre San Jerónimo (aunque no con su aprovechamiento): *Quid ibi laboris insumpserim, quid sustinuerim difficultatis, quoties desperaverim, quotiesque cessaverim et contentione discendi rursus inceperim; testis est conscientia, tam mea, qui passus sum, quam eorum qui mecum duxerunt vitam.* Menos los compañeros y testigos (que aun de ese alivio he carecido), lo demás bien puedo asegurar con verdad. ¡Y que haya sido tal esta mi negra inclinación que todo lo haya vencido!

Solía sucederme que, como entre otros beneficios, debo a Dios un natural tan blando y tan afable y las religiosas me aman mucho por él (sin reparar, como buenas, en mis faltas) y con esto gustan mucho de mi compañía; conociendo esto, y movida del grande amor que las tengo, con mayor motivo que ellas a mí, gusto más de la suya; así, me solía ir los ratos que a unas y a otras nos sobraban a consolarlas y recrearme con su conversación. Reparé que en este tiempo hacía falta a mi estudio, y hacía voto de no entrar en celda alguna si no me obligase a ello la obediencia o la caridad, porque sin este freno tan duro, al de sólo propósito le rompiera el amor; y este voto (conociendo mi fragilidad) le hacía por un mes o por quince días; y dando, cuando se cumplía, un día o dos de treguas, lo volvía a renovar, sirviendo este día no tanto a mi descanso (pues nunca lo ha sido para mí el no estudiar) cuanto a que no me tuviesen por áspera, retirada e ingrata al no merecido cariño de mis carísimas hermanas.

Bien se deja en esto conocer cuál es la fuerza de mi inclinación. Bendito sea Dios, que quiso fuese hacia las letras y no hacia otro vicio que fuera en mí casi insuperable; y bien se infiere también cuán contra la corriente han navegado (o, por mejor decir, han naufragado) mis pobres estudios. Pues aún falta por referir lo más arduo de las dificultades, que las de hasta aquí sólo han sido estorbos obligatorios y casuales, que indirectamente lo son, y faltan los positivos, que directamente han tirado a estorbar y prohibir el ejercicio. ¿Quién no creerá,

know), merely the desiring to know, has been such torment that I can say, as has my Father Saint Jerome (although not with his accomplishment) . . . *my conscience is witness to what effort I have expended, what difficulties I have suffered, how many times I have despaired, how often I have ceased my labors and turned to them again, driven by the hunger for knowledge; my conscience is witness, and that of those who have lived beside me.* With the exception of the companions and witnesses (for I have been denied even this consolation), I can attest to the truth of these words. And to the fact that even so, my dark inclination has been so great that it has conquered all else!

It has been my fortune that, among other benefices, I owe to God a most tender and affable nature, and because of it my sisters (who being good women do not take note of my faults) hold me in great affection, and take pleasure in my company; and knowing this, and moved by the great love I hold for them—having greater reason than they—I enjoy even more *their* company. Thus I was wont in our rare idle moments to visit among them, offering them consolation and entertaining myself in their conversation. I could not help but note, however, that in these times I was neglecting my study, and I made a vow not to enter any cell unless obliged by obedience or charity; for without such a compelling constraint—the constraint of mere intention not being sufficient—my love would be more powerful than my will. I would (knowing well my frailty) make this vow for the period of a few weeks, or a month, and when that time had expired, I would allow myself a brief respite of a day or two before renewing it, using that time not so much for rest (for *not* studying has never been restful for me) as to assure that I not be deemed cold, remote, or ungrateful in the little-deserved affection of my dearest sisters.

In this practice one may recognize the strength of my inclination. I give thanks to God, Who willed that such an ungovernable force be turned toward letters and not to some other vice. From this it may also be inferred how obdurately against the current my poor studies have sailed (more accurately, have foundered). For still to be related is the most arduous of my difficulties—those mentioned until now, either compulsory or fortuitous, being merely tangential—and still unreported the more-directly aimed

viendo tan generales aplausos, que he navegado viento en popa
y mar en leche sobre las palmas de las aclamaciones comunes?
Pues Dios sabe que no ha sido muy así, porque entre las flores
de esas mismas aclamaciones se han levantado y despertado
tales áspides de emulaciones y persecuciones cuantas no podré
contar, y los que más nocivos y sensibles para mí han sido no
son aquellos que con declarado odio y malevolencia me han
perseguido, sino los que amándome y deseando mi bien (y por
ventura mereciendo mucho con Dios por la buena intención)
me han mortificado y atormentado más que los otros con
aquel: *No conviene a la santa ignorancia que deben, este estu-
dio; se ha de perder, se ha de desvanecer en tanta altura con su
misma perspicacia y agudeza.* ¿Qué me habrá costado resistir
esto? ¡Rara especie de martirio, donde yo era el mártir y me era
el verdugo!

Pues por la—en mí dos veces infeliz—habilidad de hacer
versos, aunque fuesen sagrados, ¿qué pesadumbres no me han
dado o cuáles no me han dejado de dar? Cierto, Señora mía,
que algunas veces me pongo a considerar que el que se señala—
o le señala Dios, que es quien sólo lo puede hacer—es recibido
como enemigo común, porque parece a algunos que usurpa los
aplausos que ellos merecen o que hace estanque de las admira-
ciones a que aspiraban, y así le persiguen.

Aquella ley políticamente bárbara de Atenas por la cual salía
desterrado de su república el que se señalaba en prendas y vir-
tudes porque no tiranizase con ellas la libertad pública todavía
dura, todavía se observa en nuestros tiempos, aunque no hay
ya aquel motivo de los atenienses; pero hay otro no menos efi-
caz, aunque no tan bien fundado, pues parece máxima del
impío Maquiavelo, que es aborrecer al que se señala porque
desluce a otros. Así sucede y así sucedió siempre.

Y si no, ¿cuál fue la causa de aquel rabioso odio de los
fariseos contra Cristo, habiendo tantas razones para lo con-
trario? Porque si miramos su presencia, ¿cuál prenda más ama-

slings and arrows that have acted to impede and prevent the exercise of my study. Who would have doubted, having witnessed such general approbation, that I sailed before the wind across calm seas, amid the laurels of widespread acclaim. But our Lord God knows that it has not been so; He knows how from amongst the blossoms of this very acclaim emerged such a number of aroused vipers, hissing their emulation and their persecution, that one could not count them. But the most noxious, those who most deeply wounded me, have not been those who persecuted me with open loathing and malice, but rather those who in loving me and desiring my well-being (and who are deserving of God's blessing for their good intent) have mortified and tormented me more than those others with their abhorrence. "Such studies are not in conformity with sacred innocence; surely she will be lost; surely she will, by cause of her very perspicacity and acuity, grow heady at such exalted heights." How was I to endure? An uncommon sort of martyrdom in which I was both martyr and executioner.

And as for my (in me, twice hapless) facility in making verses, even though they be sacred verses, what sorrows have I not suffered? What sorrows not ceased to suffer? Be assured, lady, it is often that I have meditated on how one who distinguishes himself—or one on whom God chooses to confer distinction, for it is only He who may do so—is received as a common enemy, because it seems to some that he usurps the applause they deserve, or that he dams up the admiration to which they aspired, and so they persecute that person.

That politically barbaric law of Athens by which any person who excelled by cause of his natural gifts and virtues was exiled from his Republic in order that he not threaten the public freedom still endures, is still observed in our day, although not for the reasons held by the Athenians. Those reasons have been replaced by another, no less efficient though not as well founded, seeming, rather, a maxim more appropriate to that impious Machiavelli—which is to abhor one who excels, because he deprives others of regard. And thus it happens, and thus it has always happened.

For if not, what was the cause of the rage and loathing the Pharisees directed against Christ, there being so many reasons to love

ble que aquella divina hermosura? ¿Cuál más poderosa para
arrebatar los corazones? Si cualquiera belleza humana tiene ju-
risdicción sobre los albedríos y con blanda y apetecida violen-
cia los sabe sujetar, ¿qué haría aquélla con tantas prerrogativas
y dotes soberanos? ¿Qué haría, qué movería y qué no haría y
qué no movería aquella incomprensible beldad, por cuyo her-
moso rostro, como por un terso cristal, se estaban trans-
parentando los rayos de la Divinidad? ¿Qué no movería aquel
semblante, que sobre incomparables perfecciones en lo hu-
mano señalaba iluminaciones de divino? Si el de Moisés, de
sólo la conversación con Dios, era intolerable a la flaqueza de
la vista humana, ¿qué sería el del mismo Dios humanado? Pues
si vamos a las demás prendas, ¿cuál más amable que aquella ce-
lestial modestia, que aquella suavidad y blandura derramando
misericordias en todos sus movimientos, aquella profunda
humildad y mansedumbre, aquellas palabras de vida eterna
y eterna sabiduría? Pues ¿cómo es posible que esto no les
arrebatara las almas, que no fuesen enamorados y elevados
tras él?

Dice la Santa Madre y madre mía Teresa que después que vio
la hermosura de Cristo, quedó libre de poderse inclinar a
criatura alguna, porque ninguna cosa veía que no fuese fealdad,
comparada con aquella hermosura. Pues, ¿cómo en los hom-
bres hizo tan contrarios efectos? Y ya que como toscos y viles
no tuvieran conocimiento ni estimación de sus perfecciones,
siquiera como interesables, ¿no les moviera sus propias conve-
niencias y utilidades en tantos beneficios como les hacía,
sanando los enfermos, resucitando los muertos, curando los
endemoniados? Pues ¿cómo no le amaban? ¡Ay, Dios, que por
eso mismo no le amaban, por eso mismo le aborrecían! Así lo
testificaron ellos mismos.

Júntanse en su concilio y dicen: *Quid facimus, quia hic homo
multa signa facit*? ¿Hay tal causa? Si dijeran: éste es un malhe-
chor, un transgresor de la ley, un alborotador que con engaños
alborota el pueblo, mintieran, como mintieron cuando lo
decían; pero eran causales más congruentes a lo que solicita-
ban, que era quitarle la vida; mas dar por causal que hace cosas
señaladas no parece de hombres doctos, cuales eran los

Him? If we behold His presence, what is more to be loved than that Divine beauty? What more powerful to stir one's heart? For if ordinary human beauty holds sway over strength of will, and is able to subdue it with tender and enticing vehemence, what power would Divine beauty exert, with all its prerogatives and sovereign endowments? What might move, what affect, what not move and not affect, such incomprehensible beauty, that beauteous face through which, as through a polished crystal, were diffused the rays of Divinity? What would not be moved by that semblance which beyond incomparable human perfections revealed Divine illuminations? If the visage of Moses, merely from conversation with God, caused men to fear to come near him, how much finer must be the face of God-made-flesh? And among other virtues, what more to be loved than that celestial modesty? That sweetness and kindness disseminating mercy in every movement? That profound humility and gentleness? Those words of eternal life and eternal wisdom? How therefore is it possible that such beauty did not stir their souls, that they did not follow after Him, enamored and enlightened?

The Holy Mother, my Mother Teresa, says that when she beheld the beauty of Christ, never again was she inclined toward any human creature, for she saw nothing that was not ugliness compared to such beauty. How was it then that in men it engendered such contrary reactions? For although they were uncouth and vile and had no knowledge or appreciation of His perfections, not even as they might profit from them, how was it they were not moved by the many advantages of such benefices as He performed for them, healing the sick, resurrecting the dead, restoring those possessed of the devil? How was it they did not love Him? But God is witness that it was for these very acts they did not love Him, that they despised Him. As they themselves testified.

They gather together in their council and say: *What do we? for this man doth many miracles.*[10] Can this be cause? If they had said: here is an evil-doer, a transgressor of the law, a rabble-rouser who with deceit stirs up the populace, they would have lied—as they did indeed lie when they spoke these things. But there were more apposite reasons for effecting what they desired, which was to take His life; and to give as reason that he had performed won-

fariseos. Pues así es que cuando se apasionan los hombres doctos prorrumpen en semejantes inconsecuencias. En verdad que sólo por eso salió determinado que Cristo muriese. Hombres, si es que así se os puede llamar, siendo tan brutos, ¿por qué es esa tan cruel determinación? No responden más sino que *multa signa facit.* ¡Válgame Dios, que el hacer cosas señaladas es causa para que uno muera! Haciendo reclamo este *multa signa facit* a aquel *radix Iesse, qui stat in signum populorum* y al otro *in signum cui contradicetur.* ¿Por signo? ¡Pues muera! ¿Señalado? ¡Pues padezca, que eso es el premio de quien se señala!

Suelen en la eminencia de los templos colocarse por adorno unas figuras de los Vientos y de la Fama, y por defenderlas de las aves las llenan todas de púas; defensa parece y no es sino propiedad forzosa: no puede estar sin púas que la puncen quien está en alto. Allí está la ojeriza del aire, allí es el rigor de los elementos, allí despican la cólera los rayos, allí es el blanco de piedras y flechas. ¡Oh infeliz altura, expuesta a tantos riesgos! ¡Oh signo que te ponen por blanco de la envidia y por objeto de la contradicción! Cualquiera eminencia, ya sea de dignidad, ya de nobleza, ya de riqueza, ya de hermosura, ya de ciencia, padece esta pensión; pero la que con más rigor la experimenta es la del entendimiento. Lo primero, porque es el más indefenso, pues la riqueza y el poder castigan a quien se les atreve, y el entendimiento no, pues mientras es mayor es más modesto y sufrido y se defiende menos. Lo segundo es porque, como dijo doctamente Gracián, las ventajas en el entendimiento lo son en el ser. No por otra razón es el ángel más que el hombre que porque entiende más; no es otro el exceso que el hombre hace al bruto, sino sólo entender; y así como ninguno quiere ser menos que otro, así ninguno confiesa que otro entiende más, porque es consecuencia del ser más. Sufrirá uno y confesará que otro es más noble que él, que es más rico, que es más hermoso y aun que es más docto; pero que es más entendido apenas habrá quien lo confiese; *Rarus est, qui velit cedere ingenio.* Por eso es tan eficaz la batería contra esta prenda.

drous deeds seems not befitting learned men, for such were the Pharisees. Thus it is that in the heat of passion learned men erupt with such irrelevancies; for we know it as truth that only for this reason was it determined that Christ should die. Oh, men, if men you may be called, being so like to brutes, what is the cause of so cruel a determination? Their only response is that "this man doth many miracles." May God forgive them. Then is performing signal deeds cause enough that one should die? This "he doth many miracles" evokes *the root of Jesse, who standeth for an ensign of the people,*[11] and that *and for a sign which shall be contradicted.*[12] He is a sign? Then He shall die. He excels? Then He shall suffer, for that is the reward for one who excels.

Often on the crest of temples are placed as adornment figures of the winds and of fame, and to defend them from the birds, they are covered with iron barbs; this appears to be in defense, but is in truth obligatory propriety: the figure thus elevated cannot avoid becoming the target of those barbs; there on high is found the animosity of the air, on high, the ferocity of the elements, on high is unleashed the anger of the thunderbolt, on high stands the target for slings and arrows. Oh unhappy eminence, exposed to such uncounted perils. Oh sign, become the target of envy and the butt of contradiction. Whatever eminence, whether that of dignity, nobility, riches, beauty, or science, must suffer this burden; but the eminence that undergoes the most severe attack is that of reason. First, because it is the most defenseless, for riches and power strike out against those who dare attack them; but not so reason, for while it is the greater it is more modest and long-suffering, and defends itself less. Second, as Gracian stated so eruditely, *favors in man's reason are favors in his nature.* For no other cause except that the angel is superior in reason is the angel above man; for no other cause does man stand above the beast but by his reason; and thus, as no one wishes to be lower than another, neither does he confess that another is superior in reason, as reason is a consequence of being superior. One will abide, and will confess that another is nobler than he, that another is richer, more handsome, and even that he is more learned, but that another is richer in reason scarcely any will confess: *Rare is he who will concede genius.* That is why the assault against this virtue works to such profit.

Cuando los soldados hicieron burla, entretenimiento y diversión de Nuestro Señor Jesucristo, trajeron una púrpura vieja y una caña hueca y una corona de espinas para coronarle por rey de burlas. Pues ahora la caña y la púrpura eran afrentosas, pero no dolorosas; pues ¿por qué sólo la corona es dolorosa? ¿No basta que, como las demás insignias, fuese de escarnio e ignominia, pues ése era el fin? No, porque la sagrada cabeza de Cristo y aquel divino cerebro eran depósito de la sabiduría; y cerebro sabio en el mundo no basta que esté escarnecido, ha de estar también lastimado y maltratado; cabeza que es erario de sabiduría no espere otra corona que de espinas. ¿Cuál guirnalda espera la sabiduría humana si ve la que obtuvo la divina? Coronaba la soberbia romana las diversas hazañas de sus capitanes también con diversas coronas: ya con la cívica al que defendía al ciudadano, ya con la castrense al que entraba en los reales enemigos, ya con la mural al que escalaba el muro, ya con la obsidional al que libraba la ciudad cercada o el ejército sitiado o el campo o en los reales; ya con la naval, ya con la oval, ya con la triunfal otras hazañas, según refieren Plinio y Aulo Gelio; mas viendo yo tantas diferencias de coronas, dudaba de cuál especie sería la de Cristo, y me parece que fue obsidional, que (como sabéis, Señora) era la más honrosa y se llamaba obsidional de *obsidio,* que quiere decir cerco; la cual no se hacía de oro ni de plata, sino de la misma grana o yerba que cría el campo en que se hacía la empresa. Y como la hazaña de Cristo fue hacer levantar el cerco al Príncipe de las Tinieblas, el cual tenía sitiada toda la tierra, como lo dice en el libro de Job: *Circuivi terram et ambulavi per eam* y de él dice San Pedro: *Circuit, quaerens quem devoret;* y vino nuestro caudillo y le hizo levantar el cerco: *nunc princeps huius mundi eiicietur foras,* así los soldados le coronaron no con oro ni plata, sino con el fruto natural que producía el mundo que fue el campo de la lid, el cual, después de la maldición, *spinas et tribulos germinabit tibi,* no producía otra cosa que espinas; y así fue propísima corona de ellas en el valeroso y sabio vencedor con que le coronó su madre la Sinagoga; saliendo a ver el doloroso

When the soldiers mocked, made entertainment and diversion of our Lord Jesus Christ, they brought Him a worn purple garment and a hollow reed, and a crown of thorns to crown Him King of Fools. But though the reed and the purple were an affront, they did not cause suffering. Why does only the crown give pain? Is it not enough that like the other emblems the crown was a symbol of ridicule and ignominy, as that was its intent? No. Because the sacred head of Christ and His divine intellect were the depository of wisdom, and the world is not satisfied for wisdom to be the object of mere ridicule, it must also be done injury and harm. A head that is a storehouse of wisdom can expect nothing but a crown of thorns. What garland may human wisdom expect when it is known what was bestowed on that divine wisdom? Roman pride crowned the many achievements of their Captains with many crowns: he who defended the city received the civic crown; he who fought his way into the hostile camp received the camp crown; he who scaled the wall, the mural; he who liberated a besieged city, or any army besieged either in the field or in their encampment, received the obsidional, the siege, crown; other feats were crowned with naval, ovation, or triumphal crowns, as described by Pliny and Aulus Gellius. Observing so many and varied crowns, I debated as to which Christ's crown must have been, and determined that it was the siege crown, for (as well you know lady) that was the most honored crown and was called obsidional after *obsidio*, which means siege; which crown was made not from gold, or silver, but from the leaves and grasses flourishing on the field where the feat was achieved. And as the heroic feat of Christ was to break the siege of the Prince of Darkness, who had laid siege to all the earth, as is told in the Book of Job, quoting Satan: *I have gone round about the earth, and walked through it,*[13] and as St. Peter says: *As a roaring lion, goeth about seeking whom he may devour.*[14] And our Master came and caused him to lift the siege: *Now shall the prince of this world be cast out.*[15] So the soldiers crowned Him not with gold or silver but with the natural fruit of the world, which was the field of battle—and which, after the curse *Thorns also and thistles shall it bring forth to thee,*[16] produced only thorns—and thus it was a most fitting crown for the courageous and wise Conqueror, with which His mother Syna-

triunfo, como la del otro Salomón festivas, a éste llorosas las hijas de Sión, porque es el triunfo de sabio obtenido con dolor y celebrado con llanto, que es el modo de triunfar la sabiduría; siendo Cristo, como rey de ella, quien estrenó la corona, porque santificada en sus sienes, se quite el horror a los otros sabios y entiendan que no han de aspirar a otro honor.

Quiso la misma Vida ir a dar la vida a Lázaro difunto; ignoraban los discípulos el intento y le replicaron: *Rabbi, nunc quaerebant te Iudaei lapidare, et iterum vadis illuc?* Satisfizo el Redentor el temor: *Nonne duodecim sunt horae diei?* Hasta aquí parece que temían porque tenían el antecedente de quererle apedrear porque les había reprendido llamándoles ladrones y no pastores de las ovejas. Y así, temían que si iba a lo mismo (como las represiones, aunque sean tan justas, suelen ser mal reconocidas), corriese peligro su vida; pero ya desengañados y enterados de que va a dar vida a Lázaro, ¿cuál es la razón que pudo mover a Tomás para que tomando aquí los alientos que en el huerto Pedro: *Eamus et nos, ut moriamur cum eo?* ¿Qué dices, apóstol santo? A morir no va el Señor; ¿de qué es el recelo? Porque a lo que Cristo va no es a reprender, sino a hacer una obra de piedad, y por esto no le pueden hacer mal. Los mismos judíos os podían haber asegurado, pues cuando los reconvino, queriéndole apedrear: *Multa bona opera ostendi vobis ex Patre meo, propter quod eorum opus me lapidatis?*, le respondieron: *De bono opere non lapidamus te, sed de blasphemia.* Pues si ellos dicen que no le quieren apedrear por las buenas obras y ahora va a hacer una tan buena como dar la vida a Lázaro, ¿de qué es el recelo o por qué? ¿No fuera mejor decir: Vamos a gozar el fruto del agradecimiento de la buena obra que va a hacer nuestro Maestro; a verle aplaudir y rendir gracias al beneficio; a ver las admiraciones que hacen del milagro? Y no decir, al parecer una cosa tan fuera del caso como es: *Eamus et nos, ut moriamur cum eo.* Mas ¡ay! que el Santo temió como discreto y habló como apóstol. ¿No va Cristo a hacer un milagro? Pues ¿qué mayor peligro? Menos intolerable es para la soberbia oír las represiones, que para la envidia ver los mi-

gogue crowned Him. And the daughters of Zion, weeping, came out to witness the sorrowful triumph, as they had come rejoicing for the triumph of Solomon, because the triumph of the wise is earned with sorrow and celebrated with weeping, which is the manner of the triumph of wisdom; and as Christ is the King of wisdom, He was the first to wear that crown; and as it was sanctified on His brow, it removed all fear and dread from those who are wise, for they know they need aspire to no other honor.

The Living Word, Life, wished to restore life to Lazarus, who was dead. His disciples did not know His purpose and they said to Him: *Rabbi, the Jews but now sought to stone thee; and goest thou thither again?*[17] And the Redeemer calmed their fear: *Are there not twelve hours of the day?*[18] It seems they feared because there had been those who wished to stone Him when He rebuked them, calling them thieves and not shepherds of sheep. And thus the disciples feared that if He returned to the same place—for even though rebukes be just, they are often badly received—He would be risking his life. But once having been disabused and having realized that He was setting forth to raise up Lazarus from the dead, what was it that caused Thomas, like Peter in the Garden, to say *Let us also go, that we may die with him?*[19] What say you, Sainted Apostle? The Lord does not go out to die; whence your misgiving? For Christ goes not to rebuke, but to work an act of mercy, and therefore they will do Him no harm. These same Jews could have assured you, for when He reproved those who wished to stone Him, *Many good works I have shewed you from my Father; for which of those works do you stone me?*[20] they replied: *For a good work we stone thee not; but for blasphemy.*[21] And as they say they will not stone Him for doing good works, and now He goes to do a work so great as to raise up Lazarus from the dead, whence your misgiving? Why do you fear? Were it not better to say: let us go to gather the fruits of appreciation for the good work our Master is about to do; to see Him lauded and applauded for His benefice; to see men marvel at His miracle. Why speak words seemingly so alien to the circumstance as *Let us also go?* Ah, woe, the Saint feared as a prudent man and spoke as an Apostle. Does Christ not go to work a miracle? Why, what *greater* peril? It is less to be suffered that pride endure rebukes

lagros. En todo lo dicho, venerable Señora, no quiero (ni tal desatino cupiera en mí) decir que me han perseguido por saber, sino sólo porque he tenido amor a la sabiduría y a las letras, no porque haya conseguido ni uno ni otro.

Hallábase el Príncipe de los Apóstoles, en un tiempo, tan distante de la sabiduría como pondera aquel enfático: *Petrus vero sequebatur eum a longe;* tan lejos de los aplausos de docto quien tenía el título de indiscreto: *Nesciens quid diceret;* y aun examinado del conocimiento de la sabiduría dijo él mismo que no había alcanzado la menor noticia: *Mulier, nescio quid dicis. Mulier, non novi illum.* Y ¿qué le sucede? Que teniendo estos créditos de ignorante, no tuvo la fortuna, sí las aflicciones, de sabio. ¿Por qué? No se dio otra causal sino: *Et hic cum illo erat.* Era afecto a la sabiduría, llevábale el corazón, andábase tras ella, preciábase de seguidor y amoroso de la sabiduría; y aunque era tan *a longe* que no le comprendía ni alcanzaba, bastó para incurrir sus tormentos. Ni faltó soldado de fuera que no le afligiese, ni mujer doméstica que no le quejase. Yo confieso que me hallo muy distante de los términos de la sabiduría y que le he deseado seguir, aunque *a longe.* Pero todo ha sido acercarme más al fuego de la persecución, al crisol del tormento, y ha sido con tal extremo que han llegado a solicitar que se me prohíba el estudio.

Una vez lo consiguieron con una prelada muy santa y muy cándida que creyó que el estudio era cosa de Inquisición y me mandó que no estudiase. Yo la obedecí (unos tres meses que duró el poder ella mandar) en cuanto a no tomar libro, que en cuanto a no estudiar absolutamente, como no cae debajo de mi potestad, no lo pude hacer, porque aunque no estudiaba en los libros, estudiaba en todas las cosas que Dios crió, sirviéndome ellas de letras, y de libro toda esta máquina universal. Nada veía sin refleja; nada oía sin consideración, aun en las cosas más menudas y materiales; porque como no hay criatura, por baja que sea, en que no se conozca el *me fecit Deus,* no hay alguna que no pasme el entendimiento, si se considera como se debe. Así yo, vuelvo a decir, las miraba y admiraba todas; de tal ma-

than envy witness miracles. In all the above, most honored lady, I do not wish to say (nor is such folly to be found in me) that I have been persecuted for my wisdom, but merely for my love of wisdom and letters, having achieved neither one nor the other.

At one time even the Prince of the Apostles was very far from wisdom, as is emphasized in that *But Peter followed afar off.*[22] Very distant from the laurels of a learned man is one so little in his judgment that he was *Not knowing what he said.*[23] And being questioned on his mastery of wisdom, he himself was witness that he had not achieved the first measure: *But he denied him, saying: Woman, I know him not.*[24] And what becomes of him? We find that having this reputation of ignorance, he did not enjoy its good fortune, but, rather, the affliction of being taken for wise. And why? There was no other motive but: *This man also was with him.*[25] He was fond of wisdom, it filled his heart, he followed after it, he prided himself as a pursuer and lover of wisdom; and although he followed from so *afar off* that he neither understood nor achieved it, his love for it was sufficient that he incur its torments. And there was present that soldier to cause him distress, and a certain maid-servant to cause him grief. I confess that I find myself very distant from the goals of wisdom, for all that I have desired to follow it, even from *afar off.* But in this I have been brought closer to the fire of persecution, to the crucible of torment, and to such lengths that they have asked that study be forbidden to me.

At one time this was achieved through the offices of a very saintly and ingenuous Abbess who believed that study was a thing of the Inquisition, who commanded me not to study. I obeyed her (the three some months her power to command endured) in that I did not take up a book; but that I study not at all is not within my power to achieve, and this I could not obey, for though I did not study in books, I studied all the things that God had wrought, reading in them, as in writing and in books, all the workings of the universe. I looked on nothing without reflexion; I heard nothing without meditation, even in the most minute and imperfect things; because as there is no creature, however lowly, in which one cannot recognize that *God made me,* there is none that does not astound reason, if properly meditated on. Thus, I

nera que de las mismas personas con quienes hablaba, y de lo
que me decían, me estaban resaltando mil consideraciones: ¿De
dónde emanaría aquella variedad de genios e ingenios siendo
todos de una especie? ¿Cuáles serían los temperamentos y
ocultas cualidades que lo ocasionaban? Si veía una figura, es-
taba combinando la proporción de sus líneas y mediándola con
el entendimiento y reduciéndola a otras diferentes. Paseábame
algunas veces en el testero de un dormitorio nuestro (que es
una pieza muy capaz) y estaba observando que siendo las líneas
de sus dos lados paralelas y su techo a nivel, la vista fingía que
sus líneas se inclinaban una a otra y que su techo estaba más
bajo en lo distante que en lo próximo, de donde infería que las
líneas visuales corren rectas, pero no paralelas, sino que van a
formar una figura piramidal. Y discurría si sería ésta la razón
que obligó a los antiguos a dudar si el mundo era esférico o no.
Porque, aunque lo parece, podía ser engaño de la vista, de-
mostrando concavidades donde pudiera no haberlas.

Este modo de reparos en todo me sucedía y sucede siempre,
sin tener yo arbitrio en ello, que antes me suelo enfadar porque
me cansa la cabeza; y yo creía que a todos sucedía esto mismo
y el hacer versos, hasta que la experiencia me ha demostrado lo
contrario; y es de tal manera esta naturaleza o costumbre, que
nada veo sin segunda consideración. Estaban en mi presencia
dos niñas jugando con un trompo, y apenas yo vi el mo-
vimiento y la figura cuando empecé, con esta mi locura, a
considerar el fácil moto de la forma esférica y cómo duraba el
impulso ya impreso e independiente de su causa, pues distante
la mano de la niña, que era la causa motiva, bailaba el trompillo;
y no contenta con esto, hice traer harina y cernerla para que, en
bailando el trompo encima, se conociese si eran círculos per-
fectos o no los que describía con su movimiento; y hallé que no
eran sino unas líneas espirales que iban perdiendo lo circular
cuanto se iba remitiendo el impulso. Jugaban otras a los alfi-
leres (que es el más frívolo juego que usa la puerilidad); yo me
llegaba a contemplar las figuras que formaban; y viendo que
acaso se pusieron tres en triángulo, me ponía a enlazar uno en

reiterate, I saw and admired all things; so that even the very persons with whom I spoke, and the things they said, were cause for a thousand meditations. Whence the variety of genius and wit, being all of a single species? Which the temperaments and hidden qualities that occasioned such variety? If I saw a figure, I was forever combining the proportion of its lines and measuring it with my reason and reducing it to new proportions. Occasionally as I walked along the far wall of one of our dormitories (which is a most capacious room) I observed that though the lines of the two sides were parallel and the ceiling perfectly level, in my sight they were distorted, the lines seeming to incline toward one another, the ceiling seeming lower in the distance than in proximity: from which I inferred that *visual* lines run straight but not parallel, forming a pyramidal figure. I pondered whether this might not be the reason that caused the ancients to question whether the world were spherical. Because, although it so seems, this could be a deception of vision, suggesting concavities where possibly none existed.

This manner of reflection has always been my habit, and is quite beyond my will to control; on the contrary, I am wont to become vexed that my intellect makes me weary; and I believed that it was so with everyone, as well as making verses, until experience taught me otherwise; and it is so strong in me this nature, or custom, that I look at nothing without giving it further examination. Once in my presence two young girls were spinning a top and scarcely had I seen the motion and the figure described, when I began, out of this madness of mine, to meditate on the effortless *motus* of the spherical form, and how the impulse persisted even when free and independent of its cause—for the top continued to dance even at some distance from the child's hand, which was the causal force. And not content with this, I had flour brought and sprinkled about, so that as the top danced one might learn whether these were perfect circles it described with its movement; and I found that they were not, but, rather, spiral lines that lost their circularity as the impetus declined. Other girls sat playing at spillikins (surely the most frivolous game that children play); I walked closer to observe the figures they formed, and seeing that by chance three lay in a triangle, I set to joining one with another,

otro, acordándome de que aquélla era la figura que dicen tenía el misterioso anillo de Salomón, en que había unas lejanas luces y representaciones de la Santísima Trinidad, en virtud de lo cual obraba tantos prodigios y maravillas; y la misma que dicen tuvo el arpa de David, y que por eso sanaba Saúl a su sonido; y casi la misma conservan las arpas en nuestros tiempos.

Pues ¿qué os pudiera contar, Señora, de los secretos naturales que he descubierto estando guisando? Ver que un huevo se une y fríe en la manteca o aceite y, por contrario, se despedaza en el almíbar; ver que para que el azúcar se conserve fluida basta echarle una muy mínima parte de agua en que haya estado membrillo u otra fruta agria; ver que la yema y clara de un mismo huevo son tan contrarias, que en los unos, que sirven para el azúcar, sirve cada una de por sí y juntos no. Por no cansaros con tales frialdades, que sólo refiero por daros entera noticia de mi natural y creo que os causará risa; pero, señora, ¿qué podemos saber las mujeres sino filosofías de cocina? Bien dijo Lupercio Leonardo, que bien se puede filosofar y aderezar la cena. Y yo suelo decir viendo estas cosillas: Si Aristóteles hubiera guisado, mucho más hubiera escrito. Y prosiguiendo en mi modo de cogitaciones, digo que esto es tan continuo en mí que no necesito de libros; y en una ocasión que, por un grave accidente de estómago, me prohibieron los médicos el estudio, pasé así algunos días, y luego les propuse que era menos dañoso el concedérmelos, porque eran tan fuertes y vehementes mis cogitaciones que consumían más espíritus en un cuarto de hora que el estudio de los libros en cuatro días; y así se redujeron a concederme que leyese. Y más, Señora mía: que ni aun el sueño se libró de este continuo movimiento de mi imaginativa; antes suele obrar en él más libre y desembarazada, confiriendo con mayor claridad y sosiego las especies que ha conservado del día, arguyendo, haciendo versos, de que os pudiera hacer un catálogo muy grande, y de algunas razones y delgadezas que he alcanzado dormida mejor que despierta, y las dejo por no cansaros, pues basta lo dicho para que vuestra discreción y trascendencia penetre y se entere perfectamente

recalling that this was said to be the form of the mysterious ring of Solomon,[26] in which he was able to see the distant splendor and images of the Holy Trinity, by virtue of which the ring worked such prodigies and marvels. And the same shape was said to form David's harp, and that is why Saul was refreshed at its sound; and harps today largely conserve that shape.

And what shall I tell you, lady, of the natural secrets I have discovered while cooking? I see that an egg holds together and fries in butter or in oil, but, on the contrary, in syrup shrivels into shreds; observe that to keep sugar in a liquid state one need only add a drop or two of water in which a quince or other bitter fruit has been soaked; observe that the yolk and the white of one egg are so dissimilar that each with sugar produces a result not obtainable with both together. I do not wish to weary you with such inconsequential matters, and make mention of them only to give you full notice of my nature, for I believe they will be occasion for laughter. But, lady, as women, what wisdom may be ours if not the philosophies of the kitchen? Lupercio Leonardo spoke well when he said: how well one may philosophize when preparing dinner.[27] And I often say, when observing these trivial details: had Aristotle prepared victuals, he would have written more. And pursuing the manner of my cogitations, I tell you that this process is so continuous in me that I have no need for books. And on one occasion, when because of a grave upset of the stomach the physicians forbade me to study, I passed thus some days, but then I proposed that it would be less harmful if they allowed me books, because so vigorous and vehement were my cogitations that my spirit was consumed more greatly in a quarter of an hour than in four days' studying books. And thus they were persuaded to allow me to read. And moreover, lady, not even have my dreams been excluded from this ceaseless agitation of my imagination; indeed, in dreams it is wont to work more freely and less encumbered, collating with greater clarity and calm the gleanings of the day, arguing and making verses, of which I could offer you an extended catalogue, as well as of some arguments and inventions that I have better achieved sleeping than awake. I relinquish this subject in order not to tire you, for the above is sufficient to allow your discretion and acuity to penetrate perfectly and perceive my

en todo mi natural y del principio, medios y estado de mis estudios.

Si éstos, Señora, fueran méritos (como los veo por tales celebrar en los hombres), no lo hubieran sido en mí, porque obro necesariamente. Si son culpa, por la misma razón creo que no la he tenido; mas, con todo, vivo siempre tan desconfiada de mí que ni en esto ni en otra cosa me fío de mi juicio; y así remito la decisión a ese soberano talento, sometiéndome luego a lo que sentenciare, sin contradicción ni repugnancia, pues esto no ha sido más de una simple narración de mi inclinación a las letras.

Confieso también que con ser esto verdad tal que, como he dicho, no necesitaba de ejemplares, con todo no me han dejado de ayudar los muchos que he leído, así en divinas como en humanas letras. Porque veo a una Débora dando leyes, así en lo militar como en lo político, y gobernando el pueblo donde había tantos varones doctos. Veo una sapientísima reina de Sabá, tan docta que se atreve a tentar con enigmas la sabiduría del mayor de los sabios, sin ser por ello reprendida, antes por ello será juez de los incrédulos. Veo tantas y tan insignes mujeres: unas adornadas del don de profecía, como una Abigaíl; otras de persuasión, como Ester; otras de piedad, como Rahab; otras de perseverancia, como Ana, madre de Samuel, y otras infinitas en otras especies de prendas y virtudes.

Si revuelvo a los gentiles, lo primero que encuentro es con las Sibilas, elegidas de Dios para profetizar los principales misterios de nuestra Fe, y en tan doctos y elegantes versos que suspenden la admiración. Veo adorar por diosa de las ciencias a una mujer como Minerva, hija del primer Júpiter y maestra de toda la sabiduría de Atenas. Veo una Pola Argentaria, que ayudó a Lucano, su marido, a escribir la gran Batalla Farsálica. Veo a la hija del divino Tiresias, más docta que su padre. Veo a una Cenobia, reina de los Palmirenos, tan sabia como valerosa. A una Arete, hija de Aristipo, doctísima. A una Nicostrata, inventora de las letras latinas y eruditísima en las griegas. A una Aspasia Milesia que enseñó filosofía y retórica y fue maestra del filósofo Pericles. A una Hipasia, que enseñó astrología y leyó mucho tiempo en Alejandría. A una Leoncia, griega, que

nature, as well as the beginnings, the methods, and the present state of my studies.

Even, lady, were these merits (and I see them celebrated as such in men), they would not have been so in me for I cannot but study. If they are fault, then, for the same reasons, I believe I have none. Nevertheless, I live always with so little confidence in myself that neither in my study, nor in any other thing, do I trust my judgment; and thus I remit the decision to your sovereign genius, submitting myself to whatever sentence you may bestow, without controversy, without reluctance, for I have wished here only to present you with a simple narration of my inclination toward letters.

I confess, too, that though it is true, as I have stated, that I had no need of books, it is nonetheless also true that they have been no little inspiration, in divine as in human letters. Because I find a Debbora administering the law, both military and political, and governing a people among whom there were many learned men. I find a most wise Queen of Saba, so learned that she dares to challenge with hard questions the wisdom of the greatest of all wise men, without being reprimanded for doing so, but, rather, as a consequence, to judge unbelievers. I see many and illustrious women; some blessed with the gift of prophecy, like Abigail; others of persuasion, like Esther; others with pity, like Rahab; others with perseverance, like Anna, the mother of Samuel; and an infinite number of others, with divers gifts and virtues.

If I again turn to the Gentiles, the first I encounter are the Sibyls, those women chosen by God to prophesy the principal mysteries of our Faith, and with learned and elegant verses that surpass admiration. I see adored as a goddess of the sciences a woman like Minerva, the daughter of the first Jupiter and mistress over all the wisdom of Athens. I see a Polla Argentaria, who helped Lucan, her husband, write his epic *Pharsalia*. I see the daughter of the divine Tiresias, more learned than her father. I see a Zenobia, Queen of the Palmyrans, as wise as she was valiant. An Arete, most learned daughter of Aristippus. A Nicostrata, framer of Latin verses and most erudite in Greek. An Aspasia of Miletus, who taught philosophy and rhetoric, and who was a teacher of the philosopher Pericles. An Hypatia, who taught astrology, and

escribió contra el filósofo Teofrasto y le convenció. A una Ju-
cia, a una Corina, a una Cornelia; y, en fin, a toda la gran turba
de las que merecieron nombres, ya de griegas, ya de musas, ya
de pitonisas; pues todas no fueron más que mujeres doctas,
tenidas y celebradas y también veneradas de la antigüedad por
tales. Sin otras infinitas, de que están los libros llenos, pues veo
aquella egipcíaca Catarina leyendo y convenciendo todas las
sabidurías de los sabios de Egipto. Veo una Gertrudis leer, es-
cribir y enseñar. Y para no buscar ejemplos fuera de casa, veo
una santísima madre mía, Paula, docta en las lenguas hebrea,
griega y latina y aptísima para intepretar las Escrituras. ¿Y qué
más que siendo su cronista un máximo Jerónimo, apenas se
hallaba el Santo digno de serlo, pues con aquella viva pon-
deración y enérgica eficacia con que sabe explicarse dice: Si to-
dos los miembros de mi cuerpo fuesen lenguas, no bastarían a
publicar la sabiduría y virtud de Paula? Las mismas alabanzas
le mereció Blesila, viuda; y las mismas la esclarecida virgen Eus-
toquio, hijas ambas de la misma Santa; y la segunda tal que por
su ciencia era llamada Prodigio del Mundo. Fabiola, romana,
fue también doctísima en la Sagrada Escritura. Proba Falconia,
mujer romana, escribió un elegante libro con centones de Vir-
gilio, de los misterios de Nuestra Santa Fe. Nuestra reina Doña
Isabel, mujer del décimo Alfonso, es corriente que escribió de
astrología. Sin otras que omito por no trasladar lo que otros
han dicho (que es vicio que siempre he abominado), pues en
nuestros tiempos está floreciendo la gran Cristina Alejandra,
Reina de Suecia, tan docta como valerosa y magnánima, y
las Excelentísimas señoras Duquesa de Aveyro y Condesa de
Villaumbrosa.

El venerable Doctor Arce (digno profesor de Escritura por
su virtud y letras), en su *Studioso Bibliorum* excita esta
cuestión: *An liceat foeminis sacrorum Bibliorum studio incum-
bere? eaque interpretari?* Y trae por la parte contraria muchas
sentencias de santos, en especial aquello del Apóstol: *Mulieres
in Ecclesiis taceant, non enim permittitur eis loqui,* etc. Trae des-

studied many years in Alexandria. A Leontium, a Greek woman, who questioned the philosopher Theophrastus, and convinced him. A Jucia, a Corinna, a Cornelia; and, finally, a great throng of women deserving to be named, some as Greeks, some as muses, some as seers; for all were nothing more than learned women, held, and celebrated—and venerated as well—as such by antiquity. Without mentioning an infinity of other women whose names fill books. For example, I find the Egyptian Catherine, studying and influencing the wisdom of all the wise men of Egypt. I see a Gertrude studying, writing, and teaching. And not to overlook examples close to home, I see my most holy mother Paula, learned in Hebrew, Greek, and Latin, and most able in interpreting the Scriptures. And what greater praise than, having as her chronicler a Jeronimus Maximus, that Saint scarcely found himself competent for his task, and says, with that weighty deliberation and energetic precision with which he so well expressed himself: "If all the members of my body were tongues, they still would not be sufficient to proclaim the wisdom and virtue of Paula." Similarly praiseworthy was the widow Blesilla; also, the illustrious virgin Eustochium, both daughters of this same saint; especially the second, who, for her knowledge, was called the Prodigy of the World. The Roman Fabiola was most well-versed in the Holy Scripture. Proba Falconia, a Roman woman, wrote elegant centos, containing verses from Virgil, about the mysteries of Our Holy Faith. It is well-known by all that Queen Isabella, wife of the tenth Alfonso, wrote about astrology. Many others I do not list, out of the desire not merely to transcribe what others have said (a vice I have always abominated); and many are flourishing today, as witness Christina Alexandra, Queen of Sweden, as learned as she is valiant and magnanimous, and the Most Honorable Ladies, the Duquesa of Aveyro and the Condesa of Villaumbrosa.

The venerable Doctor Arce (by his virtue and learning a worthy teacher of the Scriptures) in his scholarly *Bibliorum* raises this question: *Is it permissible for women to dedicate themselves to the study of the Holy Scriptures, and to their interpretation?* and he offers as negative arguments the opinions of many saints, especially that of the Apostle: *Let women keep silence in the churches;*

pués otras sentencias, y del mismo Apóstol aquel lugar *ad Ti-
tum: Anus similiter in habitu sancto, bene docentes,* con inter-
pretaciones de los Santos Padres; y al fin resuelve, con su
prudencia, que el leer públicamente en las cátedras y predicar
en los púlpitos no es lícito a las mujeres; pero que el estudiar,
escribir y enseñar privadamente no sólo les es lícito, pero muy
provechoso y útil; claro está que esto no se debe entender con
todas, sino con aquellas a quienes hubiere Dios dotado de es-
pecial virtud y prudencia y que fueren muy provectas y erudi-
tas y tuvieren el talento y requisitos necesarios para tan sagrado
empleo. Y esto es tan justo que no sólo a las mujeres, que por
tan ineptas están tenidas, sino a los hombres, que con sólo serlo
piensan que son sabios, se había de prohibir la interpretación
de las Sagradas Letras, en no siendo muy doctos y virtuosos y
de ingenios dóciles y bien inclinados; porque de lo contrario
creo yo que han salido tantos sectarios y que ha sido la raíz de
tantas herejías; porque hay muchos que estudian para ignorar,
especialmente los que son de ánimos arrogantes, inquietos y
soberbios, amigos de novedades en la Ley (que es quien las re-
húsa); y así hasta que por decir lo que nadie ha dicho dicen una
herejía, no están contentos. De éstos dice el Espíritu Santo: *In
malevolam animam non introibit sapientia.* A éstos más daño
les hace saber que les hiciera el ignorar. Dijo un discreto que no
es necio entero el que no sabe latín, pero el que lo sabe está ca-
lificado. Y añado yo que le perfecciona (si es perfección la
necedad) el haber estudiado su poco de filosofía y teología y el
tener alguna noticia de lenguas, que con eso es necio en muchas
ciencias y lenguas, porque un necio grande no cabe en sólo la
lengua materna.

A éstos, vuelvo a decir, hace daño el estudiar, porque es
poner espada en manos del furioso; que siendo instrumento
nobilísimo para la defensa, en sus manos es muerte suya y de
muchos. Tales fueron las Divinas Letras en poder del malvado
Pelagio y del protervo Arrio, del malvado Lutero y de los
demás heresiarcas, como lo fue nuestro Doctor (nunca fue nues-
tro ni doctor) Cazalla, a los cuales hizo daño la sabiduría

for it is not permitted them to speak, etc.[28] He later cites other opinions and, from the same Apostle, verses from his letter to Titus: *The aged women in like manner, in holy attire ... teaching well,*[29] with interpretations by the Holy Fathers. Finally he resolves, with all prudence, that teaching publicly from a University chair, or preaching from the pulpit, is not permissible for women; but that to study, write, and teach privately not only is permissible, but most advantageous and useful. It is evident that this is not to be the case with all women, but with those to whom God may have granted special virtue and prudence, and who may be well advanced in learning, and having the essential talent and requisites for such a sacred calling. This view is indeed just, so much so that not only women, who are held to be so inept, but also men, who merely for being men believe they are wise, should be prohibited from interpreting the Sacred Word if they are not learned and virtuous and of gentle and well-inclined natures; that this is not so has been, I believe, at the root of so much sectarianism and so many heresies. For there are many who study but are ignorant, especially those who are in spirit arrogant, troubled, and proud, so eager for new interpretations of the Word (which itself rejects new interpretations) that merely for the sake of saying what no one else has said they speak a heresy, and even then are not content. Of these the Holy Spirit says: *For wisdom will not enter into a malicious soul.*[30] To such as these more harm results from knowing than from ignorance. A wise man has said: he who does not know Latin is not a complete fool, but he who knows it is well qualified to be. And I would add that a fool may reach perfection (if ignorance may tolerate perfection) by having studied his tittle of philosophy and theology and by having some learning of tongues, by which he may be a fool in many sciences and languages: a great fool cannot be contained solely in his mother tongue.

For such as these, I reiterate, study is harmful, because it is as if to place a sword in the hands of a madman; which, though a most noble instrument for defense, is in his hands his own death and that of many others. So were the Divine Scriptures in the possession of the evil Pelagius and the intractable Arius, of the evil Luther, and the other heresiarchs like our own Doctor (who was

porque, aunque es el mejor alimento y vida del alma, a la manera que en el estómago mal acomplexionado y de viciado calor, mientras mejores los alimentos que recibe, más áridos, fermentados y perversos son los humores que cría, así estos malévolos, mientras más estudian, peores opiniones engendran; obstrúyeseles el entendimiento con lo mismo que había de alimentarse, y es que estudian mucho y digieren poco, sin proporcionarse al vaso limitado de sus entendimientos. A esto dice el Apóstol: *Dico enim per gratiam quae data est mihi, omnibus qui sunt inter vos: Non plus sapere quam oportet sapere, sed sapere ad sobrietatem: et unicuique sicut Deus divisit mensuram fidei.* Y en verdad no lo dijo el Apóstol a las mujeres, sino a los hombres; y que no es sólo para ellas el *taceant*, sino para todos los que no fueren muy aptos. Querer yo saber tanto o más que Aristóteles o que San Agustín, si no tengo la aptitud de San Agustín o de Aristóteles, aunque estudie más que los dos, no sólo no lo conseguiré, sino que debilitaré y entorpeceré la operación de mi flaco entendimiento con la desproporción del objeto.

¡Oh, si todos—y yo la primera, que soy una ignorante—nos tomásemos la medida al talento antes de estudiar y, lo peor es, de escribir con ambiciosa codicia de igualar y aun de exceder a otros, qué poco ánimo nos quedara y de cuántos errores nos excusáramos y cuántas torcidas inteligencias que andan por ahí no anduvieran! Y pongo las mías en primer lugar, pues si conociera, como debo, esto mismo no escribiera. Y protesto que sólo lo hago por obedeceros; con tanto recelo, que me debéis más en tomar la pluma con este temor, que me debiérades si os remitiera más perfectas obras. Pero bien que va a vuestra corrección; borradlo, rompedlo y reprendedme, que eso apreciaré yo más que todo cuanto vano aplauso me pueden otros dar: *Corripiet me iustus in misericordia, et increpabit: oleum autem peccatoris non impinguet caput meum.*

Y volviendo a nuestro Arce, digo que trae en confirmación de su sentir aquellas palabras de mi Padre San Jerónimo *(ad Laetam, de institutione filiae)*, donde dice: *Adhuc tenera lingua psalmis dulcibus imbuatur. Ipsa nomina per quae consuescit*

neither ours nor a doctor) Cazalla. To these men, wisdom was harmful, although it is the greatest nourishment and the life of the soul; in the same way that in a stomach of sickly constitution and adulterated complexion, the finer the nourishment it receives, the more arid, fermented, and perverse are the humors it produces; thus these evil men: the more they study, the worse opinions they engender, their reason being obstructed with the very substance meant to nourish it, and they study much and digest little, exceeding the limits of the vessel of their reason. Of which the Apostle says: *For I say, by the grace that is given me, to all that are among you, not to be more wise than it behoveth to be wise, but to be wise unto sobriety, and according as God hath divided to every one the measure of faith.*[31] And in truth, the Apostle did not direct these words to women, but to men; and that *keep silence* is intended not only for women, but for *all* incompetents. If I desire to know as much, or more, than Aristotle or Saint Augustine, and if I have not the aptitude of Saint Augustine or Aristotle, though I study more than either, not only will I not achieve learning, but I will weaken and dull the workings of my feeble reason with the disproportionateness of the goal.

Oh, that each of us—I, being ignorant, the first—should take the measure of our talents before we study or, more important, write with the covetous ambition to equal and even surpass others, how little spirit we should have for it, and how many errors we should avoid, and how many tortured intellects of which we have experience, we should have had no experience! And I place my own ignorance in the forefront of all these, for if I knew all I should, I would not write. And I protest that I do so only to obey you; and with such apprehension that you owe me more that I have taken up my pen in fear than you would have owed had I presented you more perfect works. But it is well that they go to your correction. Cross them out, tear them up, reprove me, and I shall appreciate that more than all the vain applause others may offer. *That just men shall correct me in mercy, and shall reprove me; but let not the oil of the sinner fatten my head.*[32]

And returning again to our Arce, I say that in affirmation of his opinion he cites the words of my father, Saint Jerome: *To Leta, Upon the Education of Her Daughter.* Where he says: *Accustom*

paulatim verba contexere, non sint fortuita, sed certa, et coacervata de industria. Prophetarum videlicet, atque Apostolorum, et omnis ab Adam Patriarcharum series, de Matthaeo, Lucaque descendat, ut dum aliud agit, futurae memoriae praeparetur. Reddat tibi pensum quotidie, de Scripturarum floribus carptum. Pues si así quería el Santo que se educase una niña que apenas empezaba a hablar, ¿qué querrá en sus monjas y en sus hijas espirituales? Bien se conoce en las referidas Eustoquio y Fabiola y en Marcela, su hermana, Pacátula y otras a quienes el Santo honra en sus epístolas, exhortándolas a este sagrado ejercicio, como se conoce en la citada epístola donde noté yo aquel *reddat tibi pensum,* que es reclamo y concordante del *bene docentes* de San Pablo; pues el *reddat tibi* de mi gran Padre da a entender que la maestra de la niña ha de ser la misma Leta su madre.

¡Oh, cuántos daños se excusaran en nuestra república si las ancianas fueran doctas como Leta, y que supieran enseñar como manda San Pablo y mi Padre San Jerónimo! Y no que por defecto de esto y la suma flojedad en que han dado en dejar a las pobres mujeres, si algunos padres desean doctrinar más de lo ordinario a sus hijas, les fuerza la necesidad y falta de ancianas sabias a llevar maestros hombres a enseñar a leer, escribir y contar, a tocar y otras habilidades, de que no pocos daños resultan, como se experimentan cada día en lastimosos ejemplos de desiguales consorcios, porque con la inmediación del trato y la comunicación del tiempo, suele hacerse fácil lo que no se pensó ser posible. Por lo cual muchos quieren más dejar bárbaras e incultas a sus hijas que no exponerlas a tan notorio peligro como la familiaridad con los hombres, lo cual se excusara si hubiera ancianas doctas, como quiere San Pablo, y de unas en otras fuese sucediendo el

her tongue, still young, to the sweetness of the Psalms. Even the names through which little by little she will become accustomed to form her phrases should not be chosen by chance, but selected and repeated with care; the prophets must be included, of course, and the apostles, as well, and all the Patriarchs beginning with Adam and down to Matthew and Luke, so that as she practices other things she will be readying her memory for the future. Let your daily task be taken from the flower of the Scriptures. And if this Saint desired that a young girl scarcely beginning to talk be educated in this fashion, what would he desire for his nuns and his spiritual daughters? These beliefs are illustrated in the examples of the previously mentioned Eustochium and Fabiola, and Marcella, her sister, and Pacatula, and others whom the Saint honors in his epistles, exhorting them to this sacred exercise, as they are recognized in the epistle I cited, *Let your daily task . . .* , which is affirmation of and agreement with the aged women . . . *teaching well* of Saint Paul. My illustrious Father's *Let your daily task . . .* makes clear that the teacher of the child is to be Leta herself, the child's mother.

Oh, how much injury might have been avoided in our land if our aged women had been learned, as was Leta, and had they known how to instruct as directed by Saint Paul and by my Father, Saint Jerome. And failing this, and because of the considerable idleness to which our poor women have been relegated, if a father desires to provide his daughters with more than ordinary learning, he is forced by necessity, and by the absence of wise elder women, to bring men to teach the skills of reading, writing, counting, the playing of musical instruments, and other accomplishments, from which no little harm results, as is experienced every day in doleful examples of perilous association, because through the immediacy of contact and the intimacy born from the passage of time, what one may never have thought possible is easily accomplished. For which reason many prefer to leave their daughters unpolished and uncultured rather than to expose them to such notorious peril as that of familiarity with men, which quandary could be prevented if there were learned elder women, as Saint Paul wished to see, and if the teaching were handed down

magisterio como sucede en el de hacer labores y lo demás que es costumbre.

Porque ¿qué inconveniente tiene que una mujer anciana, docta en letras y de santa conversación y costumbres, tuviese a su cargo la educación de las doncellas? Y no que éstas o se pierden por falta de doctrina o por querérsela aplicar por tan peligrosos medios cuales son los maestros hombres, que cuando no hubiera más riesgo que la indecencia de sentarse al lado de una mujer verecunda (que aun se sonrosea de que la mire a la cara su propio padre) un hombre tan extraño, a tratarla con casera familiaridad y a tratarla con magistral llaneza, el pudor del trato con los hombres y de su conversación basta para que no se permitiese. Y no hallo yo que este modo de enseñar de hombres a mujeres pueda ser sin peligro, si no es en el severo tribunal de un confesonario o en la distante docencia de los púlpitos o en el remoto conocimiento de los libros; pero no en el manoseo de la inmediación. Y todos conocen que esto es verdad; y con todo, se permite sólo por el defecto de no haber ancianas sabias; luego es grande daño el no haberlas. Esto debían considerar los que atados al *Mulieres in Ecclesia taceant,* blasfeman de que las mujeres sepan y enseñen; como que no fuera el mismo Apóstol el que dijo: *bene docentes.* Demás de que aquella prohibición cayó sobre lo historial que refiere Eusebio, y es que en la Iglesia primitiva se ponían las mujeres a enseñar las doctrinas unas a otras en los templos; y este rumor confundía cuando predicaban los apóstoles y por eso se les mandó callar; como ahora sucede, que mientras predica el predicador no se reza en alta voz.

No hay duda de que para inteligencia de muchos lugares es menester mucha historia, costumbres, ceremonias, proverbios y aun maneras de hablar de aquellos tiempos en que se escribieron para saber sobre qué caen y a qué aluden algunas locuciones de las divinas letras. *Scindite corda vestra, et non vestimenta vestra,* ¿no es alusión a la ceremonia que tenían los hebreos de rasgar los vestidos, en señal de dolor, como lo hizo el mal pontífice cuando dijo que Cristo había blasfemado?

from one to another, as is the custom with domestic crafts and all other traditional skills.

For what objection can there be that an older woman, learned in letters and in sacred conversation and customs, have in her charge the education of young girls? This would prevent these girls being lost either for lack of instruction or for hesitating to offer instruction through such dangerous means as male teachers, for even when there is no greater risk of indecency than to seat beside a modest woman (who still may blush when her own father looks directly at her) a strange man who treats her as if he were a member of the household and with the authority of an intimate, the modesty demanded in interchange with men and in conversation with them is sufficient reason that such an arrangement not be permitted. For I do not find that the custom of men teaching women is without its peril, lest it be in the severe tribunal of the confessional, or from the remote decency of the pulpit, or in the distant learning of books—never in the personal contact of immediacy. And the world knows this is true; and, notwithstanding, it is permitted solely from the want of learned elder women. Then is it not detrimental, the lack of such women? This question should be addressed by those who, bound to that *Let women keep silence in the church,* say that it is blasphemy for women to learn and teach, as if it were not the Apostle himself who said: *The aged women . . . teaching well.* As well as the fact that this prohibition touches upon historical fact as reported by Eusebius: which is that in the early Church, women were charged with teaching the doctrine to one another in the temples and the sound of this teaching caused confusion as the Apostles were preaching and this is the reason they were ordered to be silent; and even today, while the homilist is preaching, one does not pray aloud.

Who will argue that for the comprehension of many Scriptures one must be familiar with the history, customs, ceremonies, proverbs, and even the manners of speaking of those times in which they were written, if one is to apprehend the references and allusions of more than a few passages of the Holy Word. *And rend your heart and not your garments.*[33] Is this not a reference to the ceremony in which Hebrews rent their garments as a sign of grief, as did the evil pontiff when he said that Christ had blasphemed?

Muchos lugares del Apóstol sobre el socorro de las viudas ¿no miraban también a las costumbres de aquellos tiempos? Aquel lugar de la mujer fuerte: *Nobilis in portis vir eius,* ¿no alude a la costumbre de estar los tribunales de los jueces en las puertas de las ciudades? El *dare terram Deo* ¿no significaba hacer algún voto? *Hiemantes* ¿no se llamaban los pecadores públicos, porque hacían penitencia a cielo abierto, a diferencia de los otros que la hacían en un portal? Aquella queja de Cristo al fariseo de la falta del ósculo y lavatorio de pies ¿no se fundó en la costumbre que de hacer estas cosas tenían los judíos? Y otros infinitos lugares no sólo de las letras divinas, sino también de las humanas, que se topan a cada paso, como el *adorate purpuram,* que significaba obedecer al rey; el *manumittere eum,* que significa dar libertad, aludiendo a la costumbre y ceremonia de dar una bofetada al esclavo para darle libertad. Aquel *intonuit coelum,* de Virgilio, que alude al agüero de tronar hacia occidente, que se tenía por bueno. Aquel *tu nunquam leporem edisti,* de Marcial, que no sólo tiene el donaire de equívoco en el *leporem,* sino la alusión a la propiedad que decían tener la liebre. Aquel proverbio: *Maleam legens, quae sunt domi obliviscere,* que alude al gran peligro del promonotorio de Laconia. Aquella respuesta de la casta matrona al pretensor molesto de *por mí no se untarán los quicios, ni arderán las teas,* para decir que no quería casarse, aludiendo a la ceremonia de untar las puertas con manteca y encender las teas nupciales en los matrimonios; como si ahora dijéramos: por mí no se gastarán arras ni echará bendiciones el cura. Y así hay tanto comento de Virgilio y de Homero y de todos los poetas y oradores. Pues fuera de esto, ¿qué dificultades no se hallan en los lugares sagrados, aun en lo gramatical, de ponerse el plural por singular, de pasar de segunda a tercera persona, como aquello de los Cantares: *osculetur me osculo oris sui: quia meliora sunt ubera tua vino?* Aquel poner los adjetivos en genitivo, en vez de acusativo, como *Calicem salutaris accipiam?*

In many scriptures the Apostle writes of succour for widows; did they not refer to the customs of those times? Does not the example of the valiant woman, *Her husband is honourable in the gates,*[34] allude to the fact that the tribunals of the judges were at the gates of the cities? That *Dare terram Deo,* give of your land to God, did that not mean to make some votive offering? And did they not call the public sinners *hiemantes,* those who endure the winter, because they made their penance in the open air instead of at a town gate as others did? And Christ's plaint to that Pharisee who had neither kissed him nor given him water for his feet, was that not because it was the Jews' usual custom to offer these acts of hospitality? And we find an infinite number of additional instances not only in the Divine Letters, but human as well, such as *adorate purpuram,* venerate the purple, which meant obey the King; *manumittere eum,* manumit them, alluding to the custom and ceremony of striking the slave with one's hand to signify his freedom. That *intonuit coelum,* heaven thundered, in Virgil, which alludes to the augury of thunder from the west, which was held to be good.[35] Martial's *tu nunquam leporem edisti,* you never ate hare, has not only the wit of ambiguity in its *leporem,* but, as well, the allusion to the reputed propensity of hares [to bless with beauty those who dine on them]. That proverb *maleam legens, quae sunt domi obliviscere,* to sail along the shore of Malia is to forget what one has at home, alludes to the great peril of the promontory of Laconia. That chaste matron's response to the unwanted suit of her pretender: "the hinge-pins shall not be oiled for my sake, nor shall the torches blaze," meaning that she did not want to marry, alluded to the ceremony of anointing the doorways with oils and lighting the nuptial torches in the wedding ceremony, as if now we would say, they shall not prepare the thirteen coins for my dowry, nor shall the priest invoke the blessing. And thus it is with many comments of Virgil and Homer and all the poets and orators. In addition, how many are the difficulties found even in the grammar of the Holy Scripture, such as writing a plural for a singular, or changing from the second to third persons, as in the Psalms, *Let him kiss me with the kiss of his mouth, for thy breasts are better than wine.*[36] Or placing adjectives in the genitive instead of the accusative, as in *Calicem salutaris accipiam,*

Aquel poner el femenino por masculino; y, al contrario, llamar adulterio a cualquier pecado?

Todo esto pide más lección de lo que piensan algunos que, de meros gramáticos, o cuando mucho con cuatro términos de Súmulas, quieren interpretar las Escrituras y se aferran del *Mulieres in Eclesiis taceant,* sin saber cómo se ha de entender. Y de otro lugar: *Mulier in silentio discat;* siendo este lugar más en favor que en contra de las mujeres, pues manda que aprendan, y mientras aprenden, claro está que es necesario que callen. Y también está escrito: *Audi Israel, et tace;* donde se habla con toda la colección de los hombres y mujeres, y a todos se manda callar, porque quien oye y aprende es mucha razón que atienda y calle. Y si no, yo quisiera que estos intérpretes y expositores de San Pablo me explicaran cómo entienden aquel lugar: *Mulieres in Ecclesia taceant.* Porque o lo han de entender de lo material de los púlpitos y cátedras, o de lo formal de la universalidad de los fieles, que es la Iglesia. Si lo entienden de lo primero (que es, en mi sentir, su verdadero sentido, pues vemos que, con efecto, no se permite en la Iglesia que las mujeres lean públicamente ni prediquen), ¿por qué reprenden a las que privadamente estudian? Y si lo entienden de lo segundo y quieren que la prohibición del Apóstol sea trascendentalmente, que ni en lo secreto se permita escribir ni estudiar a las mujeres, ¿cómo vemos que la Iglesia ha permitido que escriba una Gertrudis, una Teresa, una Brígida, la monja de Ágreda y otras muchas? Y si me dicen que éstas eran santas, es verdad, pero no obsta a mi argumento; lo primero, porque la proposición de San Pablo es absoluta y comprende a todas las mujeres sin excepción de santas, pues también en su tiempo lo eran Marta y María, Marcela, María madre de Jacob, y Salomé, y otras muchas que había en el fervor de la primitiva Iglesia, y no las exceptúa; y ahora vemos que la Iglesia permite escribir a las mujeres santas y no santas, pues la de Ágreda y María de la Antigua no están canonizadas y corren sus escritos; y ni cuando Santa Teresa y las demás escribieron, lo estaban: luego la prohibición de San Pablo sólo miró a la publicidad de los púlpitos,

I will take the chalice of salvation.[37] Or to replace the feminine with the masculine, and, in contrast, to call any sin adultery.

All this demands more investigation than some believe, who strictly as grammarians, or, at most, employing the four principles of applied logic, attempt to interpret the Scriptures while clinging to that *Let the women keep silence in the church,* not knowing how it is to be interpreted. As well as that other verse, *Let the women learn in silence.*[38] For this latter scripture works more to women's favor than their disfavor, as it commands them to learn; and it is only natural that they must maintain silence while they learn. And it is also written, *Hear, oh Israel, and be silent.* Which addresses the entire congregation of men and women, commanding all to silence, because if one is to hear and learn, it is with good reason that he attend and be silent. And if it is not so, I would want these interpreters and expositors of Saint Paul to explain to me how they interpret that scripture, *Let the women keep silence in the church.* For either they must understand it to refer to the material church, that is the church of pulpits and cathedras, or to the spiritual, the community of the faithful, which is the Church. If they understand it to be the former, which, in my opinion, is its true interpretation, then we see that if in fact it is not permitted of women to read publicly in church, nor preach, why do they censure those who study privately? And if they understand the latter, and wish that the prohibition of the Apostle be applied transcendentally—that not even in private are women to be permitted to write or study—how are we to view the fact that the Church permitted a Gertrude, a Santa Teresa, a Saint Birgitta, the Nun of Agreda, and so many others, to write? And if they say to me that these women were saints, they speak the truth; but this poses no obstacle to my argument. First, because Saint Paul's proposition is absolute, and encompasses all women not excepting saints, as Martha and Mary, Marcella, Mary mother of Jacob, and Salome, all were in their time, and many other zealous women of the early Church. But we see, too, that the Church allows women who are not saints to write, for the Nun of Agreda and Sor María de la Antigua are not canonized, yet their writings are circulated. And when Santa Teresa and the others were writing, they were not as yet canonized. In which case, Saint Paul's prohibition was di-

pues si el Apóstol prohibiera el escribir, no lo permitiera la Iglesia. Pues ahora, yo no me atrevo a enseñar—que fuera en mí muy desmedida presunción—; y el escribir, mayor talento que el mío requiere y muy grande consideración. Así lo dice San Cipriano: *Gravi consideratione indigent, quae scribimus.* Lo que sólo he deseado es estudiar para ignorar menos: que, según San Agustín, unas cosas se aprenden para hacer y otras para sólo saber: *Discimus quaedam, ut sciamus; quaedam, ut faciamus.* Pues ¿en qué ha estado el delito, si aun lo que es lícito a las mujeres, que es enseñar escribiendo, no hago yo porque conozco que no tengo caudal para ello, siguiendo el consejo de Quintiliano: *Noscat quisque, et non tantum ex alienis praeceptis, sed ex natura sua capiat consilium?*

Si el crimen está en la Carta Atenagórica, ¿fue aquélla más que referir sencillamente mi sentir con todas las venias que debo a nuestra Santa Madre Iglesia? Pues si ella, con su santísima autoridad, no me lo prohibe, ¿por qué me lo han de prohibir otros? ¿Llevar una opinión contraria de Vieyra fue en mí atrevimiento, y no lo fue en su Paternidad llevarla contra los tres Santos Padres de la Iglesia? Mi entendimiento tal cual ¿no es tan libre como el suyo, pues viene de un solar? ¿Es alguno de los principios de la Santa Fe, revelados, su opinión, para que la hayamos de creer a ojos cerrados? Demás que yo ni falté al decoro que a tanto varón se debe, como acá ha faltado su defensor, olvidado de la sentencia de Tito Lucio: *Artes committatur decor;* ni toqué a la Sagrada Compañía en el pelo de la ropa; ni escribí más que para el juicio de quien me lo insinuó; y según Plinio, *non similis est conditio publicantis, et nominatim dicentis.* Que si creyera se había de publicar, no fuera con tanto desaliño como fue. Si es, como dice el censor, herética, ¿por qué no la delata?, y con eso él quedará vengado y yo contenta, que aprecio, como debo, más el nombre de católica y de obediente hija de mi Santa Madre Iglesia, que todos los aplausos de docta.

rected solely to the public office of the pulpit, for if the Apostle had forbidden women to write, the Church would not have allowed it. Now I do not make so bold as to teach—which in me would be excessively presumptuous—and as for writing, that requires a greater talent than mine, and serious reflection. As Saint Cyprian says: *The things we write require most conscientious consideration.* I have desired to study that I might be ignorant of less; for (according to Saint Augustine) some things are learned to be enacted and others only to be known: *We learn some things to know them, others, to do them.* Then, where is the offense to be found if even what is licit to women—which is to teach by writing—I do not perform, as I know that I am lacking in means following the counsel of Quintilian: *Let each person learn not only from the precepts of others, but also let him reap counsel from his own nature.*

If the offense is to be found in the *Atenagórica* letter, was that letter anything other than the simple expression of my feeling, written with the implicit permission of our Holy Mother Church? For if the Church, in her most sacred authority, does not forbid it, why must others do so? That I proffered an opinion contrary to that of de Vieyra was audacious, but, as a Father, was it not audacious that he speak against the three Holy Fathers of the Church? My reason, such as it is, is it not as unfettered as his, as both issue from the same source? Is his opinion to be considered as a revelation, as a principle of the Holy Faith, that we must accept blindly? Furthermore, I maintained at all times the respect due such a virtuous man, a respect in which his defender was sadly wanting, ignoring the phrase of Titus Lucius: *Respect is companion to the arts.* I did not touch a thread of the robes of the Society of Jesus; nor did I write for other than the consideration of the person who suggested that I write. And, according to Pliny, *how different the condition of one who writes from that of one who merely speaks.* Had I believed the letter was to be published I would not have been so inattentive. If, as the censor says, the letter is heretical, why does he not denounce it? And with that he would be avenged, and I content, for, which is only seemly, I esteem more highly my reputation as a Catholic and obedient daughter of the Holy Mother Church than all the approbation

Si está bárbara—que en eso dicen bien—,ríase, aunque sea con la risa que dicen del conejo, que yo no le digo que me aplauda, pues como yo fui libre para disentir de Vieyra, lo será cualquier para disentir de mi dictamen.

Pero ¿dónde voy, Señora mía? Que esto no es de aquí, ni es para vuestros oídos, sino que como voy tratando de mis impugnadores, me acordé de las cláusulas de uno que ha salido ahora, e insensiblemente se deslizó la pluma a quererle responder en particular, siendo mi intento hablar en general. Y así, volviendo a nuestro Arce, dice que conoció en esta ciudad dos monjas: la una en el convento de Regina, que tenía el Breviario de tal manera en la memoria, que aplicaba con grandísima prontitud y propiedad sus versos, salmos y sentencias de homilías de los santos, en las conversaciones. La otra, en el convento de la Concepción, tan acostumbrada a leer las Epístolas de mi Padre San Jerónimo, y locuciones del Santo, de tal manera que dice Arce: *Hieronymum ipsum hispane loquentem audire me existimarem.* Y de ésta dice que supo, después de su muerte, había traducido dichas Epístolas en romance; y se duele de que tales talentos no se hubieran empleado en mayores estudios con principios científicos, sin decir los nombres de la una ni de la otra, aunque las trae para confirmación de su sentencia, que es que no sólo es lícito, pero utilísimo y necesario a las mujeres el estudio de las sagradas letras, y mucho más a las monjas, que es lo mismo a que vuestra discreción me exhorta y a que concurren tantas razones.

Pues si vuelvo los ojos a la tan perseguida habilidad de hacer versos—que en mí es tan natural, que aun me violento para que esta carta no lo sean, y pudiera decir aquello de *Quidquid conabar dicere, versus erat*—, viéndola condenar a tantos tanto y acriminar, he buscado muy de propósito cuál sea el daño que puedan tener, y no le he hallado; antes sí los veo aplaudidos en las bocas de las Sibilas; santificados en las plumas de los Profetas, especialmente del Rey David, de quien dice el gran expositor y amado Padre mío, dando razón de las mensuras de sus metros: *In morem Flacci et Pindari nunc iambo currit, nunc alcaico personat, nunc sapphico tumet, nunc semipede ingreditur.*

due a learned woman. If the letter is rash, and he does well to crit-
icize it, then laugh, even if with the laugh of the rabbit, for I have
not asked that he approve; as I was free to dissent from de Vieyra,
so will anyone be free to oppose my opinion.

But how I have strayed, lady. None of this pertains here, nor is
it intended for your ears, but as I was discussing my accusers I re-
membered the words of one that recently have appeared, and,
though my intent was to speak in general, my pen, unbidden,
slipped, and began to respond in particular. And so, returning to
our Arce, he says that he knew in this city two nuns: one in the
Convent of the Regina, who had so thoroughly committed the
Breviary to memory that with the greatest promptitude and pro-
priety she applied in her conversation its verses, psalms, and
maxims of saintly homilies. The other, in the Convent of the Con-
ception, was so accustomed to reading the Epistles of my Father
Saint Jerome, and the Locutions of this Saint, that Arce says, *It
seemed I was listening to Saint Jerome himself, speaking in Span-
ish.* And of this latter woman he says that after her death he
learned that she had translated these Epistles into the Spanish lan-
guage. What a pity that such talents could not have been em-
ployed in major studies with scientific principles. He does not give
the name of either, although he offers these women as confirma-
tion of his opinion, which is that not only is it licit, but most use-
ful and essential for women to study the Holy Word, and even more
essential for nuns; and that study is the very thing to which your
wisdom exhorts me, and in which so many arguments concur.

Then if I turn my eyes to the oft-chastised faculty of making
verses—which is in me so natural that I must discipline myself
that even this letter not be written in that form—I might cite
those lines, *All I wished to express took the form of verse.* And see-
ing that so many condemn and criticize this ability, I have consci-
entiously sought to find what harm may be in it, and I have not
found it, but, rather, I see verse acclaimed in the mouths of the
Sibyls, sanctified in the pens of the Prophets, especially King
David, of whom the exalted Expositor my beloved Father says
(explicating the measure of his metres): *in the manner of Horace
and Pindar, now it hurries along in iambs, now it rings in alcaic,
now swells in sapphic, then arrives in broken feet.* The greater part

Los más de los libros sagrados están en metro, como el Cántico de Moisés; y los de Job, dice San Isidoro, en sus Etimologías, que están en verso heroico. En los Epitalamios los escribió Salomón; en los Trenos, Jeremías. Y así dice Casiodoro: *Omnis poetica locutio a Divinis scripturis sumpsit exordium.* Pues nuestra Iglesia católica no sólo no los desdeña, mas los usa en sus Himnos y recita los de San Ambrosio, Santo Tomás, de San Isidoro y otros. San Buenaventura les tuvo tal afecto que apenas hay plana suya sin versos. San Pablo bien se ve que los había estudiado, pues los cita, y traduce el de Arato: *In ipso enim vivimus, et movemur, et sumus,* y alega el otro de Parménides: *Cretenses semper mendaces, malae bestiae, pigri.* San Gregorio Nacianceno disputa en elegantes versos las cuestiones de Matrimonio y la de la Virginidad. Y ¿qué me canso? La Reina de la Sabiduría y Señora nuestra, con sus sagrados labios, entonó el Cántico de la *Magníficat;* y habiéndola traído por ejemplar; agravio fuera traer ejemplos profanos, aunque sean de varones gravísimos y doctísimos, pues esto sobra para prueba; y el ver que, aunque como la elegancia hebrea no se pudo estrechar a la mensura latina, a cuya causa el traductor sagrado, más atento a lo importante del sentido, omitió el verso, con todo, retienen los Salmos el nombre y divisiones de versos; pues, ¿cuál es el daño que pueden tener ellos en sí? Porque el mal uso no es culpa del arte, sino del mal profesor que los vicia, haciendo de ellos lazos del demonio; y esto en todas las facultades y ciencias sucede.

Pues si está el mal en que los use una mujer, ya se ve cuántas los han usado loablemente; pues ¿en qué está el serlo yo? Confieso desde luego mi ruindad y vileza, pero no juzgo que se habrá visto una copla mía indecente. Demás, que yo nunca he escrito cosa alguna por mi voluntad, sino por ruegos y preceptos ajenos; de tal manera que no me acuerdo haber escrito por mi gusto si no es un papelillo que llaman *El sueño.* Esa carta que vos, Señora mía, honrasteis tanto, la escribí con más repugnancia que otra cosa; y así porque era de cosas sagradas a quienes (como he dicho) tengo reverente temor, como porque

of the Holy Books are in metre, as is the Book of Moses; and those of Job (as Saint Isidore states in his *Etymologiae*) are in heroic verse. Solomon wrote the Canticle of Canticles in verse; and Jeremiah, his *Lamentations*. And so, says Cassiodorus: *All poetic expression had as its source the Holy Scriptures.* For not only does our Catholic Church not disdain verse, it employs verse in its hymns, and recites the lines of Saint Ambrose, Saint Thomas, Saint Isidore, and others. Saint Bonaventure was so taken with verse that he writes scarcely a page where it does not appear. It is readily apparent that Saint Paul had studied verse, for he quotes and translates verses of Aratus: *For in him we live, and move, and are.*[39] And he quotes also that verse of Parmenides: *The Cretans are always liars, evil beasts, slothful bellies.*[40] Saint Gregory Nazianzen argues in elegant verses the questions of matrimony and virginity. And, how should I tire? The Queen of Wisdom, Our Lady, with Her sacred lips, intoned the Canticle of the Magnificat; and having brought forth this example, it would be offensive to add others that were profane, even those of the most serious and learned men, for this alone is more than sufficient confirmation; and even though Hebrew elegance could not be compressed into Latin measure, for which reason, although the sacred translator, more attentive to the importance of the meaning, omitted the verse, the Psalms retain the number and divisions of verses, and what harm is to be found in them? For misuse is not the blame of art, but rather of the evil teacher who perverts the arts, making of them the snare of the devil; and this occurs in all the arts and sciences.

And if the evil is attributed to the fact that a woman employs them, we have seen how many have done so in praiseworthy fashion; what then is the evil in my being a woman? I confess openly my own baseness and meanness, but I judge that no couplet of mine has been deemed indecent. Furthermore, I have never written of my own will, but under the pleas and injunctions of others; to such a degree that the only piece I remember having written for my own pleasure was a little trifle they called *El sueño*. That letter, lady, which you so greatly honored, I wrote more with repugnance than any other emotion; both by reason of the fact that it treated sacred matters, for which (as I have stated) I hold such

parecía querer impugnar, cosa a que tengo aversión natural. Y
creo que si pudiera haber prevenido el dichoso destino a que
nacía—pues, como a otro Moisés, la arrojé expósita a las aguas
del Nilo del silencio, donde la halló y acarició una princesa
como vos—, creo, vuelvo a decir, que si yo tal pensara, la aho-
gara antes entre las mismas manos en que nacía, de miedo
de que pareciesen a la luz de vuestro saber los torpes borrones
de mi ignorancia. De donde se conoce la grandeza de vuestra
bondad, pues está aplaudiendo vuestra voluntad lo que pre-
cisamente ha de estar repugnando vuestro clarísimo en-
tendimiento. Pero ya que su ventura la arrojó a vuestras
puertas, tan expósita y huérfana que hasta el nombre le pu-
sisteis vos, pésame que, entre más deformidades, llevase tam-
bién los defectos de la prisa; porque así por la poca salud que
continuamente tengo, como por la sobra de ocupaciones en
que me pone la obediencia, y carecer de quien me ayude a escri-
bir, y estar necesitada a que todo sea de mi mano y porque,
como iba contra mi genio y no quería más que cumplir con la pa-
labra a quien no podía desobedecer, no veía la hora de acabar;
y así dejé de poner discursos enteros y muchas pruebas que se
me ofrecían, y las dejé por no escribir más; que, a saber que se
había de imprimir, no las hubiera dejado, siquiera por dejar sa-
tisfechas algunas objeciones que se han excitado, y pudiera re-
mitir, pero no seré tan desatenta que ponga tan indecentes
objetos a la pureza de vuestros ojos, pues basta que los ofenda
con mis ignorancias, sin que los remita a ajenos atrevimientos.
Si ellos por sí volaren por allá (que son tan livianos que sí
harán), me ordenaréis lo que debo hacer; que, si no es inter-
viniendo vuestros preceptos, lo que es por mi defensa nunca
tomaré la pluma, porque me parece que no necesita de que otro
le responda, quien en lo mismo que se oculta conoce su error,
pues, como dice mi Padre San Jerónimo, *bonus sermo secreta
non quaerit*, y San Ambrosio: *latere criminosae est conscien-
tiae.* Ni yo me tengo por impugnada, pues dice una regla del
Derecho: *Accusatio non tenetur si non curat de persona, quae*

reverent awe, and because it seems to wish to impugn, a practice for which I have natural aversion; and I believe that had I foreseen the blessed destiny to which it was fated—for like a second Moses I had set it adrift, naked, on the waters of the Nile of silence, where you, a princess, found and cherished it—I believe, I reiterate, that had I known, the very hands of which it was born would have drowned it, out of the fear that these clumsy scribblings from my ignorance appear before the light of your great wisdom; by which one knows the munificence of your kindness, for your goodwill applauds precisely what your reason must wish to reject. For as fate cast it before your doors, so exposed, so orphaned, that it fell to you even to give it a name, I must lament that among other deformities it also bears the blemish of haste, both because of the unrelenting ill-health I suffer, and for the profusion of duties imposed on me by obedience, as well as the want of anyone to guide me in my writing and the need that it all come from my hand, and, finally, because the writing went against my nature and I wished only to keep my promise to one whom I could not disobey, I could not find the time to finish properly, and thus I failed to include whole treatises and many arguments that presented themselves to me, but which I omitted in order to put an end to the writing—many, that had I known the letter was to be printed, I would not have excluded, even if merely to satisfy some objections that have since arisen and which could have been refuted. But I shall not be so ill-mannered as to place such indecent objects before the purity of your eyes, for it is enough that my ignorance be an offense in your sight, without need of entrusting to it the effronteries of others. But if in their audacity these latter should wing their way to you (and they are of such little weight that this will happen) then you will command what I am to do; for, if it does not run contrary to your will, my defense shall be not to take up my pen, for I deem that one affront need not occasion another, if one recognizes the error in the very place it lies concealed. As my Father Saint Jerome says, *good discourse seeks not secret things,* and Saint Ambrose, *it is the nature of a guilty conscience to lie concealed.* Nor do I consider that I have been impugned, for one statute of the Law states: *An accusation will not endure unless nurtured by the person who brought it*

produxerit illam. Lo que sí es de ponderar es el trabajo que le ha costado el andar haciendo traslados. ¡Rara demencia: cansarse más en quitarse el crédito que pudiera en granjearlo! Yo, Señora mía, no he querido responder; aunque otros lo han hecho, sin saberlo yo: basta que he visto algunos papeles, y entre ellos uno que por docto os remito y porque el leerle os desquite parte del tiempo que os he malgastado en lo que yo escribo. Si vos, Señora, gustáredes de que yo haga lo contrario de lo que tenía propuesto a vuestro juicio y sentir, al menor movimiento de vuestro gusto cederá, como es razón, mi dictamen que, como os he dicho, era de callar, porque aunque dice San Juan Crisóstomo: *calumniatores convincere oportet, interrogatores docere,* veo que también dice San Gregorio: *Victoria non minor est, hostes tolerare, quam hostes vincere;* y que la paciencia vence tolerando y triunfa sufriendo. Y si entre los gentiles romanos era costumbre, en la más alta cumbre de la gloria de sus capitanes—cuando entraban triunfando de las naciones, vestidos de púrpura y coronados de laurel, tirando el carro, en vez de brutos, coronadas frentes de vencidos reyes, acompañados de los despojos de las riquezas de todo el mundo y adornada la milicia vencedora de las insignias · de sus hazañas, oyendo los aplausos populares en tan honrosos títulos y renombres como llamarlos Padres de la Patria, Columnas del Imperio, Muros de Roma, Amparos de la República y otros nombres gloriosos—, que en este supremo auge de la gloria y felicidad humana fuese un soldado, en voz alta diciendo al vencedor, como con sentimiento suyo y orden del Senado: Mira que eres mortal; mira que tienes tal y tal defecto; sin perdonar los más vergonzosos, como sucedió en el triunfo de César, que voceaban los más viles soldados a sus oídos: *Cavete romani, adducimus vobis adulterum calvum.* Lo cual se hacía porque en medio de tanta honra no se desvaneciese el vencedor, y porque el lastre de estas afrentas hiciese contrapeso a las velas de tantos aplausos, para que no peligrase la nave del juicio entre los vientos de las aclamaciones. Si esto, digo, hacían unos gentiles, con sola la luz de la Ley Natural, nosotros, católicos, con un precepto de amar a los enemigos, ¿qué mucho haremos

forth. What *is* a matter to be weighed is the effort spent in copy-
ing the accusation. A strange madness, to expend more effort in
denying acclaim than in earning it! I, lady, have chosen not to re-
spond (although others did so without my knowledge); it suffices
that I have seen certain treatises, among them, one so learned I
send it to you so that reading it will compensate in part for the
time you squandered on my writing. If, lady, you wish that I act
contrary to what I have proposed here for your judgment and
opinion, the merest indication of your desire will, as is seemly,
countermand my inclination, which, as I have told you, is to be
silent, for although Saint John Chrysostom says, *those who slan-
der must be refuted, and those who question, taught,* I know also
that Saint Gregory says, *It is no less a victory to tolerate enemies
than to overcome them.* And that patience conquers by tolerating
and triumphs by suffering. And if among the Roman Gentiles it
was the custom when their captains were at the highest peak of
glory—when returning triumphant from other nations, robed in
purple and wreathed with laurel, crowned-but-conquered kings
pulling their carriages in the stead of beasts, accompanied by the
spoils of the riches of all the world, the conquering troops
adorned with the insignia of their heroic feats, hearing the plau-
dits of the people who showered them with titles of honor and
renown such as Fathers of the Nation, Columns of the Empire,
Walls of Rome, Shelter of the Republic, and other glorious
names—a soldier went before these captains in this moment of
the supreme apogee of glory and human happiness crying out in a
loud voice to the conqueror (by his consent and order of the Sen-
ate): Behold how you are mortal; behold how you have this or
that defect, not excepting the most shameful, as happened in the
triumph of Caesar, when the vilest soldiers clamored in his ear:
Beware, Romans, for we bring you the bald adulterer. Which was
done so that in the midst of such honor the conquerers not be
swelled up with pride, and that the ballast of these insults act as
counterweight to the bellying sails of such approbation, and that
the ship of good judgment not founder amidst the winds of accla-
mation. If this, I say, was the practice among Gentiles, who knew
only the light of Natural Law, how much might we Catholics, un-
der the injunction to love our enemies, achieve by tolerating

en tolerarlos? Yo de mí puedo asegurar que las calumnias algunas veces me han mortificado, pero nunca me han hecho daño, porque yo tengo por muy necio al que teniendo ocasión de merecer, pasa el trabajo y pierde el mérito, que es como los que no quieren conformarse al morir y al fin mueren sin servir su resistencia de excusar la muerte, sino de quitarles el mérito de la conformidad, y de hacer mala la muerte que podía ser bien. Y así, Señora mía, estas cosas creo que aprovechan más que dañan, y tengo por mayor riesgo de los aplausos en la flaqueza humana, que suelen apropiarse lo que no es suyo, y es menester estar con mucho cuidado y tener escritas en el corazón aquellas palabras del Apóstol: *Quid autem habes quod non accepisti? Si autem accepisti, quid gloriaris quasi non acceperis?* para que sirvan de escudo que resista las puntas de las alabanzas, que son lanzas que, en no atribuyéndose a Dios, cuyas son, nos quitan la vida y nos hacen ser ladrones de la honra de Dios y usurpadores de los talentos que nos entregó y de los dones que nos prestó y de que hemos de dar estrechísima cuenta. Y así, Señora, yo temo más esto que aquello; porque aquello, con sólo un acto sencillo de paciencia, está convertido en provecho; y esto, son menester muchos actos reflexos de humildad y propio conocimiento para que no sea daño. Y así, de mí lo conozco y reconozco que es especial favor de Dios el conocerlo, para saberme portar en uno y en otro con aquella sentencia de San Agustín: *Amico laudanti credendum non est, sicut nec inimico detrahenti.* Aunque yo soy tal que las más veces lo debo de echar a perder o mezclarlo con tales defectos e imperfecciones, que vicio lo que de suyo fuera bueno. Y así, en lo poco que se ha impreso mío, no sólo mi nombre, pero ni el consentimiento para la impresión ha sido dictamen propio, sino libertad ajena que no cae debajo de mi dominio, como lo fue la impresión de la Carta Atenagórica; de suerte que solamente unos *Ejercicios de la Encarnación* y unos *Ofrecimientos de los Dolores,* se imprimieron con gusto mío por la pública devoción, pero sin mi nombre; de los cuales remito algunas copias, porque (si os parece) los repartáis entre nuestras hermanas las religiosas de esa santa comunidad y además de esa ciudad. De los *Dolores* va

them? And in my own behalf I can attest that calumny has often mortified me, but never harmed me, being that I hold as a great fool one who having occasion to receive credit suffers the difficulty and loses the credit, as it is with those who do not resign themselves to death, but, in the end, die anyway, their resistance not having prevented death, but merely deprived them of the credit of resignation and caused them to die badly when they might have died well. And thus, lady, I believe these experiences do more good than harm, and I hold as greater the jeopardy of applause to human weakness, as we are wont to appropriate praise that is not our own, and must be ever watchful, and carry graven on our hearts those words of the Apostle: *Or what hast thou that thou hast not received? And if thou hast received, why doest thou glory as if thou hadst not received it.*[41] so that these words serve as a shield to fend off the sharp barbs of commendations, which are as spears which when not attributed to God (whose they are), claim our lives and cause us to be thieves of God's honor and usurpers of the talents He bestowed on us and the gifts that He lent to us, for which we must give the most strict accounting. And thus, lady, I fear applause more than calumny, because the latter, with but the simple act of patience becomes gain, while the former requires many acts of reflection and humility and proper recognition so that it not become harm. And I know and recognize that it is by special favor of God that I know this, as it enables me in either instance to act in accord with the words of Saint Augustine: *One must believe neither the friend who praises nor the enemy who detracts.* Although, most often I squander God's favor, or vitiate with such defects and imperfections that I spoil what, being His, was good. And thus in what little of mine that has been printed, neither the use of my name, nor even consent for the printing, was given by my own counsel, but by the license of another who lies outside my domain, as was also true with the printing of the *Atenagórica* letter, and only a few *Exercises of the Incarnation* and *Offerings of the Sorrows* were printed for public devotions with my pleasure but without my name; of which I am sending some few copies that (if you so desire) you may distribute them among our sisters, the nuns of that holy community, as well as in that city. I send but one copy of the *Sorrows* because the

sólo uno porque se han consumido ya y no pude hallar más. Hícelos sólo por la devoción de mis hermanas, años ha, y después se divulgaron; cuyos asuntos son tan improporcionados a mi tibieza como a mi ignorancia, y sólo me ayudó en ellos ser cosas de nuestra gran Reina: que no sé qué se tiene el que en tratando de María Santísima se enciende el corazón más helado. Yo quisiera, venerable Señora mía, remitiros obras dignas de vuestra virtud y sabiduría; pero como dijo el Poeta:

> *Ut desint vires, tamen est laudanda voluntas:*
> *hac ego contentos, auguror esse Deos.*

Si algunas otras cosillas escribiere, siempre irán a buscar el sagrado de vuestras plantas y el seguro de vuestra corrección, pues no tengo otra alhaja con que pagaros, y en sentir de Séneca, el que empezó a hacer beneficios se obligó a continuarlos; y así os pagará a vos vuestra propia liberalidad, que sólo así puedo yo quedar dignamente desempeñada, sin que caiga en mí aquello del mismo Séneca: *Turpe est beneficiis vinci.* Que es bizarría del acreedor generoso dar al deudor pobre, con que pueda satisfacer la deuda. Así lo hizo Dios con el mundo imposibilitado de pagar: diole a su Hijo propio para que se le ofreciese por digna satisfacción.

Si el estilo, venerable Señora mía, de esta carta no hubiere sido como a vos es debido, os pido perdón de la casera familiaridad o menos autoridad de que tratándoos como a una religiosa de velo, hermana mía, se me ha olvidado la distancia de vuestra ilustrísima persona, que a veros yo sin velo, no sucediera así; pero vos, con vuestra cordura y benignidad, supliréis o enmendaréis los términos y si os pareciere incongruo el *Vos* de que yo he usado por parecerme que para la reverencia que os debo es muy poca reverencia la *Reverencia,* mudadlo en el que os pareciere decente a lo que vos merecéis, que yo no me he atrevido a exceder de los límites de vuestro estilo ni a romper el margen de vuestra modestia.

Y mantenedme en vuestra gracia, para impetrarme la divina,

others have been exhausted and I could find no other copy. I wrote them long ago, solely for the devotions of my sisters, and later they were spread abroad; and their contents are disproportionate as regards my unworthiness and my ignorance, and they profited that they touched on matters of our exalted Queen; for I cannot explain what it is that inflames the coldest heart when one refers to the Most Holy Mary. It is my only desire, esteemed lady, to remit to you works worthy of your virtue and wisdom; as the poet said:

> Though strength may falter, good will must be praised.
> In this, I believe, the gods will be content.

If ever I write again, my scribbling will always find its way to the haven of your holy feet and the certainty of your correction, for I have no other jewel with which to pay you, and, in the lament of Seneca, he who has once bestowed benefices has committed himself to continue; and so you must be repaid out of your own munificence, for only in this way shall I with dignity be freed from debt and avoid that the words of that same Seneca come to pass: *It is contemptible to be surpassed in benefices.* For in his gallantry the generous creditor gives to the poor debtor the means to satisfy his debt. So God gave His gift to a world unable to repay Him: He gave His son that He be offered a recompense worthy of Him.

If, most venerable lady, the tone of this letter may not have seemed right and proper, I ask forgiveness for its homely familiarity, and the less than seemly respect in which by treating you as a nun, one of my sisters, I have lost sight of the remoteness of your most illustrious person; which, had I seen you without your veil, would never have occurred; but you in all your prudence and mercy will supplement or amend the language, and if you find unsuitable the *Vos* of the address I have employed, believing that for the reverence I owe you, Your Reverence seemed little reverent, modify it in whatever manner seems appropriate to your due, for I have not dared exceed the limits of your custom, nor transgress the boundary of your modesty.

And hold me in your grace, and entreat for me divine grace, of

de que os conceda el Señor muchos aumentos y os guarde, como le suplico y he menester. De este convento de N. Padre San Jerónimo de Méjico, a primero día del mes de marzo de mil seiscientos y noventa y un años. B. V. M. vuestra más favorecida

JUANA INÉS DE LA CRUZ

which the Lord God grant you large measure, and keep you, as I pray Him, and am needful. From this convent of our Father Saint Jerome in México City, the first day of the month of March of sixteen hundred and ninety-one. Allow me to kiss your hand, your most favored

JUANA INÉS DE LA CRUZ

FIRST I DREAM

El Sueño

Piramidal, funesta, de la tierra
nacida sombra, al Cielo encaminaba
de vanos obeliscos punta altiva,
escalar pretendiendo las Estrellas;
si bien sus luces bellas
—exentas siempre, siempre rutilantes—
la tenebrosa guerra
que con negros vapores le intimaba
la pavorosa sombra fugitiva
burlaban tan distantes,
que su atezado ceño
al superior convexo aun no llegaba
del orbe de la Diosa
que tres veces hermosa
con tres hermosos rostros ser ostenta,
quedando sólo dueño
del aire que empañaba
con el aliento denso que exhalaba;
y en la quietud contenta
de imperio silencioso,
sumisas sólo voces consentía
de las nocturnas aves,
tan obscuras, tan graves,
que aun el silencio no se interrumpía.
    Con tardo vuelo y canto, del oído
mal, y aun peor del ánimo admitido,
la avergonzada Nictimene acecha
de las sagradas puertas los resquicios,
o de las claraboyas eminentes
los huecos más propicios
que capaz a su intento le abren brecha,
y sacrílega llega a los lucientes
faroles sacros de perenne llama
que extingue, si no infama,
en licor claro la materia crasa
consumiendo, que el árbol de Minerva

First I Dream

Pyramidal, doleful, mournful shadow
born of the earth, the haughty culmination
of vain obelisks thrust toward the Heavens,
attempting to ascend and touch the Stars
whose resplendent glow
(unobscured, eternal scintillation)
mocked from afar
the tenebrous war
blackly intimated in the vapors
10   of the awesome, fleeting adumbration;
this glowering shadow
touched the edge but did not wholly absorb
the Goddess's orb
(three, Diana's faces
that show her beauteous being in three phases),
but conquered only air,
misted the atmosphere
that darkened densely with each exhalation;
and in the quietude
20   of this silent kingdom
only muted voices could be heard
from nocturnal birds,
so solemn and subdued
the muffled sound did not disturb the silence.
    In flight and song ungraceful, dull of ear,
and poorer still in quality of soul,
humiliated, poor Nyctímene
lurks, hidden, at the chinks in sacred doors,
hovers at a high clerestory,
30   seeks the propitious rift
that will intrigue to open to her scheme,
and sacrilegiously draws near the gleam
of holy lamps where burn eternal flames
that she extinguishes,
if not defames, imbibing as a clear
liquor the heavy oil unwillingly

de su fruto, de prensas agravado,
congojoso sudó y rindió forzado.
      Y aquellas que su casa
campo vieron volver, sus telas hierba,
a la deidad de Baco inobedientes
—ya no historias contando diferentes,
en forma sí afrentosa transformadas—,
segunda forman niebla,
ser vistas aun temiendo en la tiniebla,
aves sin pluma aladas:
aquellas tres oficïosas, digo,
atrevidas Hermanas,
que el tremendo castigo
de desnudas les dió pardas membranas
alas tan mal dispuestas
que escarnio son aun de las más funestas:
éstas, con el parlero
ministro de Plutón un tiempo, ahora
supersticioso indicio al agorero,
solos la no canora
componían capilla pavorosa,
máximas, negras, longas entonando,
y pausas más que voces, esperando
a la torpe mensura perezosa
de mayor proporción tal vez, que el viento
con flemático echaba movimiento,
de tan tardo compás, tan detenido,
que en medio se quedó tal vez dormido.
      Este, pues, triste són intercadente
de la asombrada turba temerosa,
menos a la atención solicitaba
que al sueño persuadía;
antes sí, lentamente,
su obtusa consonancia espacïosa
al sosiego inducía
y al reposo los miembros convidaba
—el silencio intimando a los vivientes,
uno y ótro sellando labio obscuro

40

50

60

70

relinquished, its fruit oppressed by presses,
the tortured sweat wrung from Minerva's tree.
 And those women, three,
40 their home become a field, their weaving, weeds,
for want of faith in Bacchus's deity
(no longer telling of heroic deeds,
but by dishonor hideously transformed)
now form a second fog,
fearful, even by dark, to be perceived,
winged, denuded birds;
these three of whom I speak, diligent,
audacious Sisters,
as dreadful punishment
50 with dark membranous pinions were aggrieved,
wings monstrously conceived,
a mockery, but also piteous;
they, and that Ascalaphus,
once Pluto's loose-tongued minister, but now
a sign most sinister to augurers,
among them formed
a tuneless and appalling a capella,
black maximas and longas they intoned,
their singing, though, more silences than sound,
60 hoping, perhaps, the apathetic drone
might quicken in intensity, or else,
phlegmatically, the wind might stir to song,
a tempo so lethargically composed
that halfway through, the wind itself might doze.
 This gloomy, then, and fluctuating strain
from the penumbrous, awe-inspiring throng,
less than a summoning to wakefulness,
persuasion was to sleep;
but first, and slowly,
70 the prolonged and consonant refrain
invited peacefulness,
lulling the body gently to its rest
—and there, sealing all lips, imposing quiet,
his will conveyed to every living thing,

con indicante dedo,
Harpócrates, la noche, silencioso;
a cuyo, aunque no duro,
si bien imperïoso
precepto, todos fueron obedientes—.

80   El viento sosegado, el can dormido,
éste yace, aquél quedo
los átomos no mueve,
con el susurro hacer temiendo leve,
aunque poco, sacrílego rüido,
violador del silencio sosegado.
El mar, no ya alterado,
ni aun la instable mecía
cerúlea cuna donde el Sol dormía;
y los dormidos, siempre mudos, peces,
90   en los lechos lamosos
de sus obscuros senos cavernosos,
mudos eran dos veces;
y entre ellos, la engañosa encantadora
Alcione, a los que antes
en peces transformó, simples amantes,
transformada también, vengaba ahora.

    En los del monte senos escondidos,
cóncavos de peñascos mal formados
—de su aspereza menos defendidos
100   que de su obscuridad asegurados—,
cuya mansión sombría
ser puede noche en la mitad del día,
incógnita aún al cierto
montaraz pie del cazador experto
—depuesta la fiereza
de unos, y de otros el temor depuesto—
yacía el vulgo bruto,
a la Naturaleza
el de su potestad pagando impuesto,
110   universal tributo;
y el Rey, que vigilancias afectaba,
aun con abiertos ojos no velaba.

his finger cautioning,
Harpokrates, the god of silence, night;
and to what if not
unjust, might well be thought
imperious command, all did attend.

80   The breeze becalmed, the tranquil dog adoze,
both at rest, such is the mood
the still air not an atom moves
for fear its faintest murmur might disclose
an innocent but sacrilegious hum,
a profanation of the soothing calm.
A settled, stable sea,
the cerulean cradle
of the deep unrocked, the sun asleep;
the fish forever dumb, and somnolent,
90   idle in dark ooze
within a caverned, murky firmament,
were twice, were doubly mute;
and found among them was Alcyone,
the artful sorceress
who having changed her suitors into fish
was herself transmuted in redress.

    In the hidden bosom of the mountain,
uneven domes of concave, rugged stone
(far less against adversity insured
100   than of continuing obscurity assured),
in this somber mansion
where night may fall while day is at the noon,
a landscape still unknown
to even skilled and practiced forest huntsmen
(the hunted without fear,
the stalker from ferocity released)
lay a noble beast,
and in obeisance,
the brute consigned the just tribute
110   to Nature's worldly sovereignty;
and though this king affected vigilance,
sleeping with open eyes, it did not see.

El de sus mismos perros acosado,
monarca en otro tiempo esclarecido,
tímido ya venado,
con vigilante oído,
del sosegado ambiente
al menor perceptible movimiento
que los átomos muda,
120   la oreja alterna aguda
y el leve rumor siente
que aun lo altera dormido.
Y en la quietud del nido,
que de brozas y lodo instable hamaca
formó en la más opaca
parte del árbol, duerme recogida
la leve turba, descansando el viento
del que le corta, alado movimiento.
De Júpiter el ave generosa
130   —como al fin Reina—, por no darse entera
al descanso, que vicio considera
si de preciso pasa, cuidadosa
de no incurrir de omisa en el exceso,
a un solo pie librada fía el peso,
y en otro guarda el cálculo pequeño
—despertador reloj del leve sueño—,
porque, si necesario fué admitido,
no pueda dilatarse continuado,
antes interrumpido
140   del regio sea pastoral cuidado.
¡ Oh de la Majestad pensión gravosa,
que aun el menor descuido no perdona!
Causa, quizá, que ha hecho misteriosa,
circular, denotando, la corona,
en círculo dorado,
que el afán es no menos continuado.
El sueño todo, en fin, lo poseía;
todo, en fin, el silencio lo ocupaba:
aun el ladrón dormía;
150   aun el amante no se desvelaba.

Actaeon, now by his own hounds harassed,
in other days a monarch much revered,
a timid deer become
vigilant to sounds of danger
in this calm atmosphere,
toward the least perceptible disturbance
stirring the atoms
120   flicks one and then the other pointed ear,
senses the hushed rustle
that, even in his sleep, he hears.
And in the quiet of the nest,
swaying, fragile hammocks of brush and mud
constructed in the darkest
branches of the tree, sleeps, in blest proximity,
the airy multitude—the very wind
no more by wingèd movement cleft, at rest.
For Jupiter the noble bird and Queen,
130   for never wholly yielding to repose,
which it knows only as offense
when rest exceeds the requisite, the eagle,
watchful not to sin with indolence,
to a single foot entrusts its weight
and in the other tightly grasps a stone
—a sharp alarm to startle fretful sleep—
for even should that respite be condoned
it cannot linger in its slumber but
needs must stir to fill
140   its pastoral yet regal obligation.
O Majesty, how onerous the burden
that will not countenance distraction!
Cause, perhaps, of why the crown is round,
denoting in its mystery that,
like the ring of gold,
the sovereign's duty must remain unbroken.
Sleep, in summary, now possessed all things,
all things were now by silence overtaken:
even the brigand slept,
150   even the slumberous lover did not waken.

El conticinio casi ya pasando
iba, y la sombra dimidiaba, cuando
de las diurnas tareas fatigados
—y no sólo oprimidos
del afán ponderoso
del corporal trabajo, mas cansados
del deleite también (que también cansa
objeto continuado a los sentidos
aun siendo deleitoso:
que la Naturaleza siempre alterna   160
ya una, ya otra balanza,
distribuyendo varios ejercicios,
ya al ocio, ya al trabajo destinados,
en el fiel infiel con que gobierna
la aparatosa máquina del mundo)—;
así, pues, de profundo
sueño dulce los miembros ocupados,
quedaron los sentidos
del que ejercicio tienen ordinario
—trabajo, en fin pero trabajo amado,   170
si hay amable trabajo—,
si privados no, al menos suspendidos,
y cediendo al retrato del contrario
de la vida, que—lentamente armado—
cobarde embiste y vence perezoso
con armas soñolientas,
desde el cayado humilde al cetro altivo,
sin que haya distintivo
que el sayal de la púrpura discierna:
pues su nivel, en todo poderoso,   180
gradúa por exentas
a ningunas personas,
desde la de a quien tres forman coronas
soberana tïara,
hasta la que pajiza vive choza;
desde la que el Danubio undoso dora,
a la que junco humilde, humilde mora;
y con siempre igual vara

    Nearly past, the darkest hour of the night,
shadow marking midpoint to the dawn,
relieved of his diurnal tasks, man welcomes
reprieve, fatigued, not only
by the cumbrous toll of
physical exertion, but also by the
pleasant toil of delectation (for any
action, overly repeated, may tire the
senses, even pleasure;

160   persistently, Nature lifts and lowers
one, and then the other, of her pans,
distributing her several chores—now
restful leisure, now gainful activity—
on the imbalanced balance with which she
rules the world's complex machinery);
being, then, the body
engaged by deep and welcome sleep, and,
if not ended what
might be thought the normal occupation

170   of the senses (work, after all, but
well-belovèd work
—if labor may be savored), at least
this while suspended and surrendered to the image
of the antipode to life, as sopor
(oblivion its weapon) furtively attacks
and indolently quells
the humble shepherd and the royal prince,
marking no difference between
the silk of kings and peasant's woolen stuff,

180   for slumber's strickle, in its omnipotence,
grants no favor to
any living being,
from Pope whose sovereign tiara is from
three golden circlets cast
to lowly rustic in his hut of thatch,
from Emperor in his Danube palace
to laborer beneath a roof of reeds,
as, with undiscriminating rule,

(como, en efecto, imagen poderosa
190   de la muerte) Morfeo
el sayal mide igual con el brocado.

   El alma, pues, suspensa
del exterior gobierno—en que ocupada
en material empleo,
o bien o mal da el día por gastado—,
solamente dispensa
remota, si del todo separada
no, a los de muerte temporal opresos
lánguidos miembros, sosegados huesos,
200   los gajes del calor vegetativo,
el cuerpo siendo, en sosegada calma,
un cadáver con alma,
muerto a la vida y a la muerte vivo,
de lo segundo dando tardas señas
el del reloj humano
vital volante que, si no con mano,
con arterial concierto, unas pequeñas
muestras, pulsando, manifiesta lento
de su bien regulado movimiento.

210   Este, pues, miembro rey y centro vivo
de espíritus vitales,
con su asociado respirante fuelle
—pulmón, que imán del viento es atractivo,
que en movimientos nunca desiguales
o comprimiendo ya, o ya dilatando
el musculoso, claro arcaduz blando,
hace que en él resuelle
el que lo circunscribe fresco ambiente
que impele ya caliente,
220   y él venga su expulsión haciendo activo
pequeños robos al calor nativo,
algún tiempo llorados,
nunca recuperados,
si ahora no sentidos de su dueño,
que, repetido, no hay robo pequeño—;
éstos, pues, de mayor, como ya digo,

Morpheus (infamous image of
190   eternal death) equates
the roughest homespun cloth with fine brocade.
The soul, then, freed from
governing the senses (by which endeavor
and activity it
deems the day is well or poorly spent)
now, it seems, does but
administer (remote, if not completely
disconnected from the temporary
death of languid limbs and inert bones)
200   the gift of vegetative warmth, the mortal
shell in restful lassitude, cadaver,
yet with a soul imbued,
dead in life, but living still in death,
and, of life's continuation giving
silent indication,
the vital mainspring of the human clock:
its movement marked not by hands but
harmony of vein and artery, the
slow, pulsing, regulation of the heart.
210   This, then, sovereign organ and lively
core of vital spirits,
paired with the auxiliary bellows of
the lungs, like a magnet attracting air
in constant, unvarying, to and fro,
contracting first, and then expanding
the muscular conduit of the throat
wherein the breath resounds,
cool air from the surrounding atmosphere,
a moment held and then expelled as warmth,
220   avenges its summary expulsion
with incessant theft of body heat,
only briefly wept
but never more retrieved,
losses that, though scarcely now perceived,
repeated teach no theft of life is small;
these, then, to review, exceptional two

excepción, uno y otro fiel testigo,
la vida aseguraban,
mientras con mudas voces impugnaban
230 la información, callados, los sentidos
—con no replicar sólo defendidos—,
y la lengua que, torpe, enmudecía,
con no poder hablar los desmentía.

    Y aquella del calor más competente
científica oficina,
próvida de los miembros despensera,
que avara nunca y siempre diligente,
ni a la parte prefiere más vecina
ni olvida a la remota,
240 y en ajustado natural cuadrante
las cuantidades nota
que a cada cuál tocarle considera,
del que alambicó quilo el incesante
calor, en el manjar que—medianero
piadoso—entre él y el húmedo interpuso
su inocente substancia,
pagando por entero
la que, ya piedad sea, o ya arrogancia,
al contrario voraz, necia, lo expuso
250 —merecido castigo, aunque se excuse,
al que en pendencia ajena se introduce—;
ésta, pues, si no fragua de Vulcano,
templada hoguera del calor humano,
al cerebro envïaba
húmedos, mas tan claros los vapores
de los atemperados cuatro humores,
que con ellos no sólo no empañaba
los simulacros que la estimativa
dió a la imaginativa
260 y aquésta, por custodia más segura,
en forma ya más pura
entregó a la memoria que, oficiosa,
grabó tenaz y guarda cuidadosa,
sino que daban a la fantasía

(both heart and lung impeccable informants),
affirmed that life went on,
while the senses, with their silence, impugned
230   that affirmation, all sound withdrawn
(quiescence implying refutation),
and the tongue, clumsy, muted by sleep,
wordlessly voiced its contradiction.
        That most competent and scientific
laboratory,
dispensing warmth to all the body,
withholding never, ever diligent,
neither to neighbor showing preference
nor slighting one remote,
240   with nature's instrument is taking note
of precise measurements
of chyme it will assign throughout the soma,
distilled by unremitting heat, and then,
in selfless sacrifice (benevolent
its intercession) between Humidity
and fire impose itself, and, paying the price,
give up its substance,
whether from true compassion or senseless
arrogance, in total abnegation
250   —expected punishment, although forgiven,
for one who intervenes in others' quarrels;
this, then, if not Vulcan's furnace, the
candent, bubbling, cauldron of human heat,
transmitted to the brain
misty, yet so transparent, vapors
from the fluid store of humors, four,
their presence did not obscure or blur
the simulacra reason forwarded
to the imagination,
260   it, in turn, for safer preservation,
surrendered them to memory, now in
their purest form, to be
punctiliously graved and guarded,
offering to fantasy

lugar de que formase
imágenes diversas. Y del modo
que en tersa superficie, que de Faro
cristalino portento, asilo raro
fué, en distancia longísima se vían
270   (sin que ésta le estorbase)
del reino casi de Neptuno todo
las que distantes lo surcaban naves
—viéndose claramente
en su azogada luna
el número, el tamaño y la fortuna
que en la instable campaña transparente
arresgadas tenían,
mientras aguas y vientos dividían
sus velas leves y sus quillas graves—:
280   así ella, sosegada, iba copiando
las imágenes todas de las cosas,
y el pincel invisible iba formando
de mentales, sin luz, siempre vistosas
colores, las figuras
no sólo ya de todas la criaturas
sublunares, mas aun también de aquéllas
que intelectuales claras son Estrellas,
y en el modo posible
que concebirse puede lo invisible,
290   en sí, mañosa, las representaba
y al alma las mostraba.

    La cual, en tanto, toda convertida
a su inmaterial sér y esencia bella,
aquella contemplaba,
participada de alto Sér, centella
que con similitud en sí gozaba;
y juzgándose casi dividida
de aquella que impedida
siempre la tiene, corporal cadena,
300   que grosera embaraza y torpe impide
el vuelo intelectual con que ya mide
la cuantidad inmensa de la Esfera,

occasion to release
its many images. And in the way
that on a glossy surface—that vitreous,
wondrous, mirror of Pharos signaling
safe harbor—ships, at farthest distances
270   (but not for that eclipsed),
breasting the waves of Neptune's far-flung sphere
could be observed as clearly as if near,
every particular
in that quicksilvered mirror,
the number, size, and fate of caravels
that risked, within that storm-tossed, transparent
bell, its muted tolling,
as billowing sail and ponderous keel
parted a course through swelling wind and sea;
280   similarly, Fantasy, in repose,
her fictive brush, though immaterial,
composing images of all being,
painting in brilliant colors, even
without light, figures of
not only all the earthly creatures, but
also features of those stars we know
as concepts of the intellect, and,
as far as possible
for the invisible to be conceived
290   in fancy, she limned them, artfully, and
revealed them to the soul.

    The Soul, in turn, transmuted into
beauteous essence and discarnate being,
absorbs these offerings,
made in His image, and treasuring
the spark of the Divine she bears within,
judging she is nearly free of all
that binds her, keeps her from liberty,
the corporeal chains
300   that vulgarly restrain and clumsily
impede the soaring intellect that now,
unchecked, measures the vastness of the Sphere,

ya el curso considera
regular, con que giran desiguales
los cuerpos celestiales
—culpa si grave, merecida pena
(torcedor del sosiego, riguroso)
de estudio vanamente judicioso—,
puesta, a su parecer, en la eminente
310   cumbre de un monte a quien el mismo Atlante
que preside gigante
a los demás, enano obedecía,
y Olimpo, cuya sosegada frente,
nunca de aura agitada
consintió ser violada,
aun falda suya ser no merecía:
pues las nubes—que opaca son corona
de la más elevada corpulencia,
del volcán más soberbio que en la tierra
320   gigante erguido intima al cielo guerra—,
apenas densa zona
de su altiva eminencia,
o a su vasta cintura
cíngulo tosco son, que—mal ceñido—
o el viento lo desata sacudido,
o vecino el calor del Sol lo apura.

    A la región primera de su altura
(ínfima parte, digo, dividiendo
en tres su continuado cuerpo horrendo),
330   el rápido no pudo, el veloz vuelo
del águila—que puntas hace al Cielo
y al Sol bebe los rayos pretendiendo
entre sus luces colocar su nido—
llegar; bien que esforzando
más que nunca el impulso, ya batiendo
las dos plumadas velas, ya peinando
con las garras el aire, ha pretendido,
tejiendo de los átomos escalas,
que su inmunidad rompan sus dos alas.

340   Las Pirámides dos—ostentaciones

observes the harmonious,
though richly various, rotation
of heavenly bodies
—a grave offense and deserved punishment
(and severe torment to tranquillity)
when used to speculate on destiny—
high, she deems, upon a towering mountain
310   beside which the mighty Titan, Atlas,
himself a giant tall
above all mortal men, an elf became,
and Mount Olympus, whose noble countenance
the breeze had never touched,
humbled itself, feeling
too small to stand beside such eminence,
for lowering clouds (opaque crown of the
loftiest, most substantial mountain
and of the haughtiest volcano that
320   rises to do battle with the sky)
are barely high enough
to ring its corpulence,
or form a tattered
cingulum about its waist that, loosely tied,
is all too easily undone by
howling winds or nearby, blazing Sun.
     Of these heights, even the lowest cliffs
(those which—if divided into three
that awesome majesty—composed the base)
330   rose far above the purview of the
eagle—swift and powerful of flight,
rising toward the Sun, drinking its rays,
trying to build its nest in golden light;
however great its labor
however strong the thrust of two great
feathered sails, the force of fearsome talons
combing the fibers of the air, striving
from the very atoms to weave stairs,
wings could not breach the impregnable.
340   The two Pyramids (splendor of a

de Menfis vano, y de la Arquitectura
último esmero, si ya no pendones
fijos, no tremolantes—, cuya altura
coronada de bárbaros trofeos
tumba y bandera fué a los Ptolomeos,
que al viento, que a las nubes publicaba
(si ya también al Cielo no decía)
de su grande, su siempre vencedora
ciudad—ya Cairo ahora—
350   las que, porque a su copia enmudecía,
la Fama no cantaba
Gitanas glorias, Ménficas proezas,
aun en el viento, aun en el Cielo impresas: :
        éstas—que en nivelada simetría
su estatura crecía
con tal diminución, con arte tanto,
que (cuanto más al Cielo caminaba)
a la vista, que lince la miraba,
entre los vientos se desparecía,
360   sin permitir mirar la sutil punta
que el primer Orbe finge que se junta,
hasta que fatigada del espanto,
no descendida, sino despeñada
se hallaba al pie de la espaciosa basa,
tarde o mal recobrada
del desvanecimiento
que pena fué no escasa
del visüal alado atrevimiento—,
cuyos cuerpos opacos
370   no al Sol opuestos, antes avenidos
con sus luces, si no confederados
con él (como, en efecto, confinantes),
tan del todo bañados
de su resplandor eran, que—lucidos—
nunca de calorosos caminantes
al fatigado aliento, a los pies flacos,
ofrecieron alfombra
aun de pequeña, aun de señal de sombra: :

vain Memphis, and of Architecture
the supreme cynosure, triangular
pennons, steadfast, not by the zephyr blown)
whose heights, crowned with barbaric trophies,
tomb and banner were to noble Ptolemies,
apices that to wind and cloud proclaimed
(if to the Heavens not directly told) news
of their grand, ever victorious city,
Cairo now its name,
350 'Gyptian glories and Memphistean feats,
though on the wind and in the Heavens scribed,
Fame failed to celebrate
(so great the truth, the copy stilled the tongue);
    these two, which, in their paired symmetry,
increased in stature as
they decreased in girth, both with such artistry
that (the farther they ascended toward the Sky)
despite a lynx-eyed observation,
they vanished, lost high among the winds;
360 their tips, twinned, appeared to touch the nearest
star so far from view, the questing eye,
exhausted now, and overcome with awe,
succumbed, eschewing gradual descent,
and plunged back earthward, to the base, where
it awakened, more or less,
from not insubstantial
dizziness, a punishment
for having ventured to give vision wings;
these opaque structures were
370 not at odds but, rather, in active
complicity, enjoying such close
proximity to the Sun, and being
so absolutely bathed
in its effulgence, echoing its rays,
that the sun-baked traveler, however
dazed and footsore, from them
won no indulgence, no intimation,
no sign, of grace of shade or shadow;

éstas, que glorias ya sean Gitanas,
380 o elaciones profanas,
bárbaros jeroglíficos de ciego
error, según el Griego
ciego también, dulcísimo Poeta
—si ya, por las que escribe
Aquileyas proezas
o marciales de Ulises sutilezas,
la unión no lo recibe
de los Historiadores, o lo acepta
(cuando entre su catálogo lo cuente)
390 que gloria más que número le aumente—,
de cuya dulce serie numerosa
fuera más fácil cosa
al temido Tonante
el rayo fulminante
quitar, o la pesada
a Alcides clava herrada,
que un hemistiquio solo
de los que le dictó propicio Apolo: :
según de Homero, digo, la sentencia,
400 las Pirámides fueron materiales
tipos solos, señales exteriores
de las que, dimensiones interiores,
especies son del alma intencionales:
que como sube en piramidal punta
al Cielo la ambiciosa llama ardiente,
así la humana mente
su figura trasunta,
y a la Causa Primera siempre aspira
—céntrico punto donde recta tira
410 la línea, si ya no circunferencia,
que contiene, infinita, toda esencia—.
Estos, pues, Montes dos artificiales
(bien maravillas, bien milagros sean),
y aun aquella blasfema altiva Torre
de quien hoy dolorosas son señales
—no en piedras, sino en lenguas desiguales,

these two, though they be 'Gyptian or profane and
pompous exaltations,
blind deviations and barbaric
hieroglyphs, according
to the dulcet Poet, also blind
—who, for having written of Ulysses's
martial stratagems, and
for having chronicled Achilles's feats,
was by Historians
not welcomed to their guild—although, when
included in that category,
rather than number, increased their glory;
his bounteous poetry remains unchanged,
for it is far easier
to steal the lightning bolt
from the dreaded Thunderer,
or from mighty Hercules
seize the studded club, than
to eliminate a
single line dictated by Apollo;
    it was, then, Homer's judgment that
the Pyramids were but material
symbols, whereon were shown the outward signs
of inner dimensions in the image
of the will, that is, the soul's intentions,
and that as the striving flame burns upward
toward the Heavens, a blazing pyramid,
so, too, the human mind
mimics that model
and climbs, eternally,
toward the Prime Mover—the central point toward which
all lines are drawn, if not infinite
circumference that contains all essence.
    These, then, two artificial Mountains
(marvelous, nearly miraculous)
and even that blasphemous, arrogant
Tower, dolorous signs of which today
(not ruins, but asymmetries of language

porque voraz el tiempo no las borre—
los idiomas diversos que escasean
el socïable trato de las gentes
420   (haciendo que parezcan diferentes
los que unos hizo la Naturaleza,
de la lengua por sólo la extrañeza),
si fueran comparados
a la mental pirámide elevada
donde—sin saber cómo—colocada
el Alma se miró, tan atrasados
se hallaran, que cualquiera
gradüara su cima por Esfera:
pues su ambicioso anhelo,
430   haciendo cumbre de su propio vuelo,
en la más eminente
la encumbró parte de su propia mente,
de sí tan remontada, que creía
que a otra nueva región de sí salía.

En cuya casi elevación inmensa,
gozosa mas suspensa,
suspensa pero ufana,
y atónita aunque ufana, la suprema
de lo sublunar Reina soberana,
440   la vista perspicaz, libre de anteojos,
de sus intelectuales bellos ojos
(sin que distancia tema
ni de obstáculo opaco se recele,
de que interpuesto algún objeto cele),
libre tendió por todo lo crïado:
cuyo inmenso agregado,
cúmulo incomprehensible,
aunque a la vista quiso manifiesto
dar señas de posible,
450   a la comprehensión no, que—entorpecida
con la sobra de objetos, y excedida
de la grandeza de ellos su potencia—
retrocedió cobarde.
Tanto no, del osado presupuesto,

that a voracious time does not erase)
are the many tongues that complicate
cordial exchange among communities
420   (with the result that those whom Nature
conceived as equals should be different
solely for lingual disparities),
these, then, if set beside
the sublime pyramid of the mind,
in which—knowing not how—the Soul had
perceived her dwelling, each of these would
realize how far below
they stood and take her summit for a Sphere,
for the Soul's aspiring flight,
430   ever higher through the atmosphere,
consigned of its own mind a portion
to heaven's farthest heights,
ascending so far above itself, it
fancied it soared to some new region.
    At this near immeasurable pinnacle,
joyful, but marveling,
marveling, yet well content,
still, even though content, astonished, the
supreme and sovereign Queen of all the earth,
440   —free of the obstacle of spectacles,
the vision of her beautiful and
intellectual eyes
unclouded by any fear of distance
or resistance of opaque obstructions—
cast her gaze across all creation;
this vast aggregate,
this enigmatic whole,
although to sight seeming to signal
possibility, denied
450   such clarity to comprehension,
which (bewildered by such rich profusion,
its powers vanquished by such majesty)
with cowardice, withdrew.
    Thus a repentant vision was now

revocó la intención, arrepentida,
la vista que intentó descomedida
en vano hacer alarde
contra objeto que excede en excelencia
las líneas visüales
460   —contra el Sol, digo, cuerpo luminoso,
cuyos rayos castigo son fogoso,
que fuerzas desiguales
despreciando, castigan rayo a rayo
el confiado, antes atrevido
y ya llorado ensayo
(necia experiencia que costosa tanto
fué, que Ícaro ya, su propio llanto
lo anegó enternecido)—,
como el entendimiento, aquí vencido
470   no menos de la inmensa muchedumbre
de tanta maquinosa pesadumbre
(de diversas especies conglobado
esférico compuesto),
que de las cualidades
de cada cual, cedió: tan asombrado,
que—entre la copia puesto,
pobre con ella en las neutralidades
de un mar de asombros, la elección confusa—,
equívoco las ondas zozobraba;
480   y por mirarlo todo, nada vía,
ni discernir podía
(bota la facultad intelectiva
en tanta, tan difusa
incomprehensible especie que miraba
desde el un eje en que librada estriba
la máquina voluble de la Esfera,
al contrapuesto polo)
las partes, ya no sólo,
que al universo todo considera
490   serle perfeccionantes,
a su ornato, no más, pertenecientes;
mas ni aun las que integrantes

compelled to abnegate its daring
proposition, its immoderate
attempt to vaunt its strength
against the supreme creator of
irradiating beams,
460   —against, that is, the Sun, that blazing body
whose rays are punishment intolerant
of lesser forces,
castigating, blast after blast, both
that ancient, arrogant, once daring but
now lamented challenge
(that demented experiment of
Icarus, who, for his audacity, drowned
in the sea of his own tears)—
and, just as insistently, understanding,
470   conquered no less by the immensity
of such a massive mechanism,
a sphere of multifarious, conglobed,
entities composed,
than by the properties
of each of them; and thus it acquiesced,
so awestruck that,
surrounded by such bounty, afloat upon
the neutrality of a sea of wonder,
indecisive, it feared that it might founder;
480   by observing everything, it saw nothing,
nor could it separate
(its intellectual faculties dulled
before the great, diffuse,
and incomprehensible variety
it beheld, from one axis upon which rests
the revolving machinery of the Sphere
to its diametric pole)
discrete parts—not only
those the universe considers to be
490   perfecting (that is,
reflecting beauty and embellishment),
but even those that are constituent

miembros son de su cuerpo dilatado,
proporcionadamente competentes.
    Mas como al que ha usurpado
diuturna obscuridad, de los objetos
visibles los colores,
si súbitos le asaltan resplandores,
con la sobra de luz queda más ciego
500 —que el exceso contrarios hace efectos
en la torpe potencia, que la lumbre
del Sol admitir luego
no puede por la falta de costumbre—,
y a la tiniebla misma, que antes era
tenebroso a la vista impedimento,
de los agravios de la luz apela,
y una vez y otra con la mano cela
de los débiles ojos deslumbrados
los rayos vacilantes,
510 sirviendo ya—piadosa medianera—
la sombra de instrumento
para que recobrados
por grados se habiliten,
porque después constantes
su operación más firmes ejerciten
—recurso natural, innata ciencia
que confirmada ya de la experiencia,
maestro quizá mudo,
retórico ejemplar, inducir pudo
520 a uno y otro Galeno
para que del mortífero veneno,
en bien proporcionadas cantidades
escrupulosamente regulando
las ocultas nocivas cualidades,
ya por sobrado exceso
de cálidas o frías,
o ya por ignoradas simpatías
o antipatías con que van obrando
las causas naturales su progreso
530 (a la admiración dando, suspendida,

components, the basic elements,
of the very structure of the cosmos.
      But in the way that one
whose ambience has been bled of color
by darkness will,
when suddenly assailed by radiance,
be blinded by that extravagance of light
500   —just the opposite of sight, the consequence
of excess on that weakened faculty,
which, unaccustomed,
cannot endure the Sun's candescent fire—
and will appeal to those same shadows,
once themselves the obstacle to vision,
to help withstand the light's aggression,
and, with one protesting hand, repeatedly,
shade her weak, bedazzled eyes against
the dancing, blazing rays,
510   the darkness, now a benign mediator,
the facilitator
to swift recovery,
so that, gradually,
eyes may adjust, and then
more diligently perform their function
—a natural recourse, the instinctive science
that experience has now confirmed,
enabling Galen,
a silent master, though exemplary
520   orator, to direct
disciples to extract from lethal poisons,
in carefully apportioned quantities,
their hidden, noxious qualities,
scrupulously measured, whether for an
already known excess
of heat or cold, or for
other, as yet unknown, antipathies
and sympathies with which natural causes
give confirmation of their progress
530   (offering, for our admiration,

efecto cierto en causa no sabida,
con prolijo desvelo y remirada
empírica atención, examinada
en la bruta experiencia,
por menos peligrosa),
la confección hicieran provechosa,
último afán de la Apolínea ciencia,
de admirable trïaca,
¡que así del mal el bien tal vez se saca!—: :
540   no de otra suerte el Alma, que asombrada
de la vista quedó de objeto tanto,
la atención recogió, que derramada
en diversidad tanta, aun no sabía
recobrarse a sí misma del espanto
que portentoso había
su discurso calmado,
permitiéndole apenas
de un concepto confuso
el informe embrïón que, mal formado,
550   inordinado caos retrataba
de confusas especies que abrazaba
—sin orden avenidas,
sin orden separadas,
que cuanto más se implican combinadas
tanto más se disuelven desunidas,
de diversidad llenas—,
ciñendo con violencia lo difuso
de objeto tanto, a tan pequeño vaso
(aun al más bajo, aun al menor, escaso).
560   Las velas, en efecto, recogidas,
que fió inadvertidas
traidor al mar, al viento ventilante
—buscando, desatento,
al mar fidelidad, constancia al viento—,
mal le hizo de su grado
en la mental orilla
dar fondo, destrozado,
al timón roto, a la quebrada entena,

sure effects from causes not yet explained,
but gained through wakeful nights and scrupulous,
empirical attention, then verified
on animals—that
being less dangerous)
and concoct a compound to denote
the goal of Apollonian science:
a wondrous antidote,
that, from the fatal, blessing be obtained,
540   so, too, the Soul, dazed by the enormity
of all that lay before her eyes, regained
her concentration, although, embracing
such diversity, unable still
to rid herself of the prodigious awe
that had paralyzed
her reason, admitting
only, of a blurry
concept, the hazy
embryo, ineptly formed, sketching
550   the disorienting chaos of the
confusing images her eyes beheld
—anarchic, whether
joined or separate,
and, the more together and complete they seemed,
the more discrete and disparate their state:
innate variety—
trying to contain such diversity
in a container far too small
for even the lowest entity.
560   In that tempest, the Soul's ship, sails furled,
heedlessly entrusted
to swirling winds and tossing, storm-whipped waves
—in naive expectation of calm seas
and steady breezes—
ran hard aground, to her
dismay, stranding her
upon the mental shore,
rudder shattered, mast badly splintered,

besando arena a arena
570   de la playa el bajel, astilla a astilla,
donde—ya recobrado—
el lugar usurpó de la carena
cuerda refleja, reportado aviso
de dictamen remiso:
que, en su operación misma reportado,
más juzgó conveniente
a singular asunto reducirse,
o separadamente
una por una discurrir las cosas
580   que vienen a ceñirse
en las que artificiosas
dos veces cinco son Categorías: :
        reducción metafísica que enseña
(los entes concibiendo generales
en sólo unas mentales fantasías
donde de la materia se desdeña
el discurso abstraído)
ciencia a formar de los universales,
reparando, advertido,
590   con el arte el defecto
de no poder con un intüitivo
conocer acto todo lo crïado,
sino que, haciendo escala, de un concepto
en otro va ascendiendo grado a grado,
y el de comprender orden relativo
sigue, necesitado
del del entendimiento
limitado vigor, que a sucesivo
discurso fía su aprovechamiento: :
600   cuyas débiles fuerzas, la doctrina
con doctos alimentos va esforzando,
y el prolijo, si blando,
continuo curso de la disciplina,
robustos le va alientos infundiendo,
con que más animoso
al palio glorïoso

        battered keel kissing,
570   one by one, innumerable grains of sand,
        where—reason recovered—
        sane reflection took the place of errant
        judgment, and with circumspection
        redressed a lack of care:
        there, thwarted in her operation,
        it seemed advisable
        to narrow her attention to one theme,
        or, in a different plan,
        ponder, one by one, the things combined
580   within ingenious
        Categories, ten
        in Aristotle's postulation,
        metaphysical reduction teaching
        (the type and genus of all entities
        established solely in mental fantasies,
        in which abstract reasoning prizes
        essence above matter)
        how science is educed from universals,
        and, with experience,
590   emends the defect
        of the inability to comprehend
        through intuition all creation
        and, instead, constructs a ladder leading
        from one concept to another, step by step,
        ascending to the order, relative, of
        comprehension imposed
        by limitations
        of human intellect, which entrusts
        its progress to sequential reasoning;
600   doctrine nurtures these feeble forces
        with nourishment of erudition
        and persevering,
        punctilious, but pleasant, discipline,
        instilling vigorous encouragement,
        with which, emboldened,
        the Soul, to the most

del empeño más arduo, altivo aspira,
los altos escalones ascendiendo
—en una ya, ya en otra cultivado
610   facultad—, hasta que insensiblemente
la honrosa cumbre mira
término dulce de su afán pesado
(de amarga siembra, fruto al gusto grato,
que aun a largas fatigas fué barato),
y con planta valiente
la cima huella de su altiva frente.
       De esta serie seguir mi entendimiento
el método quería,
o del ínfimo grado
620   del sér inanimado
(menos favorecido,
si no más desvalido,
de la segunda causa productiva),
pasar a la más noble jerarquía
que, en vegetable aliento,
primogénito es, aunque grosero,
de Thetis—el primero
que a sus fértiles pechos maternales,
con virtud atractiva,
630   los dulces apoyó manantïales
de humor terrestre, que a su nutrimento
natural es dulcísimo alimento—,
y de cuatro adornada operaciones
de contrarias acciones,
ya atrae, ya segrega diligente
lo que no serle juzga conveniente,
ya lo superfluo expele, y de la copia
la substancia más útil hace propia;
       y—ésta ya investigada—
640   forma inculcar más bella
(de sentido adornada,
y aun más que de sentido, de aprehensiva
fuerza imaginativa),
que justa puede ocasionar querella

golden laurels may aspire, ascend
the soaring rungs of the most arduous
devoir—calling on one, and then another
610   branch of knowledge—until, surprised,
she spies the lauded crest,
the treasured terminus to her endeavor
(from bitter sowing, gratifying fruit,
reward far outweighing her long labors)
and with triumphant tread
steps onto the mountain's lofty heights.
    Of this progression, my reason wished to
imitate the method,
that is, from the least
620   of the inanimate
(not unprotected
but less favored by
the second originating cause)
pass to the vegetal, a more noble
hierarchy, with
its green breath, though rudimentary,
the first of Thetis's
progeny—at her maternal breast
a suckling child that,
630   drawing from the humors of the earth,
expressed sweet, flowing streams that are its
natural, dulcet nourishment—
an order graced with four distinctive
functions to effect:
to extract these humors, then carefully
reject those deemed not beneficial,
to discard the unessential, and
replicate the ones it finds most useful;
then, passing that order, my Reason
640   longed to ponder one more elegant
(one that was sentient,
and, more than that, endowed with powers
of imagination),
one that may occasion jealousy

—cuando afrenta no sea—
de la que más lucida centellea
inanimada Estrella,
bien que soberbios brille resplandores
—que hasta a los Astros puede superiores,
650   aun la menor criatura, aun la más baja,
ocasionar envidia, hacer ventaja—;
   y de este corporal conocimiento
haciendo, bien que escaso, fundamento,
al supremo pasar maravilloso
compuesto triplicado,
de tres acordes líneas ordenado
y de las formas todas inferiores
compendio misterioso:
bisagra engazadora
660   de la que más se eleva entronizada
Naturaleza pura
y de la que, criatura
menos noble, se ve más abatida:
no de las cinco solas adornada
sensibles facultades,
mas de las interiores
que tres rectrices son, ennoblecida
—que para ser señora
de las demás, no en vano
670   la adornó Sabia Poderosa Mano—:
fin de Sus obras, círculo que cierra
la Esfera con la tierra,
última perfección de lo crïado
y último de su Eterno Autor agrado,
en quien con satisfecha complacencia
Su inmensa descansó magnificencia: :
   fábrica portentosa
que, cuanto más altiva al Cielo toca,
sella el polvo la boca
680   —de quien ser pudo imagen misteriosa
la que Águila Evangélica, sagrada
visión en Patmos vió, que las Estrellas

—if not offense—
in an insensate Star, however
brightly it may glow
or scintillating its resplendent light,
for even the least, the most benighted
650   creature (for harboring the vital spark)
will kindle envy in the highest star,
    and using information of these bodies
as foundation, however minimal,
pass to the supreme and marvelous
triadic combination
of three harmonious lines devised,
a mysterious compendium comprising
all inferior forms:
the articulation
660   between, high on its celestial throne,
pure Nature, spirit,
and, of all creation,
lacking life, the least noble order;
this being, favored not only with
sensory faculties
is ennobled too
by inner qualities (will, reason,
memory), propitiously
bestowed by the hand
670   of an Omnipotent Deity—
the culmination of His works, the circle
joining Heaven with Earth,
utmost perfection, manifested,
and ultimate fulfillment of the
Three-in-One, the Wondrous Maker who,
his work on earth complete, then rested,
having created
the being that in its Heavenward thrust
seals its return to dust
680   —one for whom the metaphor might be
the mystery, the vision, seen in Patmos
by the Evangel Angel, St. John Apostle,

midió y el suelo con iguales huellas,
o la estatua eminente
que del metal mostraba más preciado
la rica altiva frente,
y en el más desechado
material, flaco fundamento hacía,
con que a leve vaivén se deshacía—:
690   el Hombre, digo, en fin, mayor portento
que discurre el humano entendimiento;
compendio que absoluto
parece al Ángel, a la planta, al bruto;
cuya altiva bajeza
toda participó Naturaleza.
¿Por qué? Quizá porque más venturosa
que todas, encumbrada
a merced de amorosa
Unión sería. ¡Oh, aunque repetida,
700   nunca bastantemente bien sabida
merced, pues ignorada
en lo poco apreciada
parece, o en lo mal correspondida!
     Estos, pues, grados discurrir quería
unas veces. Pero otras, disentía,
excesivo juzgando atrevimiento
el discurrirlo todo,
quien aun la más pequeña,
aun la más fácil parte no entendía
710   de los más manüales
efectos naturales;
quien de la fuente no alcanzó risueña
el ignorado modo
con que el curso dirige cristalino
deteniendo en ambages su camino
—los horrorosos senos
de Plutón, las cavernas pavorosas
del abismo tremendo,
las campañas hermosas,
720   los Elíseos amenos,

the mighty angel whose feet of fire
trod earth and star alike,
or the towering statue whose haughty brow
gave forth a golden glow
but, as we know, stood
uncertainly upon two feet of clay
that crumbled with the slightest trepidation.
690   Man, in sum, the greatest marvel
posed to human comprehension,
a synthesis composed
of qualities of angel, plant, and beast,
whose elevated baseness
shows traits of each of these.
And why? Perhaps more blessed than other forms
it was designed that
Man, through loving Union,
should join with the Divine. A favor
700   never fully fathomed, and, were we
to judge by how it is
reciprocated,
insufficiently appreciated!
     These, then, were the steps I wished to follow,
even repeat, but others of my
sisters disagreed, decreed it was
too bold for one who
understood so little
of the least, of the most tractable,
710   of natural effects
to ponder greater things
while ignorant of how Arethusa
curved her crystalline
course beneath the deepest seas, paused to
swirl through subterranean cavities
—the awesome bosom
of the deep, the yawning chasms of
Pluto's daunting caverns—
meandered through meadows,
720   Elysian fields,

tálamo ya de su triforme esposa,
clara pesquisidora registrando
(útil curiosidad, aunque prolija,
que de su no cobrada bella hija
noticia cierta dió a la rubia Diosa,
cuando montes y selvas trastornando,
cuando prados y bosques inquiriendo,
su vida iba buscando
y del dolor su vida iba perdiendo)—;

730   quien de la breve flor aun no sabía
por qué ebúrnia figura
circunscribe su frágil hermosura:
mixtos, por qué, colores
—confundiendo la grana en los albores—
fragrante le son gala:
ámbares por qué exhala,
y el leve, si más bello
ropaje al viento explica,
que en una y otra fresca multiplica
740   hija, formando pompa escarolada
de dorados perfiles cairelada,
que—roto del capillo el blanco sello—
de dulce herida de la Cipria Diosa
los despojos ostenta jactanciosa,
si ya el que la colora,
candor al alba, púrpura al aurora
no le usurpó y, mezclado,
purpúreo es ampo, rosicler nevado:
tornasol que concita
750   los que del prado aplausos solicita:
preceptor quizá vano
—si no ejemplo profano—
de industria femenil que el más activo
veneno, hace dos veces ser nocivo
en el velo aparente
de la que finge tez resplandeciente.

    Pues si a un objeto solo—repetía
tímido el pensamiento—

the nuptial bed for a wife thrice mythified,
then continued, limpid seeker and,
eventually, deliverer of
tidings of the beauteous, long-lost daughter
of that distraught blond goddess Ceres
who, tirelessly, had sought Persephone
in meadows, woods, and mountains, searching
with desperation,
her life ebbing into desolation.
730   And what of one still ignorant of why
the fragile beauty
of a flower is sometimes limned in pearl,
yet others, robed
—like streaks of carmine in the dawning sky—
in fragrant scarlet,
why it exhales
its sweet perfume,
why it unfurls
its petals to the breeze,
740   bloom upon bloom, each exquisite,
a frilly ruff, a gorget edged in gold,
that—once broken the pale bud's seal—unfolds
to bare, with boastful ostentation,
the red of Venus's blood, colors
appropriating
from the dawn its milky light as well as
rosy beam, creating
crimson snow and silvery vermillion
iridescence
750   that puts to shame the meadow's pretty show,
a vain preceptor
—if not profane example—
of female industry that makes of
noxious poisons potions doubly vile,
powders to mask the truth,
paints for those who would recapture youth.
For if before a single object
—my intellect

huye el conocimiento
760   y cobarde el discurso se desvía;
si a especie segregada
—como de las demás independiente,
como sin relación considerada—
da las espaldas el entendimiento,
y asombrado el discurso se espeluza
del difícil certamen que rehusa
acometer valiente,
porque teme—cobarde—
comprehenderlo o mal, o nunca, o tarde,
770   ¿cómo en tan espantosa
máquina inmensa discurrir pudiera,
cuyo terrible incomportable peso
—si ya en su centro mismo no estribara—
de Atlante a las espaldas agobiara,
de Alcides a las fuerzas excediera;
y el que fué de la Esfera
bastante contrapeso,
pesada menos, menos ponderosa
su máquina juzgara, que la empresa
780   de investigar a la Naturaleza?
      Otras—más esforzado—,
demasiada acusaba cobardía
el lauro antes ceder, que en la lid dura
haber siquiera entrado;
y al ejemplar osado
del claro joven la atención volvía
—auriga altivo del ardiente carro—,
y el, si infeliz, bizarro
alto impulso, el espíritu encendía:
790   donde el ánimo halla
—más que el temor ejemplos de escarmiento—
abiertas sendas al atrevimiento,
que una ya vez trilladas, no hay castigo
que intento baste a remover segundo
(segunda ambición, digo).
      Ni el panteón profundo

reflected—reason
760   ignobly flees from confrontation
and, from a single
species—independent of all others and
free of any obvious relation—
comprehension turns away, dismayed
while, dreading failure, acumen evades
the daunting challenge, loath to embark upon
such an endeavor,
given its fear of
understanding badly, late, or never,
770   then how could one
deliberate on the complexities
of a mechanism so immense
that—when not sustained by Providence—
it bows the straining back of Atlas
and surmounts the strength of Hercules?
And how could he who
serves as bearer of the
Sphere judge any lighter, any less
severe, his burden than that incurred in
780   probing and investigating Nature?
    Other times—to a more
determined mind—it seemed faint-hearted
meekly to yield the laurel wreath before
the battle started;
and once again foremost
in my thought was that illustrious youth
—bold charioteer who tried to guide the sun—
whose brave, if hapless
paradigm fired my will to persevere
790   in that realm where
the spirit finds—more lesson learned than cause
for fear—paths toward daring that once
traveled cannot present sufficient danger
to prevent a second journey, that is,
a second try.
    Neither the watery tomb,

—cerúlea tumba a su infeliz ceniza—,
ni el vengativo rayo fulminante
mueve, por más que avisa,
800   al ánimo arrogante
que, el vivir despreciando, determina
su nombre eternizar en su rüina.
Tipo es, antes, modelo:
ejemplar pernicioso
que alas engendra a repetido vuelo,
del ánimo ambicioso
que—del mismo terror haciendo halago
que al valor lisonjea—,
las glorias deletrea
810   entre los caracteres del estrago.
O el castigo jamás se publicara,
porque nunca el delito se intentara:
político silencio antes rompiera
los autos del proceso
—circunspecto estadista—;
o en fingida ignorancia simulara
o con secreta pena castigara
el insolente exceso,
sin que a popular vista
820   el ejemplar nocivo propusiera:
que del mayor delito la malicia
peligra en la noticia,
contagio dilatado trascendiendo;
porque singular culpa sólo siendo,
dejara más remota a lo ignorado
su ejecución, que no a lo escarmentado.

    Mas mientras entre escollos zozobraba
confusa la elección, sirtes tocando
de imposibles, en cuantos intentaba
830   rumbos seguir—no hallando
materia en que cebarse
el calor ya, pues su templada llama
(llama al fin, aunque más templada sea,
que si su activa emplea

—blue sepulcher to his ill-starred ashes—
nor vengeful, lethal, lightning flashes
deter, despite their warning,
800   the haughty spirit that,
scorning life, rashly will seek his doom
in order to immortalize his name.
Instead, that figure serves
as perilous exemplar,
kindling in an ambitious spirit
ardor to soar again,
and, making of fear a form of flattery
to nurture courage,
transcribes glory
810   from letters that spell out tragedy.
O that the punishment were never known,
that the offense not be repeated;
rather, that prudent silence—judicious
statesman—muffle tidings
of the consequence,
or, feigning ignorance, dissimulate,
and castigate with secret penalty
the brazen excess,
shielding from public view
820   all evidence of such examples.
For news of a compelling action is
its greatest danger,
as contagion spreads with every telling:
far better that the deed remain unsung
and not taught as admonition;
less heeded, less the chance of repetition.
    But as my powers of selection sailed
blindly through the reefs, thwarted by shoals
that altered the direction of my goals,
830   and, lacking fuel
on which to feed,
the body's heat, its flame abated
(yet still a flame, even if dimmed, for
in the interim

operación, consume, si no inflama)
sin poder excusarse
había lentamente
el manjar trasformado,
propia substancia de la ajena haciendo:
840   y el que hervor resultaba bullicioso
de la unión entre el húmedo y ardiente,
en el maravilloso
natural vaso, había ya cesado
(faltando el medio), y consiguientemente
los que de él ascendiendo
soporíferos, húmedos vapores
el trono racional embarazaban
(desde donde a los miembros derramaban
dulce entorpecimiento),
840   a los suaves ardores
del calor consumidos,
las cadenas del sueño desataban:
y la falta sintiendo de alimento
los miembros extenuados,
del descanso cansados,
ni del todo despiertos ni dormidos,
muestras de apetecer el movimiento
con tardos esperezos
ya daban, extendiendo
860   los nervios, poco a poco, entumecidos,
y los cansados huesos
(aun sin entero arbitrio de su dueño)
volviendo al otro lado—,
a cobrar empezaron los sentidos,
dulcemente impedidos
del natural beleño,
su operación, los ojos entreabriendo.
      Y del cerebro, ya desocupado,
las fantasmas huyeron,
870   y—como de vapor leve formadas—
en fácil humo, en viento convertidas,
su forma resolvieron.

its moderated fires burn on)
instinctively,
slowly and steadily,
transformed aliment,
brewing from foodstuffs its own nourishment;
840   the boisterous boilings that ensued,
born of the union of Humidity
and heat in Nature's
marvelous retort, by now had gently ceased
(for want of fodder), and, consequently,
moist and soporific
vapors were released to issue upward
and assail the throne of reason (whence
sweet torpor was dispensed, making its way
to every limb)
850   and where, consumed by
warmth's soft ardor,
the chains of sleep began to slip away;
enervated limbs, feeling the loss
of sustenance,
weary of weariness,
not awake, but neither somnolent,
gave indication of pending movement
with slow stretching,
bending, then gradual
860   extending of nerves benumbed by sleep,
as rest-racked bones
(without their owner's express volition)
shifted position;
senses sweetly impeded by a
natural potion
recuperated,
stirred slightly, as eyes fluttered open.
    And from the Brain, thus liberated,
the ghostly figures fled
870   and, as if composed of misty vapors
or blown away like wind or smoke,
forms dissipated.

Así linterna mágica, pintadas
representa fingidas
en la blanca pared varias figuras,
de la sombra no menos ayudadas
que de la luz: que en trémulos reflejos
los competentes lejos
guardando de la docta perspectiva,
en sus ciertas mensuras
de varias experiencias aprobadas,
la sombra fugitiva,
que en el mismo esplendor se desvanece,
cuerpo finge formado,
de todas dimensiones adornado,
cuando aun ser superficie no merece.
En tanto, el Padre de la Luz ardiente,
de acercarse al Oriente
ya el término prefijo conocía,
y al antípoda opuesto despedía
con transmontantes rayos:
que—de su luz en trémulos desmayos—
en el punto hace mismo su Occidente,
que nuestro Oriente ilustra luminoso.
Pero de Venus, antes, el hermoso
apacible lucero
rompió el albor primero,
y del viejo Tithón la bella esposa
—amazona de luces mil vestida,
contra la noche armada,
hermosa si atrevida,
valiente aunque llorosa—,
su frente mostró hermosa
de matutinas luces coronada,
aunque tierno preludio, ya animoso
del Planeta fogoso,
que venía las tropas reclutando
de bisoñas vislumbres
—las más robustas, veteranas lumbres
para la retaguardia reservando—,

880

890

900

910

In this same way, the magic lantern throws
on a white wall
the contours of delineated figures
in thrall as much to shadow as to light,
trembling reflections maintained by guarding
a proper distance
according to the precepts of perspective
880   and precise measurements
derived from various experiments:
this fleeting shadow
dissolved by day's illumination
feigns solid form
as if adorned with all dimensions
though not deserving claim even to one.
        Meanwhile, the blazing Father of Light,
nearing the East,
complies with predetermined codes and,
890   with waning rays, signals farewell to
distant antipodes:
at some common point—from trembling light—
creating their darkening Occident
and our luminescent Orient.
But first to pierce the darkness of the sky
was Venus, the gentle,
beauteous morning star,
and with her Dawn, wife of Tithonus
—an Amazon robed in a thousand lights
900   to vanquish night,
comely though bold,
brave, if dewy-eyed—
who revealed a brow
crowned with a matutinal glow,
a gentle though resolute prelude
to the Orb of Fire
that now appeared, mustering his troops
of pale recruits
—reserving his most resplendent and
910   robust veterans to reinforce the rear—

contra la que, tirana usurpadora
del imperio del día,
negro laurel de sombras mil ceñía
y con nocturno cetro pavoroso
las sombras gobernaba,
de quien aun ella misma se espantaba.
   Pero apenas la bella precursora
signífera del Sol, el luminoso
en el Oriente tremoló estandarte,
920 tocando al arma todos los süaves
si bélicos clarines de las aves
(diestros, aunque sin arte,
trompetas sonorosos),
cuando—como tirana al fin, cobarde,
de recelos medrosos
embarazada, bien que hacer alarde
intentó de sus fuerzas, oponiendo
de su funesta capa los reparos,
breves en ella de los tajos claros
930 heridas recibiendo
(bien que mal satisfecho su denuedo,
pretexto mal formado fué del miedo,
su débil resistencia conociendo)—,
a la fuga ya casi cometiendo
más que a la fuerza, el medio de salvarse,
ronca tocó bocina
a recoger los negros escuadrones
para poder en orden retirarse,
cuando de más vecina
940 plenitud de reflejos fué asaltada,
que la punta rayó más encumbrada
de los del Mundo erguidos torreones.
   Llegó, en efecto, el Sol cerrando el giro
que esculpió de oro sobre azul zafiro:
de mil multiplicados
mil veces puntos, flujos mil dorados
—líneas, digo, de luz clara—salían
de su circunferencia luminosa,

still near, the tyrannical usurper
of Day's empire,
head bound with laurel wreath of shadows,
caliginous scepter in her hand,
sent forth the shades of night
that even to her inky heart struck fear.
      But no sooner had the beauteous ensign
of the Sun unfurled her luminous,
trembling pennon on the horizon, as
920   the at once sweet and martial clarion
of the birds sounded a call to arms
(tuneful, if artless,
dawn trumpeting),
than—a tyrant after all, a coward slowed
by craven fear
and braggadocio, making a show
of awesome regiments, but scurrying
to mend the rents slit in her stygian,
once impenetrable cape by blades
930   of piercing rays,
her vaunted bravery mere bravura
masking her pusillanimity—
acknowledging the certainty of fading
strength, and recognizing flight, not force,
as her best course of preservation,
she raised her horn,
and with one hoarse blast massed her squadrons
to effect an orderly retreat,
but in the act
940   she was attacked by spreading radiance,
incandescence streaking the lofty peaks
of the World's most majestic mountains.
      In sum, the Sun had risen, closing
a circle sketched of gold on sapphire blue:
a thousand thousand
sparkling motes and spokes of fire
—lines, I say, of purest light—beamed
from its luminous circumference,

pautando al Cielo la cerúlea plana;
950 y a la que antes funesta fué tirana
de su imperio, atropadas embestían:
que sin concierto huyendo presurosa
—en sus mismos horrores tropezando—
su sombra iba pisando,
y llegar al Ocaso pretendía
con el (sin orden ya) desbaratado
ejército de sombras, acosado
de la luz que el alcance le seguía.

    Consiguió, al fin, la vista del Ocaso
960 el fugitivo paso,
y—en su mismo despeño recobrada
esforzando el aliento en la rüina—
en la mitad del globo que ha dejado
el Sol desamparada,
segunda vez rebelde determina
mirarse coronada,
mientras nuestro Hemisferio la dorada
ilustraba del Sol madeja hermosa,
que con luz judiciosa
970 de orden distributivo, repartiendo
a las cosas visibles sus colores
iba, y restituyendo
entera a los sentidos exteriores
su operación, quedando a luz más cierta
el Mundo iluminado, y yo despierta.

etching the sky's cerulean expanse;
950 these golden legions put to flight the one
who once had ruled the realm of night:
now in precipitous, headlong retreat
—trampling roughshod over murky horrors—
she trod upon
her very shadow, racing to overtake
the fleeting dusk with the ragtag, tattered
band of warriors hoping to outrun
the sun following so close upon their heels.
    Gaining, in harum-scarum flight, glimpses
960 of darkest night,
and by her westward plunge revived
—impending doom a catalyst to action—
the umbrageous, rebellious empress
again connived
to don her crown and rule the darkened realm
the Sun abandoned,
while our Hemisphere was inundated
by a flood of gold that radiated
from a solar
970 aureole that impartially restored
color to all things visible, and
gradually,
reactivated the external
senses, an affirmation that left
the World illuminated, and me awake.

ROMANCES

Octosyllabic lines with second
and fourth lines in assonant rhyme

Prólogo al lector

Estos Versos, lector mío,
que a tu deleite consagro,
y sólo tienen de buenos
conocer yo que son malos,
    ni disputártelos quiero
ni quiero recomendarlos,
porque eso fuera querer
hacer de ellos mucho caso.

    No agradecido te busco:
pues no debes, bien mirado,
estimar lo que yo nunca
juzgué que fuera a tus manos.

    En tu libertad te pongo,
si quisieres censurarlos;
pues de que, al cabo, te estás
en ella, estoy muy al cabo.

    No hay cosa más libre que
el entendimiento humano;
¿pues lo que Dios no violenta,
por qué yo he de violentarlo?

    Di cuanto quisieres de ellos,
que, cuando más inhumano
me los mordieres, entonces
me quedas más obligado,
    pues le debes a mi Musa
el más sazonado plato
(que es el murmurar), según
un adagio cortesano.

    Y siempre te sirvo, pues
o te agrado, o no te agrado:
si te agrado, te diviertes;
murmuras, si no te cuadro.

    Bien pudiera yo decirte
por disculpa, que no ha dado
lugar para corregirlos
la prisa de los traslados;

Prologue to the Reader

These poems, Dear Reader, I give you
with hopes your pleasure they ensure,
though all that may speak well of them
is that I know them to be poor;
    I do not wish to argue them,
nor of their worth give evidence,
for such attention to these lines
would seem to lend them consequence.

    Nor do I seek your good esteem,
for, after all, no one demands
you value what I never thought
would find its way into your hands.
    If you should wish to criticize,
I place you in full liberty,
as I am free now to conclude,
you may conclude that you are free.

    We know nothing as unbound
as our human intellect;
and what God never violates,
should I not honor and respect?
    Say of these verses what you will,
the more that you are inhumane,
and at them cruelly bite and gnaw,
the more my debtor you remain,

    for in the Court it is well known
that only through my Muse's grace
do you enjoy that richest dish,
the spiteful chatter you embrace.
    How well I serve you, at all times,
in pleasing you or pleasing not;
you are diverted if I please,
and gossip if I come to naught.

    In asking pardon, I might say
I hoped some poems to remedy,
but due to haste in copying,
had little opportunity;

que van de diversas letras,
y que algunas, de muchachos,
matan de suerte el sentido
que es cadáver el vocablo;

y que, cuando los he hecho,
ha sido en el corto espacio
que ferian al ocio las
precisiones de mi estado;

que tengo poca salud
y continuos embarazos,
tales, que aun diciendo esto,
llevo la pluma trotando.

Pero todo eso no sirve,
pues pensarás que me jacto
de que quizás fueran buenos
a haberlos hecho despacio;

y no quiero que tal creas,
sino sólo que es el darlos
a la luz, tan sólo por
obedecer un mandato.

Esto es, si gustas creerlo,
que sobre eso no me mato,
pues al cabo harás lo que
se te pusiere en los cascos.

Y a Dios, que esto no es más de
darte la muestra del paño:
si no te agrada la pieza,
no desenvuelvas el fardo.

they come in many different hands
and some, where little lads have erred,
do kill the sense, and you will see
cadavers made of living words,

    besides which, when I wrote these lines,
they were composed in those rare fêtes
when leisure called a holiday
amidst the duties of my state;

    for I suffer from ill-health,
my life, with obstacles is fraught,
so many, even as I write,
my pen is racing at a trot.

    But pay no heed to what I say,
lest you think I vaunt my rhymes,
suggesting that they would be good
had I but had sufficient time;

    I would not have you so believe,
for their life, their imminence,
the cause for bringing them to light,
was dutiful obedience.

    And so it is, think as you will,
I do not die to have them read,
and you are free to do with them
whatever comes into your head.

    Godspeed to you, all I do here
is show a piece, but not the whole:
so if you do not like the cloth,
the bolt were better left unrolled.

48

Respondiendo a un Caballero del Perú, que le envió
unos Barros diciéndole que se volviese hombre

Señor: para responderos
todas las Musas se eximen,
sin que haya, ni aun de limosna,
una que ahora me dicte;
   y siendo las nueve Hermanas
madres del donaire y chiste,
no hay, oyendo vuestros versos,
una que chiste ni miste.

   Apolo absorto se queda
tan elevado de oírle,
que para aguijar el Carro,
es menester que le griten.

   Para escucharlo, el Pegaso
todo el aliento reprime,
sin que mientras lo recitan
tema nadie que relinche.

   Pára, contra todo el orden,
de sus cristales fluxibles
los gorjeos Helicona,
los murmurios Aganipe:

   porque sus murmurios viendo,
todas las Musas coligen
que, de vuestros versos, no
merecen ser aprendices.

   Apolo suelta la vara
con que los compases rige,
porque reconoce, al veros,
que injustamente preside.

   Y así, el responderos tengo
del todo por imposible,
si compadecido acaso
vos no tratáis de inflüirme.

   Sed mi Apolo, y veréis que
(como vuestra luz me anime)

48

*In Reply to a Gentleman from Peru, Who Sent Her Clay
Vessels While Suggesting She Would Better Be a Man*

Kind Sir, while wishing to reply,
my Muses all have taken leave,
and none, even for charity,
will aid me now I wish to speak;
    and though we know these Sisters nine
good mothers are of wit and jest,
not one, once having heard your verse,
will dare to jest at my behest.

The God Apollo listens, rapt,
and races on, so high aloft
that those who guide his Chariot
must raise their voices to a shout.

To hear your lines, fleet Pegasus
his lusty breathing will retain,
that no one fear his thunderous neigh
as your verses are declaimed.

Checking, against nature's order,
altering crystalline watercourse,
Helicon stays its gurgling water,
Agannipe, her murmuring source:
    for, having heard your murmuring,
the Nine Daughters all concede,
beside your verses they are wanting,
unfit to study at your feet.

Apollo sets aside the wand
that he employs to mark the beat,
because, on seeing you, he knows
he cannot justly take the lead.

And thus, acknowledge it I must,
I cannot scribe the verses owed
unless, perhaps, compassionate,
keen inspiration you bestow.

Be my Apollo, and behold
(as your light illumines me)

mi lira sonante escuchan
los dos opuestos confines.

Mas ¡oh cuánto poderosa
es la invocación humilde,
pues ya, en nuevo aliento, el pecho
nuevo espíritu concibe!

De extraño ardor inflamado,
hace que incendios respire;
y como de Apolo, de,
Navarrete se reviste.

Nuevas sendas al discurso
hace, que elevado pise,
y en nuevos conceptos hace
que él a sí mismo se admire.

Balbuciente con la copia,
la lengua torpe se aflige:
mucho ve, y explica poco;
mucho entiende, y poco dice.

Pensaréis que estoy burlando;
pues mirad, que el que me asiste
espíritu, no está a un
dedo de que profetice.

Mas si es querer alabaros
tan reservado imposible,
que en vuestra pluma, no más,
puede parecer factible,

¿de qué me sirve emprenderlo,
de qué intentarlo me sirve,
habiendo plumas que en agua
sus escarmientos escriben?

Dejo ya vuestros elogios
a que ellos solos se expliquen:
pues los que en sí sólo caben,
consigo sólo se miden.

Y paso a estimar aquellos
hermosamente sutiles
Búcaros, en quien el Arte
hace al apetito brindis:

how my lyre will then be heard
the length and breadth of land and sea.
    Though humble, oh, how powerful
my invocation's consequence,
I find new valor in my breast,
new spirit given utterance!
    Ignited with unfamiliar fervor,
my pen bursting into flame,
while giving due to famed Apollo
I honor Navarrete's name.
    Traveling where none has trod,
expression rises to new heights,
and, reveling in new invention,
finds in itself supreme delight.
    Stammering with such abundance
my clumsy tongue is tied with pain:
much is seen, but little spoken,
some is known, but none explained.
    You will think that I make mock;
no, nothing further from the truth,
to prophesy, my guiding spirit
is lacking but a fine hair's breadth.
    But if I am so little able
to offer you sufficient praise,
to form the kind of compliment
that only your apt pen may phrase,
    what serve me then to undertake it?
to venture it, what good will serve?
if mine be pens that write in water,
recording lessons unobserved.
    That they themselves elucidate,
I now leave your eulogies:
as none to their measure correspond,
none can match them in degree,
    and I turn to giving thanks
for your fair gifts, most subtly made;
Art lifts a toast to appetite
in lovely Vessels of fragrant clay.

Barros en cuyo primor
ostenta soberbio Chile,
que no es la plata, no el oro,
lo que tiene más plausible,

   pues por tan baja materia
hace que se desestimen
doradas Copas que néctar
en sagradas mesas sirven.

   Bésoos las manos por ellos,
que es cierto que tanto filis
tienen los Barros, que juzgo
que sois vos quien los hicisteis.

   Y en el consejo que dais,
yo os prometo recibirle
y hacerme fuerza, aunque juzgo
que no hay fuerzas que entarquinen:

   porque acá Sálmacis falta,
en cuyos cristales dicen
que hay no sé qué virtud de
dar alientos varoniles.

   Yo no entiendo de esas cosas;
sólo sé que aquí me vine
porque, si es que soy mujer,
ninguno lo verifique.

   Y también sé que, en latín,
sólo a las casadas dicen
úxor, o mujer, y que
es común de dos lo Virgen.

   Con que a mí no es bien mirado
que como a mujer me miren,
pues no soy mujer que a alguno
de mujer pueda servirle;

   y sólo sé que mi cuerpo,
sin que a uno u otro se incline,
es neutro, o abstracto, cuanto
sólo el Alma deposite.

   Y dejando esta cuestión
para que otros la ventilen,

Earthenware, so exquisite
that Chile properly is proud,
though it is not gold or silver
that gives your gift its wide renown

but, rather, from such lowly matter
forms emerge that put to shame
the brimming Goblets made of gold
from which Gods their nectar drained.

Kiss, I beg, the hands that made them,
though judging by the Vessels' charm
—such grace can surely leave no doubt—
yours were the hands that gave them form.

As for the counsel that you offer,
I promise you, I will attend
with all my strength, although I judge
no strength on earth can en-Tarquin:

for here we have no Salmacis,
whose crystal water, so they tell,
to nurture masculinity
possesses powers unexcelled.

I have no knowledge of these things,
except that I came to this place
so that, if true that I am female,
none substantiate that state.

I know, too, that they were wont
to call wife, or woman, in the Latin
uxor, only those who wed,
though wife or woman might be virgin.

So in my case, it is not seemly
that I be viewed as feminine,
as I will never be a woman
who may as woman serve a man.

I know only that my body,
not to either state inclined,
is neuter, abstract, guardian
of only what my Soul consigns.

Let us renounce this argument,
let others, if they will, debate;

porque en lo que es bien que ignore,
no es razón que sutilice
    generoso Perüano
que os lamentáis de infelice,
¿que Lima es la que dejasteis,
si acá la *lima* os trajisteis?

    Bien sabéis la ley de Atenas,
con que desterró a Aristides:
que aun en lo bueno, es delito
el que se singularice.

    Por bueno lo desterraron,
y a otros varones insignes;
porque el exceder a todos,
es delito irremisible.

    El que a todos se aventaja,
fuerza es que a todos incite
a envidia, pues el lucir
a todos juntos impide.

    Al paso que la alabanza
a uno para blanco elige,
a ese mismo paso trata
la envidia de perseguirle.

    A vos de Perú os destierran
y nuestra Patria os admite,
porque nos da el Cielo acá
la dicha que allá despiden.

    Bien es que vuestro talento
diversos climas habite:
que los que nacen tan grandes,
no sólo para sí viven.

some matters better left unknown
no reason can illuminate.

 Generous gentleman from Peru,
proclaiming such unhappiness,
did you leave Lima any art,
given the art you brought to us?

 You must know that law of Athens
by which Aristides was expelled:
it seems that, even if for good,
it is forbidden to excel.

 He was expelled for being good,
and other famous men as well;
because to tower over all
is truly unforgiveable.

 He who always leads his peers
will by necessity invite
malicious envy, as his fame
will rob all others of the light.

 To the degree that one is chosen
as the target for acclaim,
to that same measure, envy trails
in close pursuit, with perfect aim.

 Now you are banished from Peru
and welcomed in my Native Land,
we see the Heavens grant to us
the blessing that Peru declined.

 But it is well that such great talent
live in many different zones,
for those who are with greatness born
should live not for themselves alone.

57

Mientras la Gracia me excita
por elevarme a la Esfera,
más me abate a lo profundo
el peso de mis miserias.

La virtud y la costumbre
en el corazón pelean,
y el corazón agoniza
en tanto que lidian ellas.

Y aunque es la virtud tan fuerte,
temo que tal vez la venzan,
que es muy grande la costumbre
y está la virtud muy tierna.

Obscurécese el discurso
entre confusas tinieblas;
pues ¿quién podrá darme luz
si está la razón a ciegas?

De mí mesma soy verdugo
y soy cárcel de mí mesma.
¿Quién vio que pena y penante
una propia cosa sean?

Hago disgusto a lo mismo
que más agradar quisiera;
y del disgusto que doy,
en mí resulta la pena.

Amo a Dios y siento en Dios;
y hace mi voluntad mesma
de lo que es alivio, cruz,
del mismo puerto, tormenta.

Padezca, pues Dios lo manda;
mas de tal manera sea,
que si son penas las culpas,
que no sean culpas las penas.

57

While by Grace I am inspired,
'tis then I near the precipice,
I would ascend unto the Sphere,
but am dragged down to the abyss.

Virtue and custom are at odds,
and deep within my heart contend,
my anguished heart will agonize
until the two their combat end.

I fear that virtue will be crushed,
though all know its just repute,
for custom is long flourishing,
and virtue, tender as a shoot.

My thinking often is obscured,
among dark shadows ill-defined,
then who is there to give me light,
when reason falters as if blind?

Of myself I am the gaoler,
I, executioner of me,
who can know the painful pain,
who can know the tragedy?

I cause displeasure to the One
I most desire to gratify,
and from displeasure that I give,
the one who suffers most is I.

I love and find myself in God,
but my will His grace transforms,
turning solace to a cross,
quitting port to seek the storm.

Then suffer, it is God's command,
but let this be the paradigm,
that though your sins cause suffering,
your suffering not be seen as sin.

REDONDILLAS

Octosyllabic quatrains, usually rhyming abba

92
Sátira filosófica

Arguye de inconsecuentes el gusto y la censura de los
hombres que en las mujeres acusan lo que causan

Hombres necios que acusáis
a la mujer sin razón,
sin ver que sois la ocasión
de lo mismo que culpáis:

si con ansia sin igual
solicitáis su desdén,
¿por qué queréis que obren bien
si las incitáis al mal?

Combatís su resistencia
y luego, con gravedad,
decís que fue liviandad
lo que hizo la diligencia.

Parecer quiere el denuedo
de vuestro parecer loco,
al niño que pone el coco
y luego le tiene miedo.

Queréis, con presunción necia,
hallar a la que buscáis,
para prentendida, Thais,
y en la posesión, Lucrecia.

¿Qué humor puede ser más raro
que el que, falto de consejo,
él mismo empaña el espejo,
y siente que no esté claro?

Con el favor y el desdén
tenéis condición igual,
quejándoos, si os tratan mal,
burlándoos, si os quieren bien.

Opinión, ninguna gana;
pues la que más se recata,
si no os admite, es ingrata,
y si os admite, es liviana.

92
A Philosophical Satire

*She proves the inconsistency of the caprice and criticism
of men who accuse women of what they cause*

Misguided men, who will chastise
a woman when no blame is due,
oblivious that it is you
who prompted what you criticize;

if your passions are so strong
that you elicit their disdain,
how can you wish that they refrain
when you incite them to their wrong?

You strive to topple their defense,
and then, with utmost gravity,
you credit sensuality
for what was won with diligence.

Your daring must be qualified,
your sense is no less senseless than
the child who calls the boogeyman,
then weeps when he is terrified.

Your mad presumption knows no bounds,
though for a wife you want Lucrece,
in lovers you prefer Thaïs,
thus seeking blessings to compound.

If knowingly one clouds a mirror
—was ever humor so absurd
or good counsel so obscured?—
can he lament that it's not clearer?

From either favor or disdain
the selfsame purpose you achieve,
if they love, they are deceived,
if they love not, hear you complain.

There is no woman suits your taste,
though circumspection be her virtue:
ungrateful, she who does not love you,
yet she who does, you judge unchaste.

Siempre tan necios andáis
que, con desigual nivel,
a una culpáis por crüel
y a otra por fácil culpáis.

¿Pues cómo ha de estar templada
la que vuestro amor pretende,
si la que es ingrate, ofende,
y la que es fácil, enfada?

Mas, entre el enfado y pena
que vuestro gusto refiere,
bien haya la que no os quiere
y quejaos en hora buena.

Dan vuestra amantes penas
a sus libertades alas,
y después de hacerlas malas
las queréis hallar muy buenas.

¿Cuál mayor culpa ha tenido
en una pasión errada:
la que cae de rogada,
o el que ruega de caído?

¿O cuál es más de culpar,
aunque cualquiera mal haga:
la que peca por la paga,
o el que paga por pecar?

Pues ¿para qué os espantáis
de la culpa que tenéis?
Queredlas cual las hacéis
o hacedlas cual las buscáis.

Dejad de solicitar,
y después, con más razón,
acusaréis la afición
de la que os fuere a rogar.

Bien con muchas armas fundo
que lidia vuestra arrogancia,
pues en promesa e instancia
juntáis diablo, carne y mundo.

You men are such a foolish breed,
appraising with a faulty rule,
the first you charge with being cruel,
the second, easy, you decree.

So how can she be temperate,
the one who would her love expend?
if not willing, she offends,
but willing, she infuriates.

Amid the anger and torment
your whimsy causes you to bear,
one may be found who does not care:
how quickly then is grievance vent.

So lovingly you inflict pain
that inhibitions fly away;
how, after leading them astray,
can you wish them without stain?

Who does the greater guilt incur
when a passion is misleading?
She who errs and heeds his pleading,
or he who pleads with her to err?

Whose is the greater guilt therein
when either's conduct may dismay:
she who sins and takes the pay,
or he who pays her for the sin?

Why, for sins you're guilty of,
do you, amazed, your blame debate?
Either love what you create
or else create what you can love.

Were not it better to forbear,
and thus, with finer motivation,
obtain the unforced admiration
of her you plotted to ensnare?

But no, I deem you still will revel
in your arms and arrogance,
and in promise and persistence
adjoin flesh and world and devil.

EPIGRAMS

In the Spirit if not the Letter

93
Con un desengaño satírico a una
Presumida de Hermosa

Que te den en la hermosura
la palma, dices, Leonor;
la de virgen es mejor,
que tu cara la asegura.

No te precies, con descoco,
que a todos robes el alma:
que si te han dado la Palma,
es, Leonor, porque eres Coco.

94
En que descubre digna estirpe
a un Borracho linajudo

Porque tu sangre se sepa,
cuentas a todos, Alfeo,
que eres de Reyes. Yo creo
que eres de muy buena cepa;

y que, pues a cuantos topas
con esos Reyes enfadas
que, más que Reyes de Espadas,
debieron de ser de Copas.

93
*Satiric Reproach to a Woman
Who Boasts of Her Beauty*

Dear Leonor, they've given you
the palm for beauty, or so you say,
but have no fear for your virtue,
that face would save you any day.

You sing your praises without qualm,
to hear you tell it, men lose their wits:
but if they've given you the palm,
it's from the date—for you're the pits.

94
*Which Reveals the Honorable Ancestry
of a High-Born Drunkard*

Alfeo claims he comes from kings,
he boasts of blood of royal hue,
he speaks of queens with *diamond* rings,
whose *hearts* pump only royal blue.

The truth is, his line brandished *clubs,*
his House is the House of Topers,
but have no doubt, when in his cups,
he's king—in *spades*—the King of Jokers.

95
Que dan el Colirio merecido a un Soberbio

El no ser de Padre honrado,
fuera defecto, a mi ver,
si como recibí el ser
de él, se lo hubiera yo dado.
    Más piadosa fue tu Madre
que hizo que a muchos sucedas:
para que, entre tantos, puedas
tomar el que más te cuadre.

96
Con advertencia moral, a un Capitán moderno

Capitán es ya Don Juan;
mas quisiera mi cuidado,
hallarle lo reformado
antes de lo Capitán.
    Porque cierto que me inquieta,
en acción tan atrevida,
ver que no sepa la brida
y se atreva a la jineta.

95
A Much-Needed Eyewash for Cleansing
the Eyes of an Arrogant Myope

Not to be born of an honorable father
would be a blemish, I must own,
if, receiving my being from no other,
I did not judge it as his alone.
Far more generous was your mother
when she arranged your ancestry,
offering many a likely father
among whom to choose your pedigree.

96
A Bit of Moral Advice for a Modern Captain

A Captain now is our Don Juan;
but I would far prefer he serve
by learning tactics of Reserve
before becoming *Capitán.*
Consider, is he not too cocky,
the man who setting out to ride will,
knowing nothing of the bridle,
spur his mare as if a jockey?

97
Que demuestran a un Sargento las
circunstancias que le faltan

De Alabarda vencedora
un tal Sargento se armó;
mas luego él y ella paró
en lo que contaré ahora:
　　a ella, una A se desvanece,
porque la *Albarda* suceda;
a él el *Sar,* en *Sarna* queda;
y el *Argento* no parece.

97
Demonstration to a Sergeant of Ills to Befall

Our Captain Cutlass took up arms one day
and with sword and scabbard set out to the fray;
but to former and latter then befell
the abhorrent fates that now I tell.
   When *sword* was *bared* what was left was the *scab*
(to cut*less* from *cutlass* would be just as bad),
with *s* cut from *sword*, the *word's* not the same
and the *sarge* has his *argent*, but only in name.

DÉCIMAS

Stanza of ten octosyllabic lines,
usual rhyme scheme, *abbaa/ccddc*

113
Asegura la confianza de que ocultará
de todo un secreto

El paje os dirá, discreto,
como, luego que leí,
vuestro secreto rompí
por no romper el secreto.
Y aun hice más, os prometo:
los fragmentos, sin desdén,
del papel, tragué también;
que secretos que venero,
aun en pedazos no quiero
que fuera del pecho estén.

126
En un Anillo retrató a la Sra.
Condesa de Paredes. Dice por qué

Este retrato que ha hecho
copiar mi cariño ufano,
es sobrescribir la mano
lo que tiene dentro el pecho:
que, como éste viene estrecho
a tan alta perfección,
brota fuera la afición;
y en el índice la emplea,
para que con verdad sea
índice del corazón.

113
She Assures That She Will Hold a Secret
in Confidence

The page, discreetly, will relate
how, the moment it was read,
I tore your secret into shreds
that shreds not be the secret's fate.
And something more, inviolate,
I swallowed what you had confessed,
the tiny fragments of your note,
to guard the secret that you wrote
and honor thus your confidence, lest
even one scrap escape my breast.

126
Accompanying a Ring Bearing the Portrait of
la Señora Condesa de Paredes. She Explains

This portrait traced by arrogance
was nonetheless by love inspired,
whereon a clumsy hand conspired
to give emotion utterance:
no bursting breast can countenance
for long the presence of perfection,
but needs must spill out its affection;
then let your index finger show
the miniature, that all may know
the ring indexes my subjection.

130
Presente en que el cariño hace regalo la llaneza

Lysi: a tus manos divinas
doy castañas espinosas,
porque donde sobran rosas
no pueden faltar espinas.
Si a su aspereza te inclinas
y con eso el gusto engañas,
perdona las malas mañas
de quien tal regalo te hizo;
perdona, pues que un erizo
sólo puede dar castañas.

132
Describe, con énfasis de no poder dar la última mano a
la pintura, el retrato de una Belleza

Tersa frente, oro el cabello,
cejas arcos, zafir ojos,
bruñida tez, labios rojos,
nariz recta, ebúrneo cuello;
talle airoso, cuerpo bello,
cándidas manos en que
el cetro de Amor se ve,
tiene Fili; en oro engasta
pie tan breve, que no gasta
ni un pie.

130
A Modest Gift by Affection Made a Treat

Lysi: into your hands divine
I give two chestnuts with thorny spines,
because where roses bloom in number,
thorns will flowers' stems encumber.
If to their spines you are inclined,
and so contrive to trick your taste,
forgive the shocking lack of grace
of one who sent you such a toy;
for if you would the meats enjoy,
then first you must the burr embrace.

132
*She Describes in Detail—Not to Give the Last
Word to Painting—The Portrait of a Beauty*

Smooth brow and golden hair,
sapphire eyes and temple fair,
glowing skin, with lips of rose,
ivory throat, a noble nose,
her form is graceful, proud her air;
and in her hands, pale and fine,
see Love's scepter proudly shine:
Fili extolled, with—shod in gold—
a foot so comely it takes only
half a line.

SONNETS

In hendecasyllabic lines
and Italianate rhyme scheme

145
Procura desmentir los elogios que a un retrato de la
Poetisa inscribió la verdad, que llama pasión

Este, que ves, engaño colorido,
que del arte ostentando los primores,
con falsos silogismos de colores
es cauteloso engaño del sentido;
    éste, en quien la lisonja ha pretendido
excusar de los años los horrores,
y venciendo del tiempo los rigores
triunfar de la vejez y del olvido,
    es un vano artificio del cuidado,
es una flor al viento delicada,
es un resguardo inútil para el hado:
    es una necia diligencia errada,
es un afán caduco y, bien mirado,
es cádaver, es polvo, es sombra, es nada.

145
She Attempts to Minimize the Praise Occasioned
by a Portrait of Herself Inscribed by
Truth—Which She Calls Ardor

This that you gaze on, colorful deceit,
that so immodestly displays art's favors,
with its fallacious arguments of colors
is to the senses cunning counterfeit,

this on which kindness practiced to delete
from cruel years accumulated horrors,
constraining time to mitigate its rigors,
and thus oblivion and age defeat,

is but an artifice, a sop to vanity,
is but a flower by the breezes bowed,
is but a ploy to counter destiny,

is but a foolish labor, ill-employed,
is but a fancy, and, as all may see,
is but cadaver, ashes, shadow, void.

146
Quéjase de la suerte: insinúa su aversión a los vicios,
y justifica su divertimiento a las Musas

En perseguirme, Mundo ¿qué interesas?
¿En qué te ofendo, cuando sólo intento
poner bellezas en mi entendimiento
y no mi entendimiento en las bellezas?

Yo no estimo tesoros ni riquezas;
y así, siempre me causa más contento
poner riquezas en mi pensamiento
que no mi pensamiento en las riquezas.

Y no estimo hermosura que, vencida,
es despojo civil de las edades,
ni riqueza me agrada fementida,

teniendo por mejor, en mis verdades,
consumir vanidades de la vida
que consumir la vida en vanidades.

146
She Laments Her Fortune, She Hints
of Her Aversion to All Vice, and Justifies
Her Diversion with the Muses

In my pursuit, World, why such diligence?
What my offense, when I am thus inclined,
insuring elegance affect my mind,
not that my mind affect an elegance?

I have no love of riches or finánce,
and thus do I most happily, I find,
expend finances to enrich my mind
and not mind expend upon finánce.

I worship beauty not, but vilify
that spoil of time that mocks eternity,
nor less, deceitful treasures glorify,

but hold foremost, with greatest constancy,
consuming all the vanity in life,
and not consuming life in vanity.

148

Escoge antes el morir que exponerse
a los ultrajes de la vejez

Miró Celia una rosa que en el prado
ostentaba feliz la pompa vana
y con afeites de carmín y grana
bañaba alegre el rostro delicado;
    y dijo:—Goza, sin temor del Hado,
el curso breve de tu edad lozana,
pues no podrá la muerte de mañana
quitarte lo que hubieres hoy gozado;
    y aunque llega la muerte presurosa
y tu fragante vida se te aleja,
no sientas el morir tan bella y moza:
    mira que la experiencia te aconseja
que es fortuna morirte siendo hermosa
y no ver el ultraje de ser vieja.

148
Better Death Than Suffer the Affronts
of Growing Old

In the gardens, Celia gazed upon a rose
that candid in its haughty ostentation,
and bright in tints of scarlet and rich crimson,
joyfully its fragile face exposed,
    and said: "Enjoy the day, fear not the blows
of Fate in this too fleeting celebration,
the death that on the morrow claims its portion,
cannot take from you the joys this day bestows;
    though the perfume of life fade on the air,
and the hour of your passing too soon toll,
fear not the death that finds you young and fair:
    take the counsel that experience extols,
to die while beautiful is finer far
than to suffer the affront of growing old."

149
Encarece de animosidad la elección
de estado durable hasta la muerte

Si los riesgos del mar considerara,
ninguno se embarcara; si antes viera
bien su peligro, nadie se atreviera
ni al bravo toro osado provocara.

Si del fogoso bruto ponderara
la furia desbocada en la carrera
el jinete prudente, nunca hubiera
quien con discreta mano lo enfrenara.

Pero si hubiera alguno tan osado
que, no obstante el peligro, al mismo Apolo
quisiese gobernar con atrevida

mano el rápido carro en luz bañado,
todo lo hiciera, y no tomara sólo
estado que ha de ser toda la vida.

149
Spiritedly, She Considers the Choice
of a State Enduring Unto Death

Were the perils of the ocean fully weighed,
no man would voyage, or, could he but read
the hidden dangers, knowingly proceed
or dare to bait the bull to frenzied rage.

Were prudent rider overly dismayed,
should he contemplate the fury of his steed
or ponder where its headlong course might lead,
there'd be no reining hand to be obeyed.

But were there one so daring, one so bold
that, heedless of the danger, he might place,
upon Apollo's reins, emboldened hand

to guide the fleeting chariot bathed in gold,
the diversity of life he would embrace
and never choose a state to last his span.

151
Sospecha crueldad disimulada,
el alivio que la Esperanza da

    Diuturna enfermedad de la Esperanza,
que así entretienes mis cansados años
y en el fiel de los bienes y los daños
tienes en equilibrio la balanza;
    que siempre suspendida, en la tardanza
de inclinarse, no dejan tus engaños
que lleguen a excederse en los tamaños
la desesperación o confianza:
    ¿quién te ha quitado el nombre de homicida?
Pues lo eres más severa, si se advierte
que suspendes el alma entretenida;
    y entre la infausta o la felice suerte,
no lo haces tu por conservar la vida
sino por dar más dilatada muerte.

151
She Distrusts, as Disguised Cruelty,
the Solace Offered by Hope

Oh, malady of Hope, your persistence
sustains the passing of my weary years,
while measuring my wishes and my fears
your balances maintain equivalence;
    deceitfully, and with what indolence,
the pans begin to tip, but as change nears
invariably your parity adheres:
despair is counterpoised by confidence.
    Still, Murderess is how you must be known,
for Murderess you are, when it is owned
how between a fate of happiness or strife
    my soul has hung suspended far too long;
you do not act thus to prolong my life
but, rather, that in life death be prolonged.

161 (III)

Inés, yo con tu amor me *refocilo,*
y viéndome querer me *regodeo;*
en mirar tu hermosura me *recreo,*
y cuando estás celosa me *reguilo.*

Si a otro miras, de celos me *aniquilo,*
y tiemblo de tu gracia y tu *meneo;*
porque sé, Inés, que tú con un *voleo*
no dejarás humor ni aun para *quilo.*

Cuando estás enojada no *resuello,*
cuando me das picones me *refino,*
cuando sales de casa no *reposo;*

y espero, Inés, que entre esto y entre *aquello,*
tu amor, acompañado de mi *vino,*
dé conmigo en la cama o en el *coso.*

161 (III)*

    Inés, dear, with your love I am *enraptured*,
and as object of your love, I am *enthralled*,
when gazing on your beauty I am *captured*,
but when I find you jealous, want to *bawl*.
    I die of jealousy if others you *entangle*,
I tremble at your grace, your step *sublime*,
because I know, Inés, that you could *mangle*,
the humors of my systematic *chyme*.
    When I hold your dainty hand, I am *aquiver*,
in your anger, feel that I must soon *expire*,
if you venture from your home I am *adither*,
    so I say, Inés, to one thing I *aspire*,
that your love and my good wine will draw you *hither*,
and to tumble you to bed I can *conspire*.

* One of Five Burlesque Sonnets in Which the Poetess Was Circumscribed by
Rhymes Which Had Been Determined; Composed in a Moment of Relaxation

164
En que satisface un recelo con la retórica del llanto

Esta tarde, mi bien, cuando te hablaba,
como en tu rostro y tus acciones veía
que con palabras no te persuadía,
que el corazón me vieses deseaba;

y Amor, que mis intentos ayudaba,
venció lo que imposible parecía:
pues entre el llanto, que el dolor vertía,
el corazón deshecho destilaba.

Baste ya de rigores, mi bien, baste;
no te atormenten más celos tiranos,
ni el vil recelo tu quietud contraste

con sombras necias, con indicios vanos,
pues ya en líquido humor viste y tocaste
mi corazón deshecho entre tus manos.

164
She Answers Suspicions In the Rhetoric of Tears

My love, this evening when I spoke with you,
and in your face and actions I could read
that arguments of words you would not heed,
my heart I longed to open to your view.

In this intention, Love my wishes knew
and, though they seemed impossible, achieved:
pouring in tears that sorrow had conceived,
with every beat my heart dissolved anew.

Enough of suffering, my love, enough:
let jealousy's vile tyranny be banned,
let no suspicious thought your calm corrupt

with foolish gloom by futile doubt enhanced,
for now, this afternoon, you saw and touched
my heart, dissolved and liquid in your hands.

165
Que contiene una fantasía contenta
con amor decente

Detente, sombra de mi bien esquivo,
imagen del hechizo que más quiero,
bella ilusión por quien alegre muero,
dulce ficción por quien penosa vivo.

Si al imán de tus gracias, atractivo,
sirve mi pecho de obediente acero,
¿para qué me enamoras lisonjero
si has de burlarme luego fugitivo?

Mas blasonar no puedes, satisfecho,
de que triunfa de mí tu tiranía:
que aunque dejas burlado el lazo estrecho

que tu forma fantástica ceñía,
poco importa burlar brazos y pecho
si te labra prisión mi fantasía.

165
*Which Recounts How Fantasy Contents Itself
with Honorable Love*

Stay, shadow of contentment too short-lived,
illusion of enchantment I most prize,
fair image for whom happily I die,
sweet fiction for whom painfully I live.

If answering your charms' imperative,
compliant, I like steel to magnet fly,
by what logic do you flatter and entice,
only to flee, a taunting fugitive?

'Tis no triumph that you so smugly boast
that I fell victim to your tyranny;
though from encircling bonds that held you fast

your elusive form too readily slipped free,
and though to my arms you are forever lost,
you are a prisoner in my fantasy.

166
Resuelve la cuestión de cuál sea pesar
más molesto en encontradas correspondencias,
amar o aborrecer

Que no me quiera Fabio, al verse amado,
es dolor sin igual en mí sentido;
mas que me quiera Silvio, aborrecido,
es menor mal, mas no menos enfado.

¿Qué sufrimiento no estará cansado
si siempre le resuenan al oído
tras la vana arrogancia de un querido
el cansado gemir de un desdeñado?

Si de Silvio me cansa el rendimiento,
a Fabio canso con estar rendida;
si de éste busco el agradecimiento,

a mí me busca el otro agradecida:
por activa y pasiva es mi tormento,
pues padezco en querer y en ser querida.

166
She Resolves the Question of Which
Be the More Trying Role in Conflicting
Relationships: To Love or to Abhor

That Fabio does not love me, though adored,
is grief unmatched by any I have known,
a lesser hurt, though no less bothersome,
is that Silvio loves me, he in turn abhorred.

What patience, sorely tried, would not deplore,
what ringing ear, assaulted, not bemoan,
the ever-plaintive sighs of one disowned,
the arrogance of a vain conqueror.

If I am bored by Silvio's submission,
it bores Fabio to tears that I submit;
if from Fabio I forever court permission,

Silvio seeks from me what I permit;
if dual torment is to be my one condition,
both of loving and being loved I would be quit.

VILLANCICO

A religious song

317
Villancico VI

· *Estribillo* ·
¡Víctor, víctor Catarina,
que con su ciencia divina
los sabios ha convencido,
y victoriosa ha salido
—con su ciencia soberana—
de la arrogancia profana
que a convencerla ha venido!
¡Víctor, víctor, víctor!

· *Coplas* ·
De una Mujer se convencen
todos los Sabios de Egipto,
para prueba de que el sexo
no es escencia en lo entendido.
¡Víctor, víctor!
    Prodigio fue, y aun milagro;
pero no estuvo el prodigio
en vencerlos, sino en que
ellos se den por vencidos.
¡Víctor, víctor!
    ¡Qué bien se ve que eran Sabios
en confesarse rendidos,
que es triunfo el obedecer
de la razón el dominio!
¡Víctor, víctor!
    Las luces de la verdad
no se obscurecen con gritos;
que su eco sabe valiente
sobresalir del rüido.
¡Víctor, víctor!
    No se avergüenzan los Sabios
de mirarse convencidos;

317
Villancico VI,
from "Santa Catarina," 1691

· *Refrain* ·

Victor! Victor! Catherine,
who with enlightenment divine
persuaded all the learned men,
she who with triumph overcame
—with knowledge truly sovereign—
the pride and arrogance profane
of those who challenged her, in vain
Victor! Victor! Victor!

· *Verses* ·

There in Egypt, all the sages
by a woman were convinced
that gender is not of the essence
in matters of intelligence.
Victor! Victor!
    A victory, a miracle;
though more prodigious than the feat
of conquering, was surely that
the men themselves declared defeat.
Victor! Victor!
    How wise they were, these Prudent Men,
acknowledging they were outdone,
for one conquers when one yields
to wisdom greater than one's own.
Victor! Victor!
    Illumination shed by truth
will never by mere shouts be drowned;
persistently, its echo rings,
above all obstacles resounds.
Victor! Victor!
    None of these Wise Men was ashamed
when he found himself convinced,

porque saben, como Sabios,
que su saber es finito.
¡Víctor, víctor!

   Estudia, arguye y enseña,
y es de la Iglesia servicio,
que no la quiere ignorante
El que racional la hizo.
¡Víctor, víctor!

   ¡Oh, qué soberbios vendrían,
al juntarlos Maximino!
Mas salieron admirados
los que entraron presumidos.
¡Víctor, víctor!

   Vencidos, con ella todos
la vida dan al cuchillo:
¡oh cuánto bien se perdiera
si Docta no hubiera sido!
¡Víctor, víctor!

   Nunca de varón ilustre
triunfo igual habemos visto;
y es que quiso Dios en ella
honrar el sexo femíneo.
¡Víctor, víctor!

   Ocho y diez vueltas del Sol,
era el espacio florido
de su edad; mas de su ciencia
¿quién podrá contar los siglos?
¡Víctor, víctor!

   Perdióse (¡oh dolor!) la forma
de sus doctos silogismos:
pero, los que no con tinta,
dejó con su sangre escritos.
¡Víctor, víctor!

   Tutelar sacra Patrona,
es de las Letras Asilo;
porque siempre ilustre Sabios,
quien Santos de Sabios hizo.
¡Víctor, víctor!

because, in being Wise, he knew
his knowledge was not infinite.
Victor! Victor!

It is of service to the Church
that women argue, tutor, learn,
for He Who granted women reason
would not have them uninformed.
Victor! Victor!

How haughtily they must have come,
the men that Maximin convened,
though at their advent arrogant,
they left with wonder and esteem.
Victor! Victor!

Persuaded, all of them, with her,
gave up their lives unto the knife:
how much good might have been lost,
were Catherine less erudite!
Victor! Victor!

No man, whatever his renown,
accomplished such a victory,
and we know that God, through her,
honored femininity.
Victor! Victor!

Too brief, the flowering of her years,
but ten and eight, the sun's rotations,
but when measuring her knowledge,
who could sum the countless ages?
Victor! Victor!

Now all her learned arguments
are lost to us (how great the grief).
But with her blood, if not with ink,
she wrote the lesson of her life.
Victor! Victor!

Tutelar and holy Patron,
Catherine, the Shrine of Arts;
long may she illumine Wise Men,
she who Wise to Saints converts.
Victor! Victor!

THEATER, SACRED
AND PROFANE

367
Loa Para el Auto sacramental de
El divino Narciso

por alegorías

Personas que hablan en ella

El Occidente	La Religión
La América	Músicos
El Celo	Soldados

367
Loa for the Auto sacramental
The Divine Narcissus

through allegories

Cast of Characters

Occident	Religion
America	Musicians
Zeal	Soldiers

· *Escena I* ·

Sale el OCCIDENTE, Indio galán, con corona, y la AMÉRICA, a su lado, de India bizarra: con mantas y huipiles, al modo que se canta el Tocotín. Siéntanse en dos sillas; y por una parte y otra bailan Indios e Indias, con plumas y sonajas en las manos, como se hace de ordinario esta Danza; y mientras bailan, canta la Música.

MÚSICA

Nobles Mejicanos,
cuya estirpe antigua,
de las claras luces
del Sol se origina:
Pues hoy es del año
el dichoso día
en que se consagra
la mayor Reliquia,
¡venid adornados
de vuestras divisas,
y a la devoción
se una la alegría:
y en pompa festiva,
celebrad al gran Dios de las Semillas!

MÚSICA

Y pues la abundancia
de nuestras provincias
se Le debe al que es
Quien las fertiliza,
ofreced devotos,
pues Le son debidas,
de los nuevos frutos
todas las primicias.
¡Dad de vuestras venas
la sangre más fina,
para que, mezclada,
a su culto sirva;

· *Scene I* ·

Enter OCCIDENT, a stately Indian wearing a crown, and AMERICA
beside him, a noble Indian woman, in the *mantas* and *huipiles*
worn when singing a *tocotín*. They sit in two chairs; several Indian
men and women dance holding feathers and rattles in their hands,
as is traditional during this celebration; as they dance, MUSIC sings:

MUSIC

Most noble Mexicans,
whose ancient origin
is found in the brilliant rays
cast like arrows by the Sun,
mark well the time of year,
this day is given to laud
and honor in our way
the highest of our gods.
Come clad in ornaments
of your station the sign,
and to your piety
let happiness be joined:
with festive pageantry
worship the all-powerful God of Seeds!

MUSIC

The riches of our lands
in copious plenteousness
are owing to the one
who makes them bounteous.
So bring your fervent thanks,
and at the harvest time,
give unto Him his due,
the first fruit of the vine.
Let flow the purest blood,
give from your own veins,
to blend with many bloods
and thus His cult sustain.

y en pompa festiva,
celebrad al gran Dios de las Semillas!

(*Siéntanse el* OCCIDENTE *y la* AMÉRICA, *y cesa la música.*)

OCCIDENTE

Pues entre todos los Dioses
que mi culto solemniza,
aunque son tantos, que sólo
en aquesta esclarecida
Ciudad Regia, de dos mil
pasan, a quien sacrifica
en sacrificios crüentos
de humana sangre vertida,
ya las entrañas que pulsan,
ya el corazón que palpita;
aunque son (vuelvo a decir)
tantos, entre todos mira
mi atención, como a mayor,
al gran Dios de las Semillas.

AMÉRICA

Y con razón, pues es solo
el que nuestra Monarquía
sustenta, pues la abundancia
de los frutos se Le aplica;
y como éste es el mayor
beneficio, en quien se cifran
todos los otros, pues lo es
el de conservar la vida,
como el mayor Lo estimamos:
pues ¿qué importara que rica
el América abundara
en el oro de sus minas,
si esterilizando el campo
sus fumosidades mismas,

With festive pageantry
worship the all-powerful God of Seeds!

(OCCIDENT *and* AMERICA *sit, as* MUSIC *ceases.*)

OCCIDENT

So great in number are the Gods
that our religion sanctifies,
so many in this place alone
the many rites we solemnize,
that this our Royal City is
the scene of cruelest sacrifice:
two thousand gods are satisfied,
but human blood must be the price;
now see the entrails that still throb,
now see hearts that redly beat,
and though the gods are myriad,
our gods so many (I repeat),
the greatest God among them all
is our Great God, the God of Seeds!

AMERICA

And rightly so, for He alone
has long sustained our Monarchy,
for all the riches of the field
we owe to Him our fealty,
and as the greatest benefice,
in which all others are contained,
is that abundance of the land,
our life and breath by it maintained,
we name Him greatest of the Gods.
What matters all the glittering gold
in which America abounds,
what value precious ores untold,
if their excrescences befoul
and sterilize a fertile earth,

no dejaran a los frutos
que en sementeras opimas
brotasen? Demás de que
su protección no limita
sólo a corporal sustento
de la material comida,
sino que después, haciendo
manjar de sus carnes mismas
(estando purificadas
antes, de sus inmundicias
corporales), de las manchas
el Alma nos purifica.
Y así, atentos a su culto,
todos conmigo repitan:

ELLOS, *y* MÚSICA

¡En pompa festiva,
celebrad al gran Dios de las Semillas!

· *Escena II* ·
(*Éntranse bailando; y salen la* RELIGIÓN CRISTIANA, *de Dama Española, y el* CELO, *de Capitán General, armado; y detrás,* SOLDADOS *Españoles.*)

RELIGIÓN

¿Cómo, siendo el Celo tú,
sufren tus cristianas iras
ver que, vanamente ciega,
celebre la Idolatría
con supersticiosos cultos
un Ídolo, en ignominia
de la Religión Cristiana?

CELO

Religión: no tan aprisa
de mi omisión te querelles,

if no fruits ripen, no maize grows,
and no tender buds spring forth?
But the protection of this God
is broader than continuance,
with the provision of our food,
of our daily sustenance,
He makes a paste of His own flesh,
and we partake with veneration
(though first the paste is purified
of bodily contamination),
and so our Soul he purifies
of all its blemishes and stains.
And thus in homage to His cult,
may everyone with me proclaim:

ALL *and* MUSIC

In festive pageantry,
worship the all-powerful God of Seeds!

· *Scene II* ·

(*They exit, dancing, and then enter* CHRISTIAN RELIGION, *as a
Spanish Lady, and* ZEAL, *as a Captain General, armed; behind
them, Spanish* SOLDIERS.)

RELIGION

How is it, then, as you are Zeal,
your Christian wrath can tolerate
that here with blind conformity
they bow before Idolatry,
and, superstitious, elevate
an Idol, with effrontery,
above our Christianity?

ZEAL

Religion, do not be dismayed:
my compassion you upbraid,

te quejes de mis caricias;
pues ya levantado el brazo,
ya blandida la cuchilla
traigo, para tus venganzas.
Tú a ese lado te retiras
mientras vengo tus agravios.

(*Salen, bailando, el* OCCIDENTE *y* AMÉRICA, *y Acompañamiento y
Música, por otro lado*)

MÚSICA

¡Y en pompa festiva,
celebrad al gran Dios de las Semillas!

CELO

Pues ya ellos salen, yo llego.

RELIGIÓN

Yo iré también, que me inclina
la piedad a llegar (antes
que tu furor los embista)
a convidarlos, de paz,
a que mi culto reciban.

CELO

Pues lleguemos, que en sus torpes
ritos está entretenida.

MÚSICA

¡Y en pompa festiva,
celebrad al gran Dios de las Semillas!

(*Llegan el* CELO *y la* RELIGIÓN)

my tolerance you disavow,
but see, I stand before you now
with arm upraised, unsheathed my blade,
which I address to your revenge.
And now, retire, your cares allayed,
as their transgressions I avenge.

(*Enter, dancing,* OCCIDENT *and* AMERICA, *and from the other side,*
MUSIC, *with accompaniment*)

MUSIC

And with festive pageantry,
worship the all-powerful God of Seeds!

ZEAL

They are here. I will approach.

RELIGION

And I as well, with all compassion,
for I would go with tones of peace
(before unleashing your aggression)
to urge them to accept my word,
and in the faith be sanctified.

ZEAL

Then let us go, for even now
they practice their revolting rite.

MUSIC

And with festive pageantry,
worship the great God of Seeds!

(ZEAL *and* RELIGION *approach*)

RELIGIÓN

Occidente poderoso,
América bella y rica,
que vivís tan miserables
entre las riquezas mismas:
dejad el culto profano
a que el Demonio os incita.
¡Abrid los ojos! Seguid
la verdadera Doctrina
que mi amor os persüade.

OCCIDENTE

¿Qué gentes no conocidas
son éstas que miro, ¡Cielos!,
que así de mis alegrías
quieren impedir el curso?

AMÉRICA

¿Qué Naciones nunca vistas
quieren oponerse al fuero
de mi potestad antigua?

OCCIDENTE

¡Oh tú, extranjera Belleza;
¡oh tú, Mujer peregrina!
Dime quién eres, que vienes
a perturbar mis delicias.

RELIGIÓN

Soy la Religión Cristiana,
que intento que tus Provincias
se reduzcan a mi culto.

RELIGION

Hear me, mighty Occident,
America, so beautiful,
your lives are led in misery
though your land is bountiful.
Abandon this unholy cult
which the Devil doth incite.
Open your eyes. Accept my word
and follow in the Path of Light,
fully persuaded by my love.

OCCIDENT

These unknown persons, who are they
who now before my presence stand?
Oh gods, who ventures thus to stay
the festive moment's rightful course?

AMERICA

What Nations these, which none has seen?
Do they come here to interfere,
my ancient power contravene?

OCCIDENT

Oh, Lovely Beauty, who are you,
fair Pilgrim from another nation?
I ask you now, why have you come
to interrupt my celebration?

RELIGION

Christian Religion is my name,
and I propose that all will bend
before the power of my word.

OCCIDENTE

¡Buen empeño solicitas!

AMÉRICA

¡Buena locura pretendes!

OCCIDENTE

¡Buen imposible maquinas!

AMÉRICA

Sin duda es loca; ¡dejadla,
y nuestros cultos prosigan!

MÚSICA *y* ELLOS

¡Y en pompa festiva,
celebrad al gran Dios de las Semillas!

CELO

¿Cómo, bárbara Occidente:
¿cómo, ciega Idolatría,
a la Religión desprecias,
mi dulce Esposa querida?
Pues mira que a tus maldades
ya has llenado la medida,
y que no permite Dios
que en tus delitos prosigas,
y me envía a castigarte.

OCCIDENTE

¿Quién eres, que atemorizas
con sólo ver tu semblante?

OCCIDENT

A great endeavor you intend!

AMERICA

A great madness you display!

OCCIDENT

The inconceivable you scheme!

AMERICA

She must be mad, ignore her now,
let them continue with our theme!

ALL *and* MUSIC

With festive pageantry,
worship the all-powerful God of Seeds!

ZEAL

How, barbaric Occident,
and you, oh blind Idolatry,
can you presume to scorn my Wife,
beloved Christianity?
For brimming to the vessel's lip
we see your sinful degradation;
the Lord our God will not allow
That you continue in transgression,
and He sends me to punish you.

OCCIDENT

And who are you, who terrorize
all those who gaze upon your face?

CELO

El Celo soy. ¿Qué te admira?
Que, cuando a la Religión
desprecian tus demasías,
entrará el Celo a vengarla
castigando tu osadía.
Ministro de Dios soy, que
viendo que tus tiranías
han llegado ya a lo sumo,
cansado de ver que vivas
tantos años entre errores,
a castigarte me envía.
Y así, estas armadas Huestes,
que rayos de acero vibran,
ministros son de Su enojo
e instrumentos de Sus iras.

OCCIDENTE

¿Qué Dios, qué error, qué torpeza,
o qué castigos me intimas?
Que no entiendo tus razones
ni aun por remotas noticias,
ni quién eres tú, que osado
a tanto empeño te animas
como impedir que mi gente
en debidos cultos diga:

MÚSICA

¡Y en pompa festiva,
celebrad al gran Dios de las Semillas!

AMÉRICA

Bárbaro, loco, que ciego,
con razones no entendidas,

ZEAL

I am Zeal. Whence your surprise?
For when Religion you would scorn
with practices of vile excess,
then Zeal must enter on the scene
to castigate your wickedness.
I am a Minister from God
Who, witnessing your tyranny,
the error of these many years
of lives lived in barbarity,
has reached the limits of His grace
and sends His punishment through me.
And thus these armed and mighty Hosts
whose gleaming blades of steel you see
are His ministers of wrath,
the instruments of Holy rage.

OCCIDENT

What god, what error, what offense,
what punishment do you presage?
I do not understand your words,
nor does your argument persuade;
I know you not, who, brazenly,
would thus our rituals invade
and with such zeal that you prevent
that in just worship people say:

MUSIC

With festive pageantry,
worship the great God of Seeds!

AMERICA

Oh, mad, blind, barbaric man,
disturbing our serenity,

quieres turbar el sosiego
que en serena paz tranquila
gozamos: ¡cesa en tu intento,
si no quieres que, en cenizas
reducido, ni aun los vientos
tengan de tu sér noticias!
Y tú, Esposo, y tus vasallos,

(*Al Occidente*)

negad el oído y vista
a sus razones, no haciendo
caso de sus fantasías:
y proseguid vuestros cultos,
sin dejar que advenedizas
Naciones, osadas quieran
intentar interrumpirlas.

MÚSICA

¡Y en pompa festiva,
celebrad al gran Dios de las Semillas!

CELO

Pues la primera propuesta
de paz desprecias altiva,
la segunda, de la guerra,
será preciso que admitas.
¡Toca al arma! ¡Guerra, guerra!

(*Suenan cajas y clarines*)

OCCIDENTE

¿Qué abortos el Cielo envía
contra mí? ¿Qué armas son éstas,
nunca de mis ojos vistas?

you bring confusing arguments
to counter our tranquillity;
you must immediately cease,
unless it is your wish to find
all here assembled turned to ash
with no trace even on the wind!
And you, Husband, and your vassals,

(*to* OCCIDENT)

you must close your ears and eyes,
do not heed their fantasies,
do not listen to their lies;
proceed, continue with your rites!
Our rituals shall not be banned
by these Nations, still unknown,
so newly come unto our land.

MUSIC

And with festive pageantry,
worship the great God of Seeds!

ZEAL

As our first offering of peace
you have so haughtily disdained,
accept the second, that of war,
from war we will not be restrained!
War! War! To arms! To arms!

(*Sound of drums and trumpets*)

OCCIDENT

What is this wrath the gods devise?
What are the weapons here displayed
that so confound my awestruck eyes?

¡Ah, de mis Guardas! ¡Soldados:
las flechas que prevenidas
están siempre, disparad!

AMÉRICA

¿Qué rayos el Cielo vibra
contra mí? ¿Qué fieros globos
de plomo ardiente graniza?
¿Qué Centauros monstrüosos
contra mis gentes militan?

(*Dentro:*)

¡Arma, arma! ¡Guerra, guerra!

(*Tocan*)

¡Viva España! ¡Su Rey viva!

(*Trabada la batalla, van entrándose por una puerta, y salen por otra huyendo los* INDIOS, *y los* ESPAÑOLES *en su alcance; y detrás, el* OCCIDENTE *retirándose de la* RELIGIÓN, *y* AMÉRICA *del* CELO.)

· *Escena III* ·

RELIGIÓN

¡Ríndete, altivo Occidente!

OCCIDENTE

Ya es preciso que me rinda
tu valor, no tu razón.

CELO

¡Muere, América atrevida!

Ho, my Soldiers, ho there, Guards!
Those arrows that you hold prepared
now send against the enemy!

AMERICA

Why have the gods their lightning bared
to strike me down? What are these spheres
that fall like fiery leaden hail?
What are these Centaurs, man and horse,
that now my followers assail?

(*Off*)

To arms! To arms! We are at war!

(*Drums and trumpets*)

Long live Spain! Her King we hail!

(*The battle is struck;* INDIANS *enter and flee across the stage, pursued by the* SPANISH; OCCIDENT *and* AMERICA *begin to retreat before* RELIGION *and* ZEAL)

· *Scene III* ·

RELIGION

Surrender, haughty Occident!

OCCIDENT

Your declarations I defy
and only to your power yield.

ZEAL

Now bold America must die!

RELIGIÓN

¡Espera, no le des muerte,
que la necesito viva!

CELO

Pues ¿cómo tú la defiendes,
cuando eres tú la ofendida?

RELIGIÓN

Sí, porque haberla vencido
le tocó a tu valentía,
pero a mi piedad le toca
el conservarle la vida:
porque vencerla por fuerza
te tocó; mas el rendirla
con razón, me toca a mí,
con suavidad persuasiva.

CELO

Si has visto ya la protervia
con que tu culto abominan
ciegos, ¿no es mejor que todos
mueran?

RELIGIÓN

            Cese tu justicia,
Celo; no les des la muerte:
que no quiere mi benigna
condición, que mueran, sino
que se conviertan y vivan.

RELIGION

Hold, Zeal, do not strike them dead,
keep America alive!

ZEAL

What, you defend America
when she has your faith reviled?

RELIGION

There is no doubt that her defeat
is owing to your bravery,
but now allowing her to live
is witness to my clemency;
it was your duty, with your force,
to conquer her; but now with reason
I, too, work to vanquish her,
but I shall win with soft persuasion.

ZEAL

But their perversion you have seen,
how they abhor and scorn your Word;
they are blind, is it not better
that they die?

RELIGION

            Put up your sword.
Forebear, Zeal, do not attack,
it is my nature to forgive,
I do not want their immolation,
but conversion, let them live.

AMÉRICA

Si el pedir que yo no muera,
y el mostrarte compasiva,
es porque esperas de mí
que me vencerás, altiva
como antes con corporales,
después con intelectivas
armas, estás engañada;
pues aunque lloro cautiva
mi libertad, ¡mi albedrío
con libertad más crecida
adorará mis Deidades!

OCCIDENTE

Yo ya dije que me obliga
a rendirme a ti la fuerza;
y en esto, claro se explica
que no hay fuerza ni violencia
que a la voluntad impida
sus libres operaciones;
y así, aunque cautivo gima,
¡no me podrás impedir
que acá, en mi corazón, diga
que venero al gran Dios de las Semillas!

· *Escena IV* ·

RELIGIÓN

Espera, que aquésta no
es fuerza, sino caricia.
¿Qué Dios es ése que adoras?

AMERICA

If in petitioning for my life,
and in exhibiting compassion,
it is your hope that I will yield,
that you will thus divert my passion,
employing arguments of words
as once before you employed arms,
then you will find yourself deceived,
for though my person come to harm,
and though I weep for liberty,
my liberty of will, will grow,
and I shall still adore my Gods!

OCCIDENT

I have told you, and all know,
that I have bowed before your might,
but this caution you must heed,
that there is no strength or might
that ever can my will impede
from its just course, free of control;
though captive I may moan in pain,
your will can never conquer mine,
and in my heart I will proclaim:
I worship the great God of Seeds!

· *Scene IV* ·

RELIGION

But wait, for what we offer here
is not might, but gentleness.
What God is this that you adore?

OCCIDENTE

Es un Dios que fertiliza
los campos que dan los frutos;
a quien los cielos se inclinan,
a Quien la lluvia obedece
y, en fin, es El que nos limpia
los pecados, y después
se hace Manjar, que nos brinda.
¡Mira tú si puede haber,
en la Deidad más benigna,
más beneficios que haga
ni más que yo te repita!

RELIGIÓN

(*Aparte*)

¡Válgame Dios! ¿Qué dibujos,
qué remedos o qué cifras
de nuestras sacras Verdades
quieren ser estas mentiras?
¡Oh cautelosa Serpiente!
¡Oh Áspid venenoso! ¡Oh Hidra,
que viertes por siete bocas,
de tu ponzoña nociva
toda la mortal cicuta!
¿Hasta dónde tu malicia
quiere remedar de Dios
las sagradas Maravillas?
Pero con tu mismo engaño,
si Dios mi lengua habilita,
te tengo de convencer.

AMÉRICA

¿En qué, suspensa, imaginas?
¿Ves cómo no hay otro Dios

OCCIDENT

The Great Lord of fruitfulness.
He makes fertile all the fields,
all the heavens bow to Him,
it is He the rain obeys,
and finally, of all our sin
He cleanses us, then of His being
makes a feast to nurture us.
Tell me whether there can be,
in a God so bounteous,
any greater benefice
than I give in this summary?

RELIGION

(*Aside*)

May God have mercy! What reflection
do I see, what counterfeit,
thus patterned in their evil lies,
to mock our holy sacred Truths?
Oh, wily Serpent, sly Reptile,
oh, venom from the Viper's tooth!
Oh, Hydra, seven-headed beast
whose seven mouths spew, lethally,
rivers of poison on our heads,
how far, and how maliciously,
can you continue in this way
God's sacred Miracles to mime?
Now if God will grace my tongue,
this same deceit I shall refine
and use your arguments to win.

AMERICA

What mischief do you fabricate?
Do you not see there is no God,

como Aquéste, que confirma
en beneficios Sus obras?

RELIGIÓN

De Pablo con la doctrina
tengo de argüir; pues cuando
a los de Atenas predica
viendo que entre ellos es ley
que muera el que solicita
introducir nuevos Dioses,
como él tiene la noticia
de que a un *Dios no conocido*
ellos un altar dedican,
les dice: "No es Deidad nueva,
sino la no conocida
que adoráis en este altar,
la que mi voz os publica?"
Así yo . . . ¡Occidente, escucha;
oye, ciega Idolatría,
pues en escuchar mis voces
consisten todas tus dichas!
    Esos milagros que cuentas,
esos prodigios que intimas,
esos visos, esos rasgos,
que debajo de cortinas
supersticiosas asoman;
esos portentos que vicias,
atribuyendo su efecto
a tus Deidades mentidas,
obras del Dios Verdadero,
y de Su sabiduría
son efectos. Pues si el prado
florido se fertiliza,
si los campos se fecundan,
si el fruto se multiplica,
si las sementeras crecen,
si las lluvias se destilan,

none other, who corroborates
in benefices all His works?

RELIGION

Then I shall be like Paul, and speak
from holy doctrine; for when he
had come to preach among the Greeks,
he found in Athens the strict law
that he who sought to introduce
an unfamiliar god, would die,
but as he knew they had the use
of faithful worship in a place
devoted to THE UNKNOWN GOD,
he said: this God I give to you
is not unknown, but One you laud,
you ignorantly worship Him,
now Him declare I unto you.
And thus do I. . . . Hear, Occident,
Idolatry, attend me, too,
for if you listen to my words
you will find salvation there.
    Those many wonders you recount,
the miracles to which you swear,
the shimmering light, the flashing gleam
you glimpsed through Superstition's veil,
the prodigies, the prophecies,
the portents we heard you detail,
attributing their consequence
to your mendacious deities,
are but the work of One True God,
His wisdom and His sovereignty.
For if the flowering meadows bloom
and gardens yield their rich supply,
if the fields are fertilized,
and if their fruits do multiply,
if the plants from seedlings grow,
and if the clouds their rain distill,

todo es obra de Su diestra;
pues ni el brazo que cultiva,
ni la lluvia que fecunda,
ni el calor que vivifica,
diera incremento a las plantas
a faltar Su productiva
Providencia, que concurre
a darles vegetativa alma.

AMÉRICA

    Cuando eso así sea,
díme: ¿Será tan propicia
esa Deidad, que se deje
tocar de mis manos mismas,
como el Ídolo que aquí
mis propias manos fabrican
de semillas y de sangre
inocente, que vertida
es sólo para este efecto?

RELIGIÓN

Aunque su Esencia Divina
es invisible e inmensa,
como Aquésta está ya unida
a nuestra Naturaleza,
tan Humana se avecina
a nosotros, que permite
que Lo toquen las indignas
manos de los Sacerdotes.

AMÉRICA

Cuanto a aqueso, convenidas
estamos, porque a mi Dios
tan raras, tan exquisitas
no hay nadie a quien se permita

all must come from His right hand,
and never will the arm that tills,
nor the rains that feed the earth,
nor the warmth that wakes the seeds,
have the power to make plants live
if Providence has not decreed
that they have life: all nature's green,
her verdant soul, is His design.

AMERICA

And if all this is as you say,
is He, tell me, so benign,
this God of yours, your Deity,
so kind that he will tolerate
that I touch Him with my hands,
like the Idol I create
from many seeds and from the blood
of innocents, blood that is shed
for this alone, this one intent?

RELIGION

Although in Essence the Godhead
is both invisible and vast,
as that Essence is combined
and with our Being bound so fast,
thus He is like to Humankind,
and His benevolence allows
that undeserving though they be,
He may be touched by hands of Priests.

AMERICA

In this much, then, we are agreed.
For of my God the same is true,
and none may touch our Deity
except for those who as His priests

tocarlo, sino a los que
de Sacerdotes Le sirvan;
y no sólo no tocarlo,
mas ni entra en Su Capilla
se permite a los seglares.

CELO

¡Oh reverencia, más digna
de hacerse al Dios verdadero!

OCCIDENTE

Y dime, aunque más me digas:
¿será ese Dios, de materias
como de sangre, que fue
en sacrificio ofrecida,
y semilla, que es sustento?

RELIGIÓN

Ya he dicho que es Su infinita
Majestad, inmaterial;
mas Su Humanidad bendita,
puesta incrüenta en el Santo
Sacrificio de la Misa,
en cándidos accidentes,
se vale de las semillas
del trigo, el cual se convierte
en Su Carne y Sangre misma;
y Su Sangre, que en el Cáliz
está, es Sangre que ofrecida
en el Ara de la Cruz,
inocente, pura y limpia,
fue la Redención del Mundo.

to serve Him have authority;
not only may He not be touched,
but neither may they enter in
His Chapel who are not ordained.

ZEAL

What reverence, whose origin
were better found in Our True God!

OCCIDENT

Then tell me, though much more you swear:
is this God formed of elements
that are as exquisite, as rare,
as that of blood shed valiantly
and offered up as sacrifice,
as well as seeds, our sustenance?

RELIGION

His Majesty, I say this twice,
is infinite and without form,
but His divine Humanity,
found in the Sacrament of Mass,
with mercy, not with cruelty,
assuming the white innocence
that in the seeds of wheat resides,
becomes incarnate in these seeds,
in Flesh and Blood is deified;
here in this Chalice is His Blood,
the Blood He sacrificed for us,
that on the Altar of the Cross,
unsullied, pure, in righteousness,
was the Redemption of the World.

AMÉRICA

Ya que esas tan inauditas
cosas quiera yo creer,
¿será esa Deidad que pintas,
tan amorosa, que quiera
ofrecérseme en comida,
como Aquésta que yo adoro?

RELIGIÓN

Sí, pues Su Sabiduría,
para ese fin solamente,
entre los hombres habita.

AMÉRICA

¿Y no veré yo a ese Dios,
para quedar convencida,

OCCIDENTE

y para que de una vez
de mi tema me desista?

RELIGIÓN

Sí, verás, como te laves
en la fuente cristalina
del Bautismo.

OCCIDENTE

              Ya yo sé
que antes que llegue a la rica
mesa, tengo de lavarme,
que así es mi costumbre antigua.

AMERICA

I stand in awe of all you say,
and hearing, I want to believe;
but could this God that you portray
be so loving that as food
He would give Himself to me,
like the God that I adore?

RELIGION

Yes, for in His Wisdom, He
came down with only this in view,
to live on earth among mankind.

AMERICA

So, may I not see this God,
that true persuasion I may find?

OCCIDENT

And I as well, thus will it be
that my obsession be forgot?

RELIGION

Oh, you will see, once you are washed
in the crystalline, holy font
of Baptism.

OCCIDENT

          Yes, this I know,
before aspiring to come near
the fruitful table, I must bathe;
that ancient rite is practiced here.

CELO

No es aquése el lavatorio
que tus manchas necesitan.

OCCIDENTE

¿Pues cuál?

RELIGIÓN

        El de un Sacramento
que con virtud de aguas vivas
te limpie de tus pecados.

AMÉRICA

Como me das las noticias
tan por mayor, no te acabo
de entender; y así, querría
recibirlas por extenso,
pues ya inspiración divina
me mueve a querer saberlas.

OCCIDENTE

Y yo; y más, saber la vida
y muerte de ese gran Dios
que estar en el Pan afirmas.

RELIGIÓN

Pues vamos. Que en una idea
metafórica, vestida
de retóricos colores,
representable a tu vista,
te la mostraré; que ya
conozco que tú te inclinas

ZEAL

That bathing for your rituals
will not cleanse you of your stains.

OCCIDENT

What bathing will?

RELIGION

                    The Sacrament,
which in pure waters like the rains
will cleanse you of your every sin.

AMERICA

The magnitude of this you bring
as notices, as yet I cannot
comprehend, of everything
I would know more, and in detail,
for I am moved by powers divine,
inspired to know all you can tell.

OCCIDENT

An even greater thirst is mine,
I would know of the Life and Death
of this great God found in the Bread.

RELIGION

That we shall do. I shall give you
a metaphor, an idea clad
in rhetoric of many colors
and fully visible to view,
this shall I show you, now I know
that you are given to imbue

a objetos visibles, más
que a lo que la Fe te avisa
por el oído; y así,
es preciso que te sirvas
de los ojos, para que
por ellos la Fe recibas.

OCCIDENTE

Así es; que más quiero verlo,
que no que tú me lo digas.

· *Escena V* ·

RELIGIÓN

Vamos, pues.

CELO

        Religión, dime:
¿en qué forma determinas
representar los Misterios?

RELIGIÓN

De un Auto en la alegoría,
quiero mostrarlos visibles,
para que quede instruída
ella, y todo el Occidente,
de lo que ya solicita
saber.

CELO

    ¿Y cómo intitulas
el Auto que alegorizas?

with meaning what is visible;
it is now clear you value less
what Faith conveys unto your ears,
thus it is better you assess
what you can see, and with your eyes
accept the lessons She conveys.

OCCIDENT

Yes, it is so, for I would see,
and not rely on what you say.

· *Scene V* ·

RELIGION

Let us begin.

ZEAL

Religion, speak,
to represent the Mysteries,
what form do you plan to employ?

RELIGION

An allegory it will be,
the better to instruct the two,
an *Auto* that will clearly show
America and Occident
all that they now beg to know.

ZEAL

This Allegory as *Auto*,
what title for it do you plan?

RELIGIÓN

Divino Narciso, porque
si aquesta infeliz tenía
un Ídolo, que adoraba,
de tan extrañas divisas,
en quien pretendió el demonio,
de la Sacra Eucaristía
fingir el alto Misterio,
sepa que también había
entre otros Gentiles, señas
de tan alta Maravilla.

CELO

¿Y dónde se representa?

RELIGIÓN

En la coronada Villa
de Madrid, que es de la Fe
el Centro, y la Regia Silla
de sus Católicos Reyes,
a quien debieron las Indias
las luces del Evangelio
que en el Occidente brillan.

CELO

¿Pues no ves la impropiedad
de que en Méjico se escriba
y en Madrid se represente?

RELIGIÓN

¿Pues es cosa nunca vista
que se haga una cosa en una
parte, porque en otra sirva?

RELIGION

Divine Narcissus, for although
America, unhappy land,
adored an Idol symbolized
by signs of such complexity
that through that Idol Satan tried
to feign the highest Mystery,
that of the Sacred Eucharist,
there was, as well, intelligence
among the Gentiles of this land
of other marvelous events.

ZEAL

And where will they enact your play?

RELIGION

In Madrid, the Royal Town,
the Center of our Holy Faith,
the Jewel in the Royal Crown,
the Seat of Catholic Kings and Queens
through whom the Indies have been sent
the blessing of Evangel Light
that shines throughout the Occident.

ZEAL

But does it not seem ill-advised
that what you write in Mexico
be represented in Madrid?

RELIGION

Oh, tell me, did you never know
an object fashioned in one place
and subsequently employed elsewhere?

Demás de que el escribirlo
no fue idea antojadiza,
sino debida obediencia
que aun a lo imposible aspira.
Con que su obra, aunque sea
rústica y poco pulida,
de la obediencia es efecto,
no parto de la osadía.

CELO

Pues dime, Religión, ya
que a eso le diste salida,
¿cómo salvas la objeción
de que introduces las Indias,
y a Madrid quieres llevarlas?

RELIGIÓN

Como aquesto sólo mira
a celebrar el Misterio,
y aquestas introducidas
personas no son más que
unos abstractos, que pintan
lo que se intenta decir,
no habrá cosa que desdiga,
aunque las lleve a Madrid:
que a especies intelectivas
ni habrá distancias que estorben
ni mares que les impidan.

CELO

Siendo así, a los Reales Pies,
en quien Dos Mundos se cifran,
pidamos perdón prostrados;

As for the act of writing it,
you find no whim or fancy there,
but only due obedience
attempting the impossible.
Therefore this work, though it may be
inelegant, its lustre dull,
is owing to obedience,
and not born of effrontery.

ZEAL

Religion, tell me, as the play
is your responsibility,
how do you counter the complaint
that in the Indies was begun
what you would carry to Madrid?

RELIGION

The drama's purpose is but one,
to celebrate the Mystery,
as to the persons introduced,
they are but abstraction,
symbolic figures who educe
the implication of the work,
and no part need be qualified
though it be taken to Madrid;
for men of reason realize
there is no distance that deters,
nor seas that interchange efface.

ZEAL

Prostrate, at the Royal Feet
that regally Two Worlds embrace,
we seek permission to proceed,

RELIGIÓN

y a su Reina esclarecida

AMÉRICA

cuyas soberanas plantas
besan humildes las Indias;

CELO

a sus Supremos Consejos;

RELIGIÓN

a las Damas, que iluminan
su Hemisferio;

AMÉRICA

        a sus Ingenios,
a quien humilde suplica
el mío, que le perdonen
el querer con toscas líneas
describir tanto Misterio.

OCCIDENTE

¡Vamos, que ya mi agonía
quiere ver cómo es el Dios
que me han de dar en comida,

(*Cantan la* AMÉRICA *y el* OCCIDENTE *y el* CELO)

diciendo que ya
conocen las Indias
al que es Verdadero
Dios de las Semillas!

RELIGION

and of the Queen, our Sovereign,

AMERICA

at whose feet the Indies kneel
to pledge obeisance once again,

ZEAL

and of her Supreme Councillors,

RELIGION

and Ladies, who illuminate
the Hemisphere;

AMERICA

                    and the Erudite
whom I most humbly supplicate
to pardon the poor lack of wit
in wishing with these clumsy lines
to treat so great a Mystery.

OCCIDENT

My agony is exquisite,
come, show me how in bread and wine
this God gives of Himself to me.

(AMERICA, OCCIDENT, *and* ZEAL *sing*)

Now are the Indies
all agreed,
there is but One
True God of Seeds!

Y en lágrimas tiernas
que el gozo destila,
repitan alegres
con voces festivas:

TODOS

¡Dichoso el día
que conocí al gran Dios de las Semillas!

(*Éntranse bailando y cantando*)

    With tender tears
by joy distilled,
raise voices high
with gladness filled:

ALL

Blessed the day
I came to know the great God of the Seeds!

(*All exit, dancing and singing*)

386
Fragmento del monólogo de Doña Leonor
en Los empeños de una casa

Si de mis sucesos quieres
escuchar los tristes casos
con que ostentan mis desdichas
lo poderoso y lo vario,
escucha, por si consigo
que divirtiendo tu agrado,
lo que fue trabajo propio
sirva de ajeno descanso,
o porque en el desahogo
hallen mis tristes cuidados
a la pena de sentirlos
el alivio de contarlos.

    Yo nací noble, éste fue
de mi mal el primer paso,
que no es pequeña desdicha
nacer noble un desdichado;
que aunque la nobleza sea
joya de precio tan alto,
es alhaja que en un triste
sólo sirve de embarazo;
porque estando en un sujeto
repugnan como contrarios,
entre plebeyas desdichas
haber respetos honrados.

    Decirte que nací hermosa
presumo que es excusado,
pues lo atestiguan tus ojos
y lo prueban mis trabajos.
Sólo diré . . . Aquí quisiera
no ser yo quien lo relato,
pues en callarlo o decirlo
dos inconvenientes hallo:
porque si digo que fui
celebrada por milagro

386
Fragment of Doña Leonor's monologue from
The Trials of a Noble House

If of my life you wish to hear
examples of adversity
in which misfortune manifests
its fury and variety,
then listen, and should I succeed
in adding slightly to your pleasure,
the catalogue of my travail
will entertain you in your leisure,
or, perhaps, as it is purged,
all my wretchedness may find
that though the living causes pain,
the telling creates peace of mind.

   I was born of noble blood,
this was the first of fortune's blows:
good fortune does not accompany birth
as any troubled noble knows,
and though few doubt that noble blood
is fortune's gift, a priceless jewel,
to one who suffers, such a gem
may seem, instead, an obstacle:
how inconsistent in one person,
battling in contradiction,
amid plebeian misery,
deference and veneration.

   To tell you I was born with beauty
is something you may well forgive,
the truth is witnessed by your eyes
as well as hardships I have lived.
I merely state, I did not wish
to be the one to tell this tale,
in telling or in keeping still
two difficulties I detail:
if I say that I was known
and celebrated for discretion,

de discreción, me desmiente
la necedad del contarlo;
y si lo callo, no informo
de mí, y en un mismo caso
me desmiento si lo afirmo,
y lo ignoras si lo callo.
Pero es preciso al informe
que de mis sucesos hago
(aunque pase la modestia
la vergüenza de contarlo)
para que entiendas la historia,
presuponer asentado
que mi discreción la causa
fue principal de mi daño.

    Inclinéme a los estudios
desde mis primeros años
con tan ardientes desvelos,
con tan ansiosos cuidados,
que reduje a tiempo breve
fatigas de mucho espacio.
Conmuté el tiempo, industriosa
a lo intenso del trabajo,
de modo que en breve tiempo
era el admirable blanco
de todas las atenciones,
de tal modo, que llegaron
a venerar como infuso
lo que fue adquirido lauro.
Era de mi patria toda
el objeto venerado
de aquellas adoraciones
que forma el común aplauso;
y como lo que decía
fuese bueno o fuese malo,
ni el rostro lo deslucía,
ni lo desairaba el garbo,
llegó la superstición
popular a empeño tanto,

I prove the very opposite
by the folly of narration;
but if silent, none will know
the truth of me; you see the question,
in silence, you are uninformed,
in speaking, I betray discretion.
But if in making this account
I must record each incident
(though in so doing, modesty
surrenders to embarrassment)
in order that you understand,
you may with confidence assume
that my discretion clearly was
the foremost reason for my doom.

   Such was my eagerness to learn,
from my earliest inclination,
that studying far into the night,
and with most eager application,
I accomplished in a briefer span
the weary toil of long endeavor,
with diligence, commuting time
through the fervor of my labor;
within a very little time
I was the target of all eyes,
admired, the center of attention,
so immoderately eulogized
that laurels won through industry
were glorified as gifts of God.
I was, through all my native land,
recipient of praise and laud,
the quality of veneration
formed by communal acclaim;
and as the things that all were saying,
to good purpose, or in vain,
by elegance of face and bearing
were not in any way gainsaid,
too soon, a general superstition
was so insistent and widespread

que ya adoraban deidad
el ídolo que formaron.
Voló la fama parlera,
discurrió reinos extraños,
y en la distancia segura
acreditó informes falsos.
La pasión se puso anteojos
de tan engañosos grados,
que a mis moderadas prendas
agrandaban los tamaños. . . .

    Entre estos aplausos yo,
con la atención zozobrando
entre tanta muchedumbre,
sin hallar seguro blanco,
no acertaba a amar alguno
viéndome amada de tantos. . . .

that the idol they'd created
now the people deified.
To foreign lands, to distant realms,
Fame spread the tidings far and wide,
and the persuasion distance lends
gave credence to these false reports.
Then Fervor, wearing spectacles
whose lens reality distorts,
saw talents of most modest worth
disproportionately magnified. . . .

   Amid such unrestrained applause
my least reflection stultified,
in all the throng I could not find
for my regard a worthy mark;
and so, belovéd of so many,
I took not one into my heart. . . .

Response to the Most Illustrious Poetess Sor Filotea de la Cruz
  1. Luke 1:43. Bracketed words have been added for clarity.
  2. I Kings 9:21.
  3. II Corinthians 12:4.
  4. John 21:25.
  5. Exodus 33:13.
  6. Psalms 49:16.
  7. II Corinthians 12:11.
  8. Job 38:31, 32.
  9. Don Juan Carlos Mero says that Sor Juana confused Kircher's *Magnes sive de arte magnetica* with *De magnete* by William Gilbert, London, 1600.
 10. John 11:47.
 11. Isaiah 11:10.
 12. Luke 2:34.
 13. Job 1:7.
 14. I Peter 5:8.
 15. John 12:31.
 16. Genesis 3:18.
 17. John 11:8.
 18. John 11:9.
 19. John 11:16.
 20. John 10:32.
 21. John 10:33.
 22. Luke 22:54.
 23. Luke 9:33.
 24. Luke 22:57.
 25. Luke 22:56.
 26. The *seal* of Solomon contains triangles in its design—it is the Star of David. Possibly the ring does as well.

27. Bartolomé, not Lupercio Leonardo.
28. I Corinthians 14:34.
29. Titus 2:3.
30. Wisdom 1:4.
31. Romans 12:3.
32. Psalms 140:5.
33. Job 2:13.
34. Proverbs 31:23.
35. This is probably an error for "thundered from the left," a reference to Virgil's *Aeneid*.
36. Canticle of Canticles 1:1.
37. Psalms 115:13.
38. Timothy 2:11.
39. Acts 17:28.
40. Titus 1:12.
41. I Corinthians 4:7.

First I Dream

27	Nyctimene was turned into an owl as punishment for an incestuous relationship with her father, a reference that appears in Ovid's *Metamorphoses*.
39 and 48	Daughters of King Minyas who refused to participate in festivities honoring Dionysus, choosing instead to continue to weave both cloth and stories to while away their time. For such daring, their weaving was destroyed and they were metamorphosed: in one version into three different creatures, a mouse, a screech owl, and an owl; here, as in Ovid, into bats.
53	Another punishment, Ascalaphus was changed into a screech owl after betraying Persephone by reporting she had eaten forbidden pomegranate seeds in Hades.
76	Son of Isis; called "the infant Horus."
93	One of the Pleiades.
113	In his notes to *El sueño*, Alfonso Méndez Plancarte (to whom I, like many before me through the years, am indebted for illumination and clarification) writes that Actaeon was not "exactly" a king, although he was the son of Cadmus, the King of Thebes. It was his misfor-

tune to have seen Diana and her nymphs bathing, and for that indiscretion was changed into a deer and pursued by his own pack of hounds.

129–42   Luis de Góngora y Argote, a Spanish poet whom Sor Juana greatly admired, referred to the eagle "as the queen of birds." Méndez Plancarte lists several authors, including Pliny, Leonardo da Vinci, and Garcilaso de la Vega, who endow the eagle with the attribute of vigilance.

235 ff.   This passage is more easily followed once the "laboratory" Sor Juana refers to is identified as the stomach, and the processes described understood as contemporary views of digestion and its related organs. *El húmedo radical*, "Humidity," is described in the Espasa Calpe dictionary as "A sweet, subtle, and balsamic lymphatic humor that gave flexibility and elasticity to the fibers of the body." It was believed that the *calor natural* (natural heat) of our body consumed the *húmedo radical* in a continuous battle between those two warring forces.

581–82   Aristotle's classifications of reality were: substance, quantity, quality, relation, action, passion, position, condition, and time and space determination.

627   Méndez Plancarte substitutes Thetis for Sor Juana's Themis, arguing that as the mother of Rivers and Oceanids the former is the more logical one to have produced "sweet, flowing streams."

710–29   Sor Juana uses several mythic references to illustrate the extent of her "ignorance," hence unfitness to aspire to higher realms of knowledge. Alpheius, smitten with Arethusa, attempted to abduct her as she was bathing in his stream, but she was changed into a fountain and swallowed by the earth. (To be united with her, he took the form of a river.)

          While in "Pluto's daunting caverns," Arethusa saw Ceres, for whose daughter, Persephone, Pluto had prepared in those Elysian fields a "nuptial bed." Among other triadic references, Persephone, as queen

of the Underworld, had attributes of the bat, the narcissus, and the pomegranate.

    Ceres eventually found her daughter and brought her to live with her aboveground, but in the four months of her return to Pluto's realm, vegetation becomes dormant.

785　　Phaëthon is a recurrent image in Sor Juana's writing, as is Icarus (line 800), two icons whose "brazen excess"—Phaëthon's hubris in believing he could control the chariot of the sun, Icarus's ambitious soaring toward the sun—was punished by crashing back to earth, a fitting metaphor for Sor Juana's very life.

898　　Tithonus is the father of Phaëthon; also called Cephalus.

959　　I hope Sor Juana would approve of this irresistible word, in use during her lifetime and, in my mind, appropriate for describing night's ragged flight.

Romances

Prologue　　Méndez Plancarte suggests that Sor Juana's "haste in copying" the poems was due to the pressures of getting them into the hands of the Marquesa de la Laguna in time for a new edition of poems published the year following *Inundación Castálida.*

48　　"en-Tarquin": is a verb invented by Sor Juana—broadly, "to turn woman into man." Her choice of model, however, must be ironic, since Lucretia's rape by Sextus, son of Tarquinius Superbus, is considered to be the cause of Tarquin's deposition.

    That Sor Juana could not be a woman "who would serve a man" as wife could be interpreted either as a reference to her state as a nun or as a disinclination to be subservient to a man. The following quartet seems more explicit: "I know only that my body,/ not to either state inclined,/ is neuter, abstract, guardian/ of only what my Soul consigns."

    The reference to Aristides, and the following lines with their allusions to envy, echo long passages in the

"Respuesta" and lines from Doña Leonor's mono-
logue in *Los empeños de una casa*.

Epigrams

93   Sor Juana calls Leonor the *Coco*, "the boogeyman."
        The pun in Spanish is with *coco*, "the coconut palm."
        The species is changed in English for the sake of a pun.

94   This is admittedly an *imitation*, not a *translation*.

95   This is the only instance in which Sor Juana alludes to
        her bastardy. Octavio Paz finds it remarkable that the
        accent is more on the question of her father's social
        rank than of her own legitimacy.

Décimas

126   This poem lends substance to the conjecture that Sor
        Juana was an accomplished artist. One of her portraits
        is believed to be a self-portrait—or a painting copied
        from a self-portrait—but there are no extant attrib-
        uted paintings.

130   Lysi and Fili are names by which Sor Juana alluded to
        the Marquesa de la Laguna.

Sonnets

161   Méndez Plancarte laments these "naughty, even gross,"
        exercises, considering them to be indecorous and un-
        worthy of Sor Juana. In explanation, he points out
        that "one must remember the times." Although her
        near-contemporaries Góngora and Quevedo and Lope
        far surpassed Sor Juana in grossness, it is true that the
        modern reader is surprised by the earthiness of this
        and the accompanying four sonnets for which Sor
        Juana was asked to fit a poem to prescribed end-
        rhymes. Is it possible that Sor Juana could not refuse
        the challenge of the game?

Villancico

317   Méndez Plancarte believes that the allusion to the sur-
        render of the "Prudent Men" inevitably recalls Sor

Juana's own triumph over the celebrated Portuguese priest Antonio de Vieyra; it was, nonetheless, a costly triumph, leading, as it did, directly to the confrontation of the "Respuesta."

Sor Juana's argument that women should "argue, tutor, learn" is a major theme of the "Respuesta."

Méndez Plancarte points out that Catherine was the patron saint of the "Royal and Pontifical University of Mexico." As Sor Juana was denied any connection with that body, I suspect that the saint's patronage was of much less interest to her than what she symbolized.

There is an ironic and tragic foreshadowing in the lines "now all her learned arguments/ are lost to us. . . ." We do have four volumes of Sor Juana's writing, but her personal papers, as well as additional literary and intellectual works, have been lost.

Theater, Sacred and Profane

367   A *loa* was a brief theatrical work which could be performed in isolation but more frequently preceded an *auto* [sacramental play] or *comedia* [profane or non-religious work].

The allusion to the Mexicans' origins in the sun, according to Méndez Plancarte, was reported by Friar Andrés de Olmos: "The Sun cast down an arrow . . . and made a hole, from which a man emerged . . . and, following, woman . . ."

The "God of the Seeds" might refer to several Aztec gods, but here is most obviously Huitzilopochtli, the most powerful of the gods of Tenochtitlán, the Aztec capital built on the site now occupied by central Mexico City. Méndez Plancarte quotes early sources recounting the rites devoted to the seed god: "They [the Indians] each year concocted the figure of Huitzilupuchtli . . . of various edible grains and seeds. . . . They ground them to form the said statue, of the size and stature of a man. The liquid with which they bound and mixed the flour was the blood of chil-

dren.... After a month's time ... they took a dag-
ger ... and struck the Idol in the breast.... They said
that they killed the God Huitzilupuchtli in order to
eat of his body ... and they divided it in very small
portions among all those of their *barrios* ... and this
was their manner of Communion ... and they called
this food *Teocualo,* which means *God is eaten.*"

AMERICA's lines, "what value precious ores untold/
if their excrescences befoul/ and sterilize a fertile
earth ..." are surely the earliest recorded comment in
this continent of environmental concerns.

Scene II

AMERICA's protest to ZEAL, calling him a "mad, blind,
barbaric man" who was "disturbing our serenity," is
very daring, considering that ZEAL is the enforcer of
the Faith.

The last lines of the scene authentically illustrate the
Indians' awe before the weapons of the Spanish, espe-
cially firearms and the horse.

Scene IV

This scene is particularly interesting. In it, Sor Juana
accurately describes the synonymies between the pre-
Columbian and the Catholic religions: the beneficence
of the Gods (rather exaggerated, considering Huit-
zilopochtli's true characteristics), the inviolability of
the Gods; the cleanliness practiced in their worship;
the Gods' blood sacrifice; and the ritual of the Mass.
Paz discusses this Jesuitical syncretic vision at length
in his *Sor Juana Inés de la Cruz* ... and the vision is
underlined in Sor Juana's quotation from Paul, argu-
ing that all along, although unknowingly, the Indians
had been worshipping the True God.

Scene V

This final scene is Sor Juana's apology and apologia.
At the same time it provides a resolution—"Now are

the Indies/ all agreed,/ there is but One/ True God of Seeds!"—that removes any possibility of criticism from her earlier defense of the customs and practices of indigenous New Spain.

386   This fragment from Doña Leonor's monologue in *Los empeños de una casa* [The Trials of a Noble House] is generally conceded to be autobiographical. With the exception of her "noble birth," Leonor does indeed seem to represent Sor Juana's not overly modest but entirely objective vision of herself.

[handwritten annotations:]

punishment
pain
sorrow
effort, trouble

suffering
love-sick
lover (m. n.)

(saw)

¿Quién vio que pena y penante
una propia cosa sean?

should be

suitable
one's own
right
natural
appropriate

Who saw that pain & suffering
should be appropriate?